John Ruffini

A quiet nook in the Jura

John Ruffini

A quiet nook in the Jura

ISBN/EAN: 9783742854636

Manufactured in Europe, USA, Canada, Australia, Japa

Cover: Foto ©Andreas Hilbeck / pixelio.de

Manufactured and distributed by brebook publishing software
(www.brebook.com)

John Ruffini

A quiet nook in the Jura

A QUIET NOOK

IN THE JURA

BY

JOHN RUFFINI

AUTHOR OF "DOCTOR ANTONIO," "LAVINIA," ETC.

COPYRIGHT EDITION.

LEIPZIG

BERNHARD TAUCHNITZ

1867.

CONTENTS.

A QUIET NOOK.

CHAPTER I.

How I stumbled upon Schrankstoinbad.

AFTER a nine months' uninterrupted enjoyment of the sweets and bitters of a great metropolis, a man, without being a misanthrope, may own to a strong inclination to wish his fellow-creatures well at a certain distance. It was in such a frame of mind that one fine day, in June, no matter the year — dates at a certain time of life become invidious witnesses, — I left town for Switzerland, in quest of a quiet nook, wherein to dream in peace, and watch leisurely some flowing stream.

Understand me, pray, *cum sale disretionis*. When I speak of a quiet nook, I mean relatively so. I am no Utopist. Give me a little space, a little air, a little privacy, with a patch of green and water, my ambition goes not beyond. A modest programme, I hope; yet, as I had to learn to my cost, not easy to realize. Not certainly at the Hydrotherapic Establishment, which I tried first, on a friend's recommendation, and where I found a house crammed to suffocation, sixty-seven crinolines, and twenty-six panamas in full array, *salon en permanence*, concerts, amateur theatricals, tombolas, and what not! Bore for bore, I might get it cheaper in town.

Equally, if not worse glutted, was the Spa, to
which I next applied, and the what-is-its-name Kulm,
up to which I climbed next. I was told at the first,
to come again within a week, and there might then be
a small room free; and, at the second, I had to fight
my way to dinner—literally fight my way through and
against hundreds of ravenous tourists, a good fourth
of them young ladies, in all the eccentricity of fashion.

Positively, Malthus is right; the world is sick of a
plethora, we are too many of us in it—and, upon this
wise conclusion, down I hurried *ab irato;* and here I
was, after four days of an odious and ignoble race,
jogging aimlessly along the rail-road, like an unmasted
vessel, and casting fond, almost envious glances at the
châlets which dot its sides, and at their happy occupants, the railway signal-men, who seemed with their
signals to sneer at the homeless wanderer.

Pretty neat cozy wooden boxes, those diminutive
homes of the Swiss railway attendants, with delightful
mosaics of pastures, and forest-covered ridges in front,
or perhaps the chain of the Alps; easy work withal on
those easy-going lines — no more than necessary to
tickle a man's conscience agreeably with the sense of
duty fulfilled; frequent contact, and near enough, with
his fellow-creatures to keep his milk of human kindness fresh and sweet — yet distant and transitory
enough to avert all danger of its turning sour. . . .

A considerable volume of tobacco-smoke, which I
happened to swallow at this point — as bad and
pungent stuff as ever came out of a pipe — startled
me out of my arcadian picture into a violent fit of
coughing. I am no new hand at smoking; I have seer
some service under the colours of the fragrant weed;

but I could not stand this. No country that I know
of can compete with Switzerland for bad and cheap
tobacco. The puff of offensive smoke came from an
old peasant in Sunday clothes, my immediate *vis-à-vis;*
his neighbour in the same seat (there are only two
places in each) was a younger peasant whose cigar was
nearly as bad as the other's pipe. Now, the wind being
against us, I and the person next to me, an old lady,
did not miss an atom of the two nuisances. The old
lady did her best, by frequent applications of her
handkerchief to her mouth and nostrils, to keep out
the infection — a poor palliative, after all, for one
must breathe.

I felt for the lady, and there was some merit in
that, for a more repulsive face I never met in my life.
Smoking being lawful in second-class carriages, remonstrating with the men was entirely out of the
question. I looked about instead in search of a less
exposed situation for my neighbour, but I saw none.
Clouds of the acrid incense whirled over every corner
of the carriage. Out of the seventeen men present
— I counted them — only four were not puffing
like chimneys. How the ladies, six in number, must
have fared in the foul atmosphere, I leave you to
imagine; one or two might be hardened to it, but the
majority were evidently ill at ease.

My dear fellow-smokers, is the cigar a new fire of
Vesta, to be kept burning for ever, or is smoking as
essential a function of life as breathing, and as such
to be necessarily indulged in at all times, and in all
places, whatever the inconvenience to others? If so, I
hold my tongue; if not, allow me to submit that a few
hours' intermission in the puffing occupation would

only enhance its pleasure for you, and prevent your spoiling that of others. Do you think that playing the part of a Westphalian-ham can be a pleasing and flattering position for a woman? The fair sex keeps us already enough at crinoline's length — is it wise, is it good policy to widen the distance between the two sexes? I know of no more active dissolvents of all social intercourse than the crinoline and the cigar. This tendency of each half of what nature ordained to form a whole, to isolate itself in its cloud of gauze or smoke, is one of the most ominous signs of the time. Let this state of things go on for ten years longer, and farewell civilisation! barbarism gets in afresh. . . .

The train had stopped at a station just as I was concluding my apostrophe. I beg pardon for my mental soliloquies and apostrophes; they are an inveterate weakness with me. I will drop them, if I can; at all events, make them short. Well — some travellers went out, my two *vis-à-vis* among others, and some came in. One of these last, a young lady in mourning, hurried in, threw on the now empty seat in front of me a small travelling-bag and her parasol, and, leaning out of the window, exchanged a few more farewells and shakings of the hand with an elderly lady and a young girl standing on the platform. Without being positively handsome, she had a very sweet countenance, and a voice to match; but what chiefly attracted me in her was her evident extreme timidity. She looked from head to foot one nervous twitch.

Presently the train moved slowly on; and, after some last flourishes of the hand, and waving of the handkerchief, the new-comer left the window, and sat down; in doing which she noticed a parasol lying upon her luggage, stared at it, took it up, went to the window, beckoned towards the platform, and, to my dismay, threw it upon the line.

I say to my dismay, because the parasol in question did not belong to the young, but to the old lady, whom, but a moment before, I had seen place it on the younger's travelling-bag.

"My parasol!" screamed the old lady; but it was too late.

"Your parasol?" echoed the young one, aghast.

"Yes, mine; why do you throw other people's things out of the window, I should like to know?"

The new-comer blushed scarlet, and stammered forth —

"I beg your pardon . . . I took it for my friend's . . . I had it in my hand upon the platform . . . it is the same colour . . . I thought I had forgotten . . . I . . I . ." and here, probably struck at once by the retrospective ludicrousness of her action, the young lady burst out laughing.

"A witty trick, in fact, and worth a good deal of merriment," resumed my exasperated neighbour; "it may cost you dear, though."

It might have cost her her life, but the lady in black could not have stopped laughing. The fit was irresistible. She covered her face with her handkerchief, and fairly gave way.

I hazarded a word of extenuation. "Madam," said I to my neighbour, "there is no offence where there is no intention of giving any, and you know that laughing is a contraction of the diaphragm quite independent of the will."

"Much obliged to you for the information," said the old lady dryly; "but with your leave it is not explanations that I want, but my parasol."

"Take mine," said the offender, who had now recovered her seriousness and speech, "or set upon yours the price you think proper, and I will pay it down."

"I want my parasol, not yours, or your money," insisted the aggrieved party.

A bright idea, if not a new one, shot through my brain at this critical juncture — to telegraph for the parasol to the station at which it had been dropped, and desire it to be sent to that where the owner was to stop. The proposal, after a little demur, was acquiesced in by the old lady, who accordingly gave her name and address, — with a very ill grace, though; a guard was called, the mistake explained to him, a telegram concocted, and, on our arrival at the nearest station, duly despatched.

I need scarcely say that the conspicuous part I enacted in the transaction had won for me from my sweet-faced *vis-à-vis* many thanks and soft smiles — a coin, this last, of which I am very greedy, especially from gentle-looking faces.

"And my ticket?" cried the old lady on a sudden.

"What ticket?" asked we.

"My railway ticket," said she; "I had put it in the folds of my parasol."

"Hang the parasol and its folds," thought I; but I only said, "You will find it with the parasol."

"Ah, indeed!" sneered the hag, "and remain a prisoner at the station till the parasol arrives, if it ever does? No such thing. This young lady must have the goodness to accompany me to —— station, and there account for my missing ticket, or pay for it."

"I'll pay for it immediately," said the young lady.

"I told you I would have no money," replied the sour-visaged one; "besides, I don't know how much they may charge — perhaps the amount of the whole line."

"But I cannot go so far as —— station," protested the young lady, now ready to cry.

"We'll see," rejoined the other.

All the little chivalry still left in my old bones stood up in arms at sight of the dewdrops gathering in the sweet eyes, which had looked upon me so gratefully; and, acting upon the impulse of the moment, I turned to her and said, "Will you empower me to act as your representative in this affair?"

"With all my heart," said she.

"Then," continued I, addressing my ill-favoured neighbour, "I'll come with you as far as —— station, and settle about the ticket in the name of this lady."

"My business is with her, and not with you," was the ungracious answer.

"It will be, in fact, with the lady," I rejoined, "since I shall only act as her proxy. Consider, madam," I went on, "that, if you have an incontestable right to recover your ticket or its price, you have none to force her out of her way, probably to her great inconvenience. If you still object to my proposal, I shall

be obliged to put the matter in the hands of the first
station-master, or whatever authority we may meet in
our way, and vindicate for this young lady her liberty
of locomotion."

My little speech obtained no other answer than a
sarcastic grin, which left me in some apprehension of
a disagreeable scene when the moment should come
for the lady in black to leave the train. My anticipations in this respect were fortunately belied by the
event. My *protégée* was allowed to alight at her own
time and place — giving me previously her address,
that I might let her know what I paid, and cordially
shaking hands with me, and renewing her apologies to
the old lady — all this without the least opposition
from the latter, who, on the contrary, wished her all
manner of happiness with an ironical emphasis.

"Why don't you go too?" asked my neighbour,
just as the train was beginning to move on, abruptly
turning upon me a set of features made ten thousand
times uglier by concentrated malice.

"Why should I?" I replied, staring my questioner
in the face.

"Youth is so charming," said she; "you seemed
mightily interested in her."

"No more interested in that young lady than in
any other of my fellow-creatures whom I take to
be good, and to be in want of some protection,"
said I.

"No more than that?" sneered she. "Well, as I
lay no claim to goodness, and I am, thank God, in no
want of protection, the sooner we part company the
better."

"I have no wish to improve your acquaintance,"

said I; "the moment I have set you right with your ticket, you may rely on my readiest obedience to your suggestion."

She grinned her ugliest grin, and said, "You are very green for a man of your time of life. Do you suppose me such a goose as to put a ticket in the folds of a parasol? I only wanted to pay off the silly minx for her impertinence, by scaring her out of her wits. Here's my ticket — you may go."

"So I will. I beg you in the meantime to receive my compliments upon your ingenuity." So saying, I bowed, and removed to a further seat.

I can bear a good deal of heat — the day was close and sultry — but the presence of this extraordinary creature, after the incredible dialogue just reported, made the carriage too hot for me. I longed to be out of it. Besides, I was thirsty and hungry; and, having no determined destination, all places were alike to me, so that I could find wherewithal to eat and drink. Accordingly, down I jumped at the next station.

The flaxen hair and the harsh sounds round me made me forthwith sensible that I was still in some part of German Switzerland. I asked, in French, of one of my many fellow-travellers who had alighted at the same place with me, if there was any hotel near at hand. The answer was a rather harsh name, whose termination in *bad* was all that I could catch. I beckoned to a boy to carry my bag, and, by a very expressive pantomime, gave him a broad hint of my wish for a meal. The boy, with a knowing nod, as much as to say, "All right," repeated the word ending in *bad*, and moved on.

An omnibus was filling fast at the back of the station — most likely for this cabalistic *bad*, as I guessed. Unluckily, I reached it just in time to see the driver, a white-haired young man in a smock-frock, bang the door to, and climb up to his seat. So on I went under a broiling sun. We cut across some fields, crossed a road, struck through some fields again, crossed another road, and entered a shady avenue, on the right of which stood a finger-post with the inscription, "Schranksteinbad, two minutes." I am just enough of a German scholar to know that *Bad* means Baths, and I was not at all sorry to acquire the certainty that I was on my way to a Spa — perhaps the very quiet nook I was sighing after; who could tell? provided, I hastened to add *in petto*, all these folks before and behind me, and those that are in the omnibus, which seems coming this way, are not bent on the same destination; for, in that case, farewell quiet nook!

Another minute brought me in sight of the Establishment, a huge long building two storeys high. There were people walking about the grounds; there were people sitting at tables in the shade. A skittle-ground in full activity appeared on my left. Worst of all, snatches of spirited dancing-music now caught my ear. Alas! alas! it was not yet my phœnix. Lucky enough if I could secure a dinner without doing battle for it, as at the what-is-its-name Kulm!

The omnibus coming up briskly, I had to jerk out of the way in some hurry, and found myself cheek-by-jowl with a man, who stood by a horse harnessed to a gig, a little to the left of the avenue, in front of the house. The man struck me instantly by the strange conformation of his head. His, and that of the horse he stood by, presented as close a likeness as the head of a human being, and that of an animal, possibly can. The similarity at all events was such as to make me stop, all flushed with heat and hurry as I was, to look a while at this natural curiosity. In both creatures the same flatness and narrowness of the upper, the same development of the lower part of the facial angle, the same tawny hue, the same immobility of features! The biped only wanted the quadruped's ears to make them a perfect pair.

It took me some effort to detach myself from this sight, and proceed to the foot of the flight of steps, where a rather rickety waiter, and a pretty-looking chambermaid — such at least I took her to be — were doing the honours of the house to the load of visitors emerging from the omnibus.

"Can I have something to eat?" I asked of the maid, when my turn came.

"Certainly," said she; "shall I take your bag?"

"Thank you. I am not sure of stopping, but if you have a spare room for me, where I can wash my hands, I shall be obliged to you."

"All the Establishment is at your disposal," returned the chambermaid courteously; "be so good as to walk this way."

I followed her steps, and said, to sound the ground, "You are very busy, I see —"

"Always more or less so on Sundays," was the answer.

"Your house is full, I suppose?"

"Pardon me," she replied, with a good-natured smile; "quite empty."

"Do you mean to say that you have no boarders at all?"

"Just so; not one as yet."

"By Jove!" cried I; "then I stay."

"You'll bring us good luck, if you do," said she.

"But all these people about?" asked I.

"Birds of passage, sir; by nightfall they'll all be gone. Will you have a room on the first or the second floor, back or front, with or without a sofa?"

I pondered a little, and replied, "On the second floor, one in front, and with a sofa."

"The floor and the look-out make no difference in the charge," explained my conductress; "but the sofa does. We charge ten centimes a day extra for that. In the beginning, we had but few of them, and everybody would have one. Now that we have plenty, many people turn up their noses at them because of the extra centimes. That is why we warn strangers beforehand."

The primitiveness of the notion, with the extreme moderateness of the extra charge, made me anticipate a homely style in the other arrangements of the house, and corresponding prices.

"Will this room suit you?" inquired my attendant, opening one. It was a neat little cell with the simplest of furniture — a red sofa, three wooden chairs, a curtainless bed, with a big eider-down quilt upon it, a small writing-table in the shape of a half-moon, a square one for washing, and a closet in the wall, instead of a chest of drawers.

"This will do perfectly," said I. "Now, will you see to my dinner, please? Anything plain and good. I'll be down in ten minutes."

"Shall I lay the cloth in the large hall, or in the breakfast-room?"

"Never mind where, provided you wait upon me."

"Willingly," said she, with a curtsey; "we must make as much as we can of our first boarder. But, then, it must be in the large hall."

Thus chance, independent of my will, had led me by the hand to the haven, which all my industry had failed to secure.

CHAPTER II.

Ueli and Suldi.

I SUPPOSE it was the vein of optimism in which my good luck had put me that made me find the dinner excellent, my waiting-maid a paragon of obligingness, and the *coup d'œil* before me full of interest. Imagine a lofty hall with plenty of people in it, bustling about in couples, in groups, some few alone, the majority sitting down to their fritters or pancakes, their wine or coffee — imagine at the end of this hall, a lesser one, thronged with dancers, waltzing or galloping to the sound of merry music; and you can form an idea of the opera-comique-like scene which enlivened my dinner, and which, according to my fair informant, graced every summer Sunday the precincts of Schrank-steinbad. Its extensive grounds and capacious accommodation indoors made it, as it seems, the favourite resort of the youth of both sexes for twenty miles round. A wide balcony, set out with tables and benches, ran all the length of the two halls.

There was not much of the picturesque in the costumes, or of prepossessing in the mien, or of refined in the manners of the company, but something very taking in the *naïve* entireness of their enjoyment. The temple of Terpsichore, in spite of Jungfrau Madeleine's repeated attempts to entice me to it (Madeleine was the name of the pretty maid), looked too chokeful to be tempting; so I reserved my visit to it for another mo-

ment, and went out instead, in quest of a little corner
in the open air, where I could sip my coffee and have
my cigar — that indispensable complement to all joys
for a true smoker. I looked round from the threshold,
and — what was the first thing I saw? My man of an
hour ago, standing on the same spot, minding the
same, or another horse and gig (to the identity of the
two latter I could not have sworn), and staring before
him.

I took my place at one of the two tables which
flanked the wicket of a garden, on the left of the
avenue, in front of where he stood, so as to command
a full view of his face, and make it my study. This
time it was less its confirmed equine character, than its
stony impassivity, which struck me. There it remained
before me, like a shut book, a perfect negation of all
thought or feeling whatever. Much and closely as I
observed it, not the least trace of impatience or weariness was visible. And yet, one does not stand at the
head of a horse for an hour and a half, as he had done,
without feeling a little impatient, if the job be unusual,
or a little weary, if it be habitual. And that it was
the last, I rather surmised, from the long row of one-
horse carriages reaching from the door of the house to
the stables — a separate building at a little distance
on the right.

Was this impassivity acquired or natural, stoicism
or dulness? Whatever it was, I began to feel it somewhat grating to my nerves. The lie is not given to
the laws of nature in our very face, without calling
forth an instinctive protest. It is the fault of the mask,
I concluded at the end of another hour; the man, if
man he be, must be fretting inwardly; let us force an

answer from this Sphinx. And with this view I spoke to him in French, expressing a misgiving that the owner of the gig might perchance have had a fit of apoplexy. The answer was what, alas! I had too well anticipated — a negative shake of the head, and "I verstoh's nitt," in the most unmitigated patois of the country.

No means of penetrating to his understanding through oral communication! I regretted it; my curiosity in the man was piqued. However, one cannot get at the gift of languages, or rather of patois, at a moment's notice. I saw no other resource but to offer him a cigar. The action of smoking might possibly break somewhat that awful blank of features. He declined my cigar; "I rauch nitt." He did not smoke; how provoking!

But thou drinkest, surely, my good fellow, thought I to myself, and, being determined to burn my vessels, in I ran and came out the next minute with a bumper of wine, which I offered to him. But I had reckoned without my host. "Danke, I trink kee wee." Here was a phenomenal Swiss indeed, one who neither smoked nor drank! At the same moment, a heavy-booted young farmer, the owner it might be of my man's gig, came down the steps of the establishment, and, going up to him at the head of the horse, gave him a string of guttural reasons, I suppose for keeping him waiting so long, which the other received with perfect calm, saying several times, "Jo, jo." After which, the young farmer went back into the house, and my neighbour resumed his passive attitude. For the nonce I lost patience, and, hurling at him an irate "blockhead," *in petto*, I got up and went away.

On my way to the hall, I met Jungfrau Madeleine, and questioned her about this man. She guessed immediately whom I meant: "He looks very odd, does he not?" and she went on to say that it was Ueli, the cowherd, also the overseer of the labourers; on Sundays he gave a hand to the stable boys; in fact, he made himself useful in all ways and at all times. Such was the substance of the information I got about this man, and in course of which I further learnt an important collateral fact, namely, that my informant and her brother Frantz were the owners of Schrankstein-bad, and of a good deal of adjoining land, which they themselves farmed; upon which I offered Jungfrau Madeleine my best apologies for having taken her for, and treated her as, a chambermaid. She answered, good-humouredly, that she hoped I would still treat her as such. She was, in fact, she said, to all practical ends and purposes, a chambermaid, and a cook, when necessary, to boot.

The character given to Ueli by my informant only served to plunge me anew into the slough of puzzle out of which I had helped myself by writing him down a blockhead. If he was not such, as evidenced by the duties he fulfilled, and the willing readiness with which he made himself useful, if he had his share of intellective and affective capabilities, by what strange perversion of physiognomic and psychologic laws was it, that nothing of the kind should ooze out of his looks? Was he playing a part? The hypothesis was inadmissible. Was he, unknown to all, under the incubus of some great misfortune? But then his countenance would bear witness to it by some sort of forlorn or stunned, or ghastly expression, while what I was finding fault with was exactly the absence of all expression.

At this point of my speculation, I could not help laughing outright at the idea of my making such a fool of myself about this cowherd of Schranksteinbad. What did it matter to me, in fact, whether he was a sphinx or an ass?

Jungfrau Madeleine had repeatedly urged me to go and have a look at the dancing-room. Besides being, perhaps, fond of dancing on her own account, Jungfrau Madeleine, as co-proprietress of the establishment, had her bit of legitimate pride in her hall, her music, and, for the time being, her crowd. Of this last item, there was no lack in the dancing-room — it was crammed to suffocation; and, had I consulted my convenience, I would, on the instant, have turned my back on it. But I was there for conscience' sake, and there I stayed.

I cannot say that I much enjoyed the sight. I confess to a sad deficiency in my organization. Dancing, as a means conducive to some end — to augment the caloric of one's body, for instance, or to exchange a few words with a pretty lass — I can readily conceive, and I have sometimes practised in my youth; but dancing, as an end in itself — that is, for its own sake — what could be the enjoyment of it I never could bring myself to understand, especially with a temperature of 90° Fahrenheit in the shade. But on this, as on many other points, I bow to universal consent, and — hold my tongue.

The room, though very capacious, was small in proportion to the number of amateurs; hence frequent stoppages, loss of the musical time, and collisions, with now and then a fall. The cavaliers, generally heavy and grave-looking, a sprinkle of them with hats on, or cigars in their mouths! The few more light and lively had a perverse knack of twisting their fair partners' arms into impossible postures, and also occasionally indulging in a sudden noisy thump with the heel of the boot, accompanied by a shrill shout, unmistakably to their own satisfaction, and seemingly to that of the public. This must be said for the dancers in general, that, good, bad, or indifferent, solemn or lively-looking, whirling round, or stretched on the ground by a false step, each and all of them, in unpretending simplicity of heart, enjoyed the sport to a high degree.

I loitered another moment in the hall, and then went out by a back-door adjoining the kitchen, and, in less than ten minutes, I was out of reach of all bustle and noise, and in as private a *tête-à-tête* with Mother Nature as one could wish. Behind the establishment stretched a cosy little dale — green as an emerald *in l'ora che si fiacca* (but newly broken) would Dante say; a dale hemmed in on all sides, like a cradle, by soft, round velvet-looking mamelons of pasture, or gently receding hillocks topped with firs and Italian pines. Here I lay down on the grass in the shade, within sound of the hum of a brook, and spent a delicious hour in a solitary reverie.

Then curiosity pushed me to go and see whether Ueli was still where I had left him, and whether there had dawned or not on his countenance anything like incipient animation or feeling. There stood my man in charge of a horse and carriage, as before, and, as before, all of one piece and impassive — the very picture of unconcerned fate in shirt-sleeves and stiff shirt-

collar. I took a lounge in the garden after supper.
Ueli was at his post, the same deadlock on his features.
I looked down from my window, before going to bed,
and I saw the black silhouette of Ueli against the
garden gate, where I had first set eyes on his face five
hours before. And the first thing I saw next morning
— the first, I should say, after the Alps, the beautiful
Alps, towering in all their glory in front of me — was
Ueli.

He was crouching on all-fours upon a plank thrown
over one of the two little pieces of artificial water before my window, and examining something very closely.
I must explain that my room formed one of the corners
of a projecting sort of gable in the centre of the building. It had, consequently, the advantage of a double
prospect; my side window looked over the avenue and
the garden already mentioned, my front one over two
small pieces of water gracefully set in a double oval
border of flowers and dwarf acacias. I immediately
guessed what kind of work Ueli was bent upon just
then. Two of the yesterday's customers, Madeleine
had informed me — overheated, let us charitably say,
by the dance — had chosen to wade their way towards
home through the cooling reservoirs, and, in doing so,
had damaged the *jets d'eau*, which Ueli was about to
repair. I took up immediately my opera glass, and
brought it to bear on his face — it was as dumb and
meaningless as ever.

I sallied forth on an exploration of my verdant
island. Madeleine had spoken truly; it was all my own.
All the throng of Sunday visitors had vanished by ten
at night, and I was the only inmate of the establishment. Well then, out I went, and — *Di pensiero in*

pensier, di monte in monte — I had a three hours' delightful ramble over hill and plain, through forest and pasture, along sweetly prattling rivulets, across meadows azure with *vergissmeinnicht*. Let scribblers in prose and verse do their worst by it, they never will succeed in unpoetizing the blue-eyed floweret. I buried myself among the blossoms, I rolled over them, I gathered loads of them. My next treat was a gentle fall of rain which overtook me on my way home. Do you know any sweeter music than the pattering of the drops on the leaves; can you dream of a more delicious sensation than the feeling of the soft dew on hands and face; or of a perfume equal to the scent of moistened earth?

Scouts were watching for me, I suppose, for I was no sooner in sight of the establishment than a tremendous peal of the bell announced *urbi et orbi* that the corps of boarders, incarnate just then in my person, was going to sit down to breakfast. You may imagine whether I did honour to it. Truth to say, the cooking might have been better, the forks of silver instead of steel, the chairs soft-cushioned rather than of slippery polished wood. I was within an ace of sliding off mine at one moment, and rolling underneath the table, without being conscious of having done anything to that end. But who could think of such small deficiencies after the joys of a ramble like mine, and with the snowy Alps in prospect all the while?

Other shortcomings I discovered in course of time, happily none trenching upon my personal comfort. The system of bed-room bells, for instance, left something to desire. First of all, they did not ring nine times out of ten. This was no inconvenience to me, who

never ring the bell, but go and fetch what I want.
There was room for improvement also in the bathing
department. The primitive wooden baths, much like
troughs, were so flat, that a bather at all afflicted with
embonpoint must give up hope of all his person lying
under water at one moment. Fortunately I am lean,
and I can manage very well with a modest depth of
water.

The day proved too hot for me to venture out of
doors. Accordingly, I did not see Ueli till near 6 P.M.,
and then in his own domain, the cow-house. I may
premise that here, as frequently in the valleys of
Switzerland, the cows are confined to the stable
during the whole season, while the grass is growing in
the open pastures, and the crops are standing in the
unenclosed ground. So here was Ueli, in the active
exercise of his functions, milking fourteen rather closely-
ranged superb animals.

Milking even fourteen cows is not a very trying
task; but doing so after mowing and carting fresh grass
enough for this number of terrible consumers (as I
afterwards perceived that Ueli did each day twice) is
warm work indeed, especially in a sweltering cow-
house. No wonder then that the veins in the man's
forehead and neck were swelled to the size of whipcord,
and the perspiration trickled down his face and breast.
Yet all this exertion imparted no animation to the negative features.

The process though might have had its interest,
had it been gone through by a man, and not by an
automaton. Ueli, tying methodically every cow's tail
to her leg previous to beginning operations, and having
not unfrequently to get up in order to swing back the

whisking brush into its hempen ring; Ueli milking
away on his milking-stool, a kind of rustic tripod,
would have been a sight worth paying for, but for that
unnatural screw, exclusive of all earthly sympathy, on
his face.

Jungfrau Madeleine in the evening gave me a few
scraps of Ueli's biography. Ueli, the patois for Ulrich,
was born in the Bernese Oberland. He spoke little,
but always to the point, and had a turn for fun. He
was a married man. He had made his matrimonial
choice, apparently, as many others have done, in a
moment of aberration; for he never alluded to his wife
but as to a babe, only fit to wear finery, and with a
sort of compassionate smile. As a workman he was
very industrious, and remarkably clever with his hands,
but very slow. Clashing as they did with all my observations of the man, these particulars were only calculated to puzzle me the more.

Returning next day from my early morning walk,
I happened to pass by the barn, a separate building
on the right of the establishment, and containing the
stables and the cow-house. I had already remarked in
one of its dependencies a carpenter's workshop with
fitting tools. As I walked by it this particular morning, my ear caught the monotonous burden of a tune,
not more musical than the buzz of a drone, which
came from the workshop. I cast my eyes into it, and
saw Ueli, plane in hand, smoothing a·plank and
humming a song. He looked up at me — judge of
my infinite surprise — with the shade of a shadow of
a smile hovering about his mouth, and returned my
"Guten Tag, Ueli," with a distinct "Guten Tag,
Herr —," pronouncing my name correctly. The

frozen features had positively thawed, the blank look was replaced by a faint gleam of self-consciousness and fellow-feeling. I was wonder-struck. What could be the occasion of this revolution? Who the Pygmalion of this statue? And in I hastened to gather data, if any could be gathered, for the solution of this new riddle.

A fine large dog, black as jet, lay stretched at full length across the threshold, sunning himself. I had no choice, in order to enter the house, but to stride over him, which I did, greatly to the quadruped's displeasure, as it seemed, inasmuch as, without deigning to budge, he set up a powerful growl like distant thunder. "What dog is that?" I asked, entering the kitchen. The kitchen, be it known, was Jungfrau Madeleine's head-quarters, and the ordinary theatre of our interviews. There was something amiss in Madeleine's generally smooth brow. She was busy plucking live pigeons' heads with the same neatness and delicacy as she would have picked roses or daisies.

"It is Suldi," said she, "our house-dog." (Suldi is patois for Sultan.)

"He seems a disagreeable customer," I observed; "he growled at me most ominously."

"Did he? I was sure he would. I wanted to warn you about the dog. Not that he bites — he never did, but he frightens people, children especially, when he is out of sorts. And he is always so, when he has fits of pain. A cart went over him when he was a puppy, and sorely damaged one of his forelegs. He is naturally very good-tempered, but, when he suffers . . . he is only a dog, you know. As it is, he has given us a deal of trouble already."

"How is it," I asked, "that I never saw him till now?"

"He was not here," was the answer; "he arrived late last night with Frantz, my brother. You must know that we had made up our minds to get rid of him. A public establishment, with hosts of children in the season, is not the place for a dog that is growing fitful. He was not so till a year or two ago. So we made up our mind to get rid of him — not by having him killed, understand; we had not the heart for that. We brought him up from a puppy, we tended him when he was all but crushed, and one gets attached to animals as well as to human beings. And then Ueli is fond of Suldi — he has not been himself ever since the dog went away — very fond, and he would never consent to his being put to death. So Frantz took Suldi with him to the Canton of Vaud, where he went to make a purchase of wine from the purveyor of the house in that article, an old friend, and who had volunteered to receive the dog and take charge of him. Now this friend, I am sorry to say, on seeing him and his ways, changed his mind; and there's Suldi on our hands again."

I must say thus much in compliment to my penetration, that I had no sooner cast eyes on Suldi, than the surmise had flashed through my mind, of his having something to do with Ueli's resurrection. Madeleine's mention of the cowherd's fondness for the dog, and of his opposition to the bare idea of his being put to death, changed my surmise into certainty. So here was the solution of the new enigma. The Pygmalion of the statue was no other than Suldi. Had any doubts on the matter remained in my mind, they would have been dispelled by a scene I witnessed in the evening of the same day — a scene that passed, about nine o'clock, in front of the barn, between Ueli and Suldi. Words cannot describe that which was a perfect dialogue in barking on one side, in guttural sounds on the other — a positive whirlwind of mad joy at being once again together — an interchange of all the endearments that a man can convey to a beast, a beast to a man.

Suldi having been my companion in many a walk, I was able to ascertain from personal observation the perfect truth of the character given him by Madeleine. Not only was Suldi not a wicked, he was positively a good and gentle and loving dog, anything but aggressive, nay, rather timid. But, as Madeleine wisely said, he was only a dog; and when his fits of pain seized him, which they did at every change of weather, no one could approach or brush by him without his growling rather unpleasantly. But I do not hesitate to assert my firm belief, that Suldi was incapable of attacking anybody, least of all children, save under strong provocation. Suldi was a noble-looking dog, powerful, brisk, and even graceful. The accident he had met with in his puppy-hood had left a slight limp in his gait.

Though Ueli's happy return to the condition of common mortality slackened, if not my interest in the man, at least my observation of him, he still attracted enough of my notice to make me sensible of the place held by Suldi in the cowman's life. Suldi was Ueli's paramount interest, the mainspring of his intelligence, his source of inspiration. Whenever Suldi was out of Ueli's sight for any considerable time (Frantz generally

took the dog with him to town on market days) the
cowman's features grew stony as of old, to revive the
moment his black friend's powerful form loomed from
afar.

Constant close communication did not appear to be
a necessity of this singular friendship. As long as
Ueli and Suldi were within sight of each other, even
at a certain distance — nay, more: as long ·as they
knew that they were within easy reach, though without
seeing each other — this was enough to make them be
and look happy.

It has amused me more than once to watch Ueli
leave his cowhouse to go a few paces to the left, where
he could command a view of the flight of steps of the
house door, and, having ascertained that Suldi was at
his post, return to his domain quite contented. Likewise,
I frequently happened to see Suldi get up all of a
sudden from a slumber in front of the establishment,
go cautiously to the cowhouse, and having satisfied
himself that Ueli was there, return to his post, with a
scarcely perceptible wag of his tail. There seemed to
exist between the two a tacit agreement to dissemble,
during broad day, the depth and extent of their affection — at least there were few outward signs of it.
Perhaps Suldi, like the intelligent watch-dog he was,
felt that he had responsible duties to perform —
squatting in front of the house, and barking at strangers
— upon which even friendship ought not to intrude;
and Ueli on his side understood and respected the
scruples of his fourfooted friend, and had some such
for himself. However this may be, the fact is that
man and dog only met on terms of unreserved demonstrativeness of an evening at dusk, in front of the

barn. It was a regular rendezvous, more or less long, but always remarkably expansive; after which Ueli retired to his room above the cowhouse, and Suldi took up his watch round the premises.

Most of the particulars I register here in a lump were of course the fruit of observations scattered over many days. It is simply in the interest of brevity and unity that I have so far deviated from chronologic order. Now to return. My island was all my own but for three days. On the fourth, Hans, the white-haired youth, deputed to drive the omnibus to the station *pro formâ*, and to drive it back as empty as it had gone, brought, to his great surprise, three passengers on his return — a lady, her little girl, and an elderly gentleman. The spell thus once broken, each consecutive day had its fresh arrivals, till, at the end of the week, we were two-and-twenty at table, a bare fifth of them mature gentlemen, the rest matrons, young ladies and children.

This influx of strangers did not cause me any uneasiness, for the style of the house and that of the new comers, as far as I could judge, gave me the best guarantee against the only great nuisance I could not put up with—I mean an invasion of town fashion, with all the absurdities, restraints, and scotches, that move in its train. And, then, by this time I knew Schranksteinbad enough, to be sure that I could here, under any circumstances, secure my three modest desiderata, — air, space, and privacy.

As the first boarder of the season, I was *de jure* and *de facto* the chairman, and sat as such at the head of the table. My immediate neighbours were, on my right, the little girl and her mother; on my left,

the elderly gentleman, the first arrivals after me. The
elderly gentleman, evidently a choleric one, was too
much taken up by eating, and grumbling at what he
ate, to have much time to give to conversation — save
when his wrath at some great culinary incongruity
sought relief in speech, and he would turn to me with
such an observation, for instance, as "could a cook in
his senses ever boil trout of this size! why, even that
child," looking across the table, "could tell that a
trout under half a pound is only eatable when fried."
Entertaining no settled opinion on the point myself, I
made no difficulty in agreeing with him that trout
under half a pound were destined *ab æterno* to be fried.
And there was an end of the colloquy.

With my next neighbour but one on the right, the
mother of the little girl, I could only communicate by
signs and good-natured nods and smiles, she speaking
no language but German. There remained the little
girl, seated between her mother and me, who spoke
both German and French; and so to her I turned.
We had made friends at once on the very day of her
arrival. I had met her labouring up the stairs with a
jug of warm water held between her tiny hands. I
took it from her to put it down at her mother's door
— the next room to mine. Shortly after a pattering
of little feet stopped at my door; then came a rap, and
vain efforts to lift the latch. I opened it, and there
stood the little curly cherub, come to thank me from
her mother for the help I had given.

I asked the little creature her name.

"Louisa," was the answer.

"A pretty name," said I.

"I will write it for you," she said, glancing at a
pen I held in my hand. "Can you write?"

I said I could a little.

"Well, so can I too, but only my name;" and,
walking deliberately to my table, she took up a pen
and dashed off an enormous charming LOUISA, and put
it gravely into my hands with "For you."

"Thank you; but do not go yet; let us have a
little talk."

She could not stay; she had her knitting and her
sampler to do, also her letters to learn. It was delightful to see the little important pout on her face, as she
enumerated the occupations which stood in the way of
her remaining with me. She promised she would come
again, if mamma would let her, and then she would
write fresh autographs for me. And so she did; for
this chance visit paved the way to many others, which
led to a closer intimacy.

We became great friends in no time. Louisa introduced me to all her dolls and playthings, initiated
me into all her little interests, but stoutly denied me
the title of her "little friend," which I besought. I
should be her big friend, if I liked, because I was big;
but a little friend she had already — a boy named
Robert — and she would have but one. I see her still,
her curly black head a little on one side, a pen between her tiny fingers, gravely scribbling her name,
and stopping now and then to look up at me, with her
large dark eyes full of interest and wonder, as I told
her the story of a hen who had swallowed lucifer
matches, and threw forth flames from her beak.

I cannot look at her autographs to this day — I
have plenty of them, done especially on rainy days —

without a thrill of tenderness. I doated on her; we doated on her; we were all her slaves. None could resist her spell, not even the choleric gentleman of the fried trout. Her gentle presence filled and enlivened the whole house; Louisa was the sunbeam, the rainbow, the charm, the pride of Schranksteinbad. Louisa was the essence of grace — a squirrel, a humming-bird, are awkward in comparison. Whatever she did, whatever she said, whatever she put on, she made a jewel of. When she went, as she used to do, and took the new arrivals by the hand, to bring them towards the company, saying, "Come, and make friends," even the most morose must needs brighten and smile. When, of an evening, worn-out by the day's sport, she would nestle into a corner of the sofa, and presently drop into slumber, a circle on tiptoe would form around the sleeping beauty, in admiration of the easy graceful *pose*, the long velvety eyelashes, the round hanging arms, or the gently crossed hands, and every one would exclaim *sotto voce*, "What a pity there is no photographist to take her picture so!"

Well, absorbed in my new passion, I had for some time almost forgotten Ueli and Suldi too, when my attention was forced back to them. Chancing one morning to pass before the workshop already mentioned, I caught sight of both of them in it, engaged in the strangest of occupations. Ueli, his shirt-sleeves tucked up to his shoulder, was presenting to Suldi's mouth, nay, forcing into it, his naked arm, exciting him all the while, with voice and gesture, to bite it. Suldi, on his side, entering fully into the spirit of what he supposed to be play, was pretending to snatch and tear at the flesh with might and main, though he left on it

no worse result than the innocuous white impress of
his teeth. Ueli looked too much in earnest to be
sporting; and yet, short of sudden madness, how suppose the man bent on getting himself bitten by the
animal? I knew not what to make of the scene; it
was the more unaccountable from a short phrase that
Ueli kept repeating with a ring of triumph. "Er bisst
nitt" was the phrase. Now, chancing to know, as I
did, that *biss* meant *bite* and *biting*, it needed no great
effort to translate the words into English, "He bites
not." But this did not help me at all to the significa-
tion of what I was witnessing.

The second bell, announcing breakfast, had long
rung, and I was half an hour past my time. I hurried
in accordingly, and, passing before the kitchen, I
thrust in my head, as usual, to wish Jungfrau Madeleine good-day. She was in tears.

"What is the matter?" I asked.

"Suldi has bitten Louisa," was she sobbing answer.

"Merciful heavens! Louisa bitten!"

The blood froze in my veins, and I sprang towards
the breakfast-room.

It presented the aspect of a sea in a tempest, but
I had no eyes but for Louisa. She lay coiled up in
her mother's lap on the sofa, as unconsciously graceful
in her paleness and tears, as she used to be in her
merriest moods. Two big drops stood on each cheek,
like dew on a white rose. Spent with emotion, she
was ready to fall asleep. I knelt down before her to
put my face on a level with hers. "Oh, my poor
child, what is it?" Louisa undid her wrapped hand,
and held it up to me. I saw the bloody marks of four

teeth on her right wrist. It was a slight wound, but, slight as it might be, a dog's bite is always a terrible thing. Who can think of the possible consequences without shuddering? I felt a knot rise in my throat; with the motion of a little kitten, Louisa put her left arm round my head, and drawing it to her, whispered gently, "Suldi is a naughty dog, but don't let him be killed."

In fact, at the moment cries not a few of "Death to Suldi," rose from the company, from the softer sex especially. Of these Louisa and her mother were alone for mercy. Poor Frantz, the only responsible power present, stood in the centre of an excited circle, a target to a German and French cross-fire of interpellations, objurgations, remonstrances, and threats of a general departure of the boarders in a body, if an example was not made of the culprit. The choleric gentleman, true to his temperament, stormed louder than all the rest together. He said it was a shame that lots of children should be enticed to a public establishment to be mangled in that way, that the police ought to interfere, that the legislature ought to be appealed to.

Nobody, as agreed on all sides, had witnessed the fatal deed, Louisa's mother and Jungfrau Madeleine being the first persons attracted to the spot by the child's cries. Yet, there were two versions current already as to the manner in which the catastrophe had been brought about. According to the first, Louisa had not so much as brushed by the animal crouching across the threshold, when he had attacked and bitten her. According to the second, backed and abetted by the majority of mothers, possessing children less popular than Louisa, this latter had given great provocation

to the dog by treading upon his tail. How they could
know she had, or had not done so, when, by common
agreement, no soul was present, none stopped to inquire.
Louisa, who could alone unloose this gordian knot,
candidly confessed to being so frightened at hearing
Suldi growl at her, when she passed by him, that she
could not tell whether she had done or not done anything to hurt him. As to me, my firm conviction was
and remains to this day, that Louisa trod on Suldi's
tail. Suldi, as I hinted before, was not the dog to bite
any one, least of all a child, without strong provocation. But this is nothing to the point.

The arrival of the doctor, fetched instantly from
the nearest village, considerably allayed the general
excitement. He examined the wound, declared it to
be a mere scratch, which would heal in a day or two,
put a little plaster upon it, cut a joke or two at Louisa,
and moved to go away. A covert hint at the possibility of the dog being mad, thrown out by the choleric
gentleman, the physician dismissed first with laughter,
and then with a grave assurance that Suldi was as
healthy a dog as could be, who ate and drank heartily,
as the doctor had seen just now.

Upon this, Louisa was carried up to her room by
her reassured mother; those of the company who had
not yet breakfasted, I among others, fell to their toast
and coffee; those who had, went out to their several
avocations. No idler remained in the room, but Frantz
and the choleric gentleman in close confabulation in a
distant corner. "Now then," I heard the latter say
after a while, motioning to Frantz to go with him.
"Now then," repeated Frantz in his turn, going. I

scented a tragedy in the wind, and followed at their heels.

"Ueli!" shouted Frantz, from the threshold of the house door. Ueli instantly obeyed the summons, followed closely by Suldi. I sought in vain on Ueli's features for any, the least trace of emotion of any kind. Nature had cast his countenance in so stiff a mould, and kneaded it in so opaque a clay, that strong indeed must be the feeling to pierce its way through it. There was nothing of the kind at work for the present; only a shade of embarrassment, as I apprehended from the long straw he held in his mouth, and used as a toothpick, instinctively with a view to give himself countenance. Such was at least my conjecture; but I might be mistaken. As to Suldi, there was no mistaking the consciousness of guilt, which weighed on his head and tail, both humbly seeking the ground.

Frantz, with a few words to Ueli, who responded "Jo," led the way to the kitchen. The choleric gentleman was there already, his legs wide apart, his hands behind his back, his back to the stoves, in the classic *pose* of a gentleman airing himself at the fire. Frantz took up his station at the big table in the middle of the room; Ueli half sat upon it, one foot resting on the floor, both confronting the choleric gentleman. Between them squatted the accused, his tail towards the latter, his head against the cowman. Jungfrau Madeleine and I, on the other side of the big table, completed the court-martial.

The proceedings being carried on in the local German, I could only get such an outline of them as my interpreter, Madeleine, could convey in a hurried whisper. They did not take long. The choleric gentleman, in a few concise phrases, began by demanding, in the name of the corps of boarders, the culprit's head. Frantz stated as briefly his acquiescence in the demand, and, turning to Ueli, asked him if he had anything to say for his client. Ueli, chewing his straw with the utmost indifference, answered "Nothing." "The heartless wretch," whispered I to Madeleine, "how coolly he sacrifices his friend!"

"Don't believe it," said she, nudging me by the elbow. "Ueli has something in his head."

Ueli in the meantime had risen up, taken Suldi by the collar, and moved towards the door. Frantz and the choleric gentleman did as much, and so did Madeleine and I. Ueli, once in the passage, halted and stooped to mend, or pretend to mend, something wrong in the dog's collar. This delayed him a few seconds, during which, Frantz and the choleric gentleman, passing by Ueli, came to the foot of the staircase leading up to the apartments inhabited by the boarders. Here the choleric gentleman stopped, and after a short further exchange of words, went up the staircase.

In the same instant, Ueli rose from his stooping posture, seized Frantz by the flap of his coat, towed him back to the kitchen, swept in Madeleine and me, who were the last to come out, and shut the door. Then in a confidential, nay, cajoling undertone, of which I should never have thought him capable, he said, "I'll tell you what *we'll* do (how I admired that *we*); *we'll* put Suldi out of the way until *der Herr* and the children are gone." Frantz met this unexpected proposal with a shake of the head, as much as to say, "It won't do."

The inarticulate objection was instantly overruled

by Ueli. "I know of a place up the mountains," said he, "where he will be as good as buried. I'll take him there at once." Still Frantz's head moved objectingly. Ueli pursued with a certain solemnity, "We must not spill the blood of any of God's creatures, except in a case of absolute necessity, and here there's none such. Trust him to me; he'll never show his face at Schranksteinbad again, I answer for it, till bidden to do so."

"And if he does?" put in Frantz.

"He won't — but, if he does, — well, then we'll have done with him." Thanks to Ueli's laconism and slow utterance, and to Jungfrau Madeleine's rapidity of translation, I lost not a syllable of the dialogue.

Frantz looked hesitating; as to me, being won over as I was to mercy's side, ever since I had heard it advocated by Louisa and her mother, I took upon myself to suggest to Mr. Frantz the advisability of having a regard to the recommendations of the two really injured parties. Though expressed in French, my appeal, its sense at least, was perfectly understood by Ueli, who rewarded me for it by a grin and a grunt expressive of gratitude. The counsels of clemency prevailed at last. Frantz was a hot-headed, but a soft-hearted fellow; besides, he was fond of the dog. In short, Ueli's request was granted on condition that the dog should be off within an hour. "And if he ever comes back!" added Frantz with an ominous gesture. Ueli wasted no time in vain protests, but hurried to his cow-house in company with the exile, put on his Sunday clothes, and both departed.

All this did not exactly give me the key of the strange scene I had seen enacted in the workshop.

Was Ueli drilling Suldi not to bite under provocation? Was he nursing himself into the delusion that a dog who could resist such a strong temptation to bite could not have bit anybody? Probably Ueli knew not himself.

It was not yet ten o'clock in the morning, when Ueli and Suldi made their exit through the avenue. All Schranksteinbad was on the look-out to see justice done, and all Schranksteinbad had the satisfaction of seeing the culprit, as they thought, on his last leg. A satisfaction, though not unmixed with pity! A knot of young ladies could not stand the melancholy sight, and looked another way. An elderly lady was heard to say to her daughter, that it was very hard. Another cried shame upon the family, who could thus sacrifice an old servant in cool blood. But no one did as much as lift a little finger practically to help the poor fellow out of jeopardy. All stood in awe of the choleric gentleman — the Tiberius of this persecution — and then you know the proverb, "Give a dog a bad name, and —"

Suldi's execution was the talk of the establishment for the rest of the day, still in the presence of Louisa and her mother the subject was universally avoided, and, when actively broached by either, it was met by charitable professions of ignorance or uncertainty of what might have become of the delinquent — a delicacy which tells much for the good-nature of the company. Louisa, by the bye, on the afternoon of this very day, was skipping and playing about the grounds as brisk as ever. Ueli's return at the end of the third day revived the topic for a short hour; his laconic answer to all questions about the dog, "he is quite safe," reconfirmed the general impression that Suldi had seen his last of this world. Another week, and poor Suldi had passed away into a mere legend, which was handed down, augmented and embellished, from the old set of children to new ones.

Schranksteinbad by this time, the first week in July, was at the height of its glory; we mean crammed to the garrets. No less than fifty-three boarders sat down every day to table in the large hall — thirty-one matrons and young ladies (half a dozen of these last, beautiful creatures), fifteen children, with a sprinkle of mature gentlemen, seven in number. We had dancing regularly every second night up to as late an hour as ten o'clock; the great scarcity of cavaliers was no check upon the sport, the ladies willingly taking each other for partners. The best understanding prevailed among the company, and various little flirtations enlivened the flitting hour. It was a small Arcadia. Frantz, as well he might, looked busy, proud, and radiant. Jungfrau Madeleine, almost out of her wits to satisfy all the demands pouring in upon her, spun round and round like a top all day.

Well, it was the sixteenth of July — I shall not easily forget that date — a very hot day it was. It might be half-past one o'clock in the afternoon. We had just done dining — the dinner hour was twelve — and were most of us sitting at our coffee under the thick-clipped silver poplars in front of the house; the children, unmindful of the sun, were at their games, sometimes in, sometimes out of sight, in the lawn yonder, on the right of the avenue. Conversation was languishing, and many an eyelid drooped under the influence of the hour, when we were startled out of

our drowsiness by the loudest of terrified screams ever
raised by ten infantine throats at one time.

A responsive scream and a rush forward of the
mothers. "What is it? what is it?" was the agitated
question of the elder party. "Suldi, Suldi," was the
cry of the fugitive little ones, Louisa foremost, still
rushing on with her companions. I am sorry to say
it, but I say it because it is the truth, the name of
Suldi, and more than that, the black silhouette of
Suldi standing in relief against the white track of the
avenue, spread such a panic in the motherly ranks,
that they instantly joined in the flight of the children,
and never stopped till they were all inside the house,
nay, up the stairs to the first storey. I need scarcely
say that we of the strong sex present, four in number,
including the narrator, did our duty by the fair ones,
first rushing forwards at their heels, then trying to stop
their mad race back, and at last covering their retreat
from the enemy — an enemy who, truth to say, looked
anything but dangerous. Poor Suldi, evidently scared
by the confusion he had created, limped on slowly
and cautiously, stopped now and then, and, whether
standing still or moving on, wagged his tail most con-
ciliatingly.

The alarm raised by the fugitives had brought the
whole household to the front door, Frantz included. I
saw him, at sight of Suldi, strike his forehead with
his clenched fist, then withdraw for an instant, and re-
appear gun in hand. Suldi no sooner saw the gun,
than he galloped away towards the cow-house. The
uncouth figure of Ueli was standing on the threshold;
Suldi sprang towards him, put his front paws on his

shoulders, and began licking his friend's face. Frantz
was upon them in a twinkling.

"Get out of the way," thundered Frantz to Ueli.

"I can't, I won't," cried Ueli.

"I'll blow your brains out if you don't," shouted
enraged Frantz.

"Do," answered Ueli, coolly, drawing the dog
closer to himself.

Frantz was exasperated; nobody can say what might
have been the consequences, if Madeleine in tears,
some of the boarders, and myself, had not interfered.
We succeeded in wringing the gun out of the maddened man's hands, while Madeleine was parleying
with Ueli. Ueli had no rebellious intentions. He
knew what he had promised, and stuck by it, only he
wanted to *do* it himself, he said, and not there.

"Will you *do* it really?" asked Frantz.

"I will."

"Upon your honour?"

"Upon my honour," affirmed the cowman, with a
motion of the right hand not wanting in nobility. Upon
this understanding Ueli was left alone, and retired with
Suldi into the cow-house. He came out of it almost immediately, looked about him for a few seconds, as if
irresolute, then struck across the fields, shunning the
avenue. His face was turned to the plain, towards the
river. He is going to drown him, thought I; the
solemnity with which Ueli had pledged himself to *do*
it, left no doubt, in my mind, as to his determination.
Drowning excluded the necessity of spilling blood, a
decisive consideration, in my mind, in favour of that
mode of execution; then, he had no weapon about him,
that I could see, not even a cudgel.

So long as they were in the grounds of the establishment, Suldi walked thoughtfully and cautiously along, turning occasionally round to see whether they were followed. The consciousness was evidently upon him that he had had a very narrow escape. But, as soon as he had crossed the road and the railway, Suldi became demonstrative, jumping for joy, barking, and barring Ueli's progress. Ueli neither encouraged nor discouraged this display of feeling; he only turned Suldi out of his own way, when necessary, and walked on fast.

We had almost all the breadth of the vale to cross in order to get to the river. It was a treeless valley, as flat as the palm of my hand, all meadows and pastures — no possible concealment even for a rabbit. Did Ueli see me following in his wake, or did he not? I don't know. If he saw me, which most likely he did, he made as though he did not. Not once did he turn his head towards me. From the day I had raised my voice in behalf of his *protégé*, I had won Ueli's heart. Even if Jungfrau Madeleine had not told me so, I should have guessed it from his never passing me without putting on what he believed his best smile, and saluting me by name.

Half-an-hour's forced march took us to the river. It was swollen by the melting of the snow — a mighty, deep, fast-darting river, with ominous eddies in the middle. Ueli sat on its raised bank, and looked down for a moment. Apparently the spot was not deep and rapid enough, for he got up and walked along the path under the stunted old willows, that darkened the water. He presently found what he wanted, and sat down

again. Suldi sat down too between Ueli's legs, his
head against Ueli's face.

The two friends looked closely at each other for
some time; then Ueli spoke. My hiding-place, behind
a tree, was near enough to hear, unfortunately, without understanding, every word he uttered, but too far
to perceive the play of his countenance. The tone of
voice was, by turns, chiding, deprecating, and tender.
I fancied that he was scolding Suldi for his dis-
obedience, which had brought them both to this pass;
that he was explaining and begging pardon for the
part of executioner he had assumed, and taking an
affectionate farewell of him. A plaintive cry of Suldi,
during the chiding period, drew forth from Ueli a passionate outburst of sensibility. It was as if I heard
him say — Oh yes, I understand what thou sayest;
thy great love of me it was that made thee come back;
I know that thou couldst not stand any longer to be
separated from thy Ueli. And I, dost thou think that
I had an easy time of it? I did nothing but pine and
pine in thy absence, but I bore it for thy sake, for thy
sake. And now!

A few seconds of silence and perfect immobility
followed the address. Ueli, as I thought, was gathering up his strength. Then a sudden jerk, a cry, and
a great splash in the water. Ueli stood alone on the
bank, his eyes riveted on the gurgling stream below.
Presently Suldi reappeared afloat, at a considerable
distance from the place where he had sunk. The
mighty current was whirling him down fast. He lifted
his head, looked at Ueli, and whined piteously. There
was something human in the sound. I could well understand Ueli's distraction at this appeal. Ueli forgot

everything, but that Suldi was in danger. His whole
soul was now bent on saving him. He hurried along
the bank, a little in advance of the dog, calling to,
and encouraging him by word and gesture. The poor
beast taking heart at this, strove with might and main,
though with little success, to get out of the current
in the direction of the bank. Ueli, in the meantime, spied a little dry indenture on the level of the
river, sprang down into it, and slipped off his smock
frock.

Suldi's strength was just then well-nigh exhausted;
a shout from Ueli revived it for a moment. The dog
pushed desperately on for a yard or so, close enough
for Ueli to wade into the water up to the chest, and
fling the smockfrock within Suldi's reach. He caught
at it with his teeth and held on fast; Ueli drew the
garment and Suldi with it towards himself. Another
moment, and rescued and rescuer lay panting by each
other on the little creek.

Ueli's success did not prove unmingled with bitterness; Suldi, as soon as he could move, withdrew from
him with distrust. This was Ueli's finishing stroke.
He sank under it. He buried his face in his hands,
and . . . I was too far to see whether he wept. Suldi
had not the heart to leave his friend long thus. He
crawled near to him, sniffed at him, whined, and licked
his hands. Ueli opened his arms to Suldi, and kept
him long embraced. What was his agony of mind
during this close embrace, God only knows. I saw him
rise on a sudden, raise his hand, and, to my horror,
strike a blow — a second, a third, a twentieth, a fiftieth
— then fall back at his full length.

Ueli's immobility made me uneasy after a time. I

crept to the spot; Ueli heard me, got up, and motioned me away with the look of a man who must be obeyed. For once there was no lack of expression in his countenance.

It was the last look I had of him. He came back late at night, as reported by Jungfrau Madeleine, informed Frantz he must go away next day, and in fact left early in the morning.

"How did he look?" I asked.

"Just as he did when you saw him first, and were so much puzzled by his appearance, like a man who takes no thought or interest in anything."

I returned on the morrow to the fatal spot. There was not the least trace of blood, or of the earth around having been dug; but on going a little farther along the bank, I found, between two willows, indications of a fresh-made grave.

Poor Suldi! poor Ueli!

CHAPTER III.

The Young Lady in Black.

MISFORTUNE never comes alone. The next corollary of the morning's alarm was Louisa's departure. Her mother had been so panic-stricken at the sight of ill-fated Suldi that she had run to her room, locked herself in, packed her things, and would have started immediately, but for the fear of finding the dog in her way.

Hearing this on my return from the fatal expedition, I hastened to the lady in the full conviction that a faithful account of the tragic transaction I had just witnessed would be more than enough to dispel her fright, and decide her to stay. But in this I was mistaken. My *de visu* evidence, interpreted to her, and backed on my side by the most expressive pantomime at my command, failed to obtain credence, either from her, or, indeed, from the interpreters. Here was the fable of the boy and the wolf realized in full. Too polite to say that she disbelieved what I said, Louisa's mother alleged the painful impressions that were associated with the place, and rendered it disagreeable for her. And she stuck to her resolution of going, which she effected the next morning.

It was a day of mourning for the establishment. Louisa's departure was a public calamity, the more keenly felt, that the only alleviating circumstance of which the case admitted — namely, a little responsive feeling from the object of all this grief — failed us

entirely. Louisa's frame of mind at leaving, I am sorry
to say, was anything but complimentary to those
she left behind. Not only was she not sorry, but
joyful, and all impatience to be gone. The excitement of the occasion, the prospect of a ride on the
railway, had put a muffler on the little pet's sensibility.
I see her still in her travelling cloak, and turned-up
hat, a leather pouch slung across her shoulders, pattering about the breakfast-room with a busy and important look; I hear her still say, in answer to those who
found fault with her for not shedding a single tear,
that it was only naughty girls that cried — the reason
accompanied by an adorable toss of the head, and demonstrative dropping of both arms, as much as to say,
There's for you! It was only on the train, that carried
her away, moving on, that Louisa realized the fact of
being about to leave behind so many friends. (All
the *personnel* of the establishment had accompanied her
to the station.) Then she looked bewildered indeed,
and her lips began to quiver . . . Alas for the little
sun of Schranksteinbad! I fear it had a rainy setting
after all.

The void left by the general favourite was incredible. An old and infirm couple, whose delight she
was, could not put up with it, and started on the next
day but one. And so did the gentleman of the fried
trout; though I must say I suspect that Louisa had
less to do with his sudden resolve than the absence of
wings from a certain dish of fowl, when the waiter
handed it to him. The fact is, that he stormed a great
deal, rose at once, asked for his bill, and departed.
Those who remained were uncomfortable; I, most of
all, who for obvious reasons felt more than any one

for the tragic end of Suldi, and for Ueli's consequent
exit from the scene. Ten to one that, had I been entirely free, I should have cut short my stay in the
country by a month or so, and returned to town: as
it was, a thread as flimsy as a gossamer, interfered
with my free-will, and held me at Schranksteinbad.

What was it? — Neither more nor less than the
hope of seeing the young lady in mourning again.
Was I then smitten with her charms? Not a bit.
Her charms were not of the smiting sort, as I told
. you already, nor is my heart of such friable stuff as
to crumble to pieces on a first notice; witness the fact,
that it remained whole and sound amid a host of fascinating young creatures, with whom I happened to
breakfast, dine, sup, and spend most of each day. No;
my interest in the young lady in black was all of a
friendly, nay of a fatherly kind — it had its roots in
the tale of sorrow which her sable garments implied,
in her extreme timidity and consequent want of protection, in her look of sincerity and gentleness. I know
very well that even out of such light materials time
can forge a solid love-chain; but I was on my guard
. . . lucky that I was so, or . . . but to the point.

That you may not take me for a still greater
dreamer than I am, you must know that my hope of
seeing the young lady again, though faint, was not entirely groundless. She had given me her address, if
you remember, that I might let her know the amount
of her debt to me; that is, the cost of the old lady's
supposed lost ticket. Accordingly, one of the first
things I did on settling at Schranksteinbad, had been
to set her heart at rest upon this matter, informing her
in a few lines of the old lady's wicked trick about the

ticket, and of the consequent issue of the affair without
any cost whatever. She wrote back to thank me, adding that, if I was going to make any stay at Schranksteinbad, she was not without hope of reiterating her
thanks personally, it not being impossible that, late in
the season, she might come to Schranksteinbad with
her aunt for a short stay. Here was the retaining
gossamer.

Well, she proved better than her word. She came
much earlier than the time she had named, and her
first words, on getting down from the omnibus, were
to ask if I was still an inmate of the house. Yes,
from behind the blinds of my window, where I had
been attracted by the sound of wheels, I heard my
name pronounced by her sweet voice! Next to the
call of the letter-carrier, the return of the omnibus
from the station was the most exciting event of the
day at our Spa. I hastened down-stairs to offer my
welcome. She was, and looked, very pleased to see
me, and said how much she and her aunt, to whom
she introduced me next, had feared disappointment in
that respect. The aunt, with an awkward curtsey in
answer to my bow, said something very commonplace
about the obligations under which she and her niece,
Maria, were to me. I confess in all humility that I
had forgotten all about the aunt, and that I had taken
her for her niece's servant. She had the *physique* and
the garb befitting the part. Mddle. Maria looked pale
and thin. I asked whether she was unwell. There
was nothing the matter, she said, only a little pain in
the back. I advised her to see the doctor; upon which
the aunt turned sharply round and said she would
have no doctoring — it was time and money thrown

away — air and rest, that was the best and cheapest physician.

I saw no more of the aunt and niece till supper-time. They, as the last arrivals, sitting at the lowest end of the table, we had all its length between us; which put out of the question all attempt at conversation from them to me, or *vice versâ*. Mdlle. Maria looked paler and thinner than ever by candle-light. I availed myself of the little confusion created by the end of the meal to approach her, and urge anew the expediency of having medical advice. She said she would when her aunt was gone, and begged me not to mention the subject again in her relative's presence — her aunt objected to . . . physicians. Was it to physicians or to fees that the lady objected? thought I; but I said nothing of the sort. Mdlle. Maria's manner was hurried and nervous in the extreme during this short colloquy; her eye was all the while on her aunt, who was talking to an elderly lady, both of whom presently joined us. I led them to the balcony, where most of the company was congregated — the moon shone beautifully — and introduced my new acquaint-ances to all the persons present.

The aunt left on the morrow after breakfast, re-commending her niece to all in general, and to me in particular. She had a concern of some kind, some-where, which could not dispense with her presence. Nobody, as far as I could see, regretted that it was so — I, least of all; though, as I learned soon after from Jungfrau Madeleine, whom the report had reached in her kitchen, she had lost no opportunity of descanting upon the great service I had rendered her niece.

Mdlle. Maria drove to the station with her aunt,

and by the same occasion called on the doctor at the
next village. The doctor treated her ailment very
lightly, and prescribed for her cold *douches* and repose.
This *fiat* of the doctor, communicated to me by Mdlle.
Maria, only half re-assured me. Considerate doctors
— and the one in question was very much so — do
not begin, of course, by frightening their patients out
of their wits, in order to effect their cure. So I resolved to question the doctor myself. Nothing more
easy; he called daily at the baths, and we were on
excellent terms with each other. I lay in wait for him
the next day, went a little way back with him, and
adroitly put him on the topic about which I wanted
enlightenment. His answer, I am glad to say, was but
a confirmation of his statement to Mdlle Maria. Her
complaint was the result of a strain made in lifting a
basket full of linen; she had injured her spine; the
hurt was happily light this time, and would entail no
bad consequences upon her; but, if they continued to
overwork her as they did, sooner or later their wash-
days would make an end of her!

"It is the pride of our housewives," continued the
doctor, "to fill their presses with heaps upon heaps of
linen, and to have in the year but two washes —
monstrous ones, of course, and enough to try the
strength of an ox. Now, Mdlle. Maria is delicate, very
delicate; I have told them so more than once, but
what is the use? So long as they can squeeze out of
her all the work that is in her, what do they care
whether she lives or dies, the miserly brutes!"

The honest indignation of the feeling practitioner
did one's heart good to see. The miserly brutes were,
of course, Mdlle. Maria's aunt that I had seen, and

this lady's worthy husband, the only near relations of
Mdlle. Maria, and with whom she had gone to stay,
ever since her father's demise, eleven months ago. The
new light of victim, under which the doctor's confidences placed my young acquaintance, was not calculated, as you may well think, to lessen my interest
in her.   .
    She did not look like a victim, though. As her
extreme timidity gradually gave way under the warmth
of the general kindness (and who could feel otherwise
than kind to the sweet-faced, sweet-mannered invalid?)
there spread over her countenance a calm serenity,
which excluded all notion of her feeling at all unhappy. Then the evident pleasure she took in constant occupation was to me another proof of her even-
ness of spirits. Mdlle. Maria was always quietly busy,
either knitting — that inexorable necessity of all Swiss
women — embroidering, sketching, or reading. When
it was too hot to sit in the open air of an afternoon,
she would quietly steal to the dancing-room, and there
play on the piano for hours, and sing (little of this
last, however, for the doctor was rather against it).
She had plenty of time for all these avocations, poor
thing, being under *veto* of taking walks of any length.
To those who congratulated her upon the variety of
her accomplishments, she simply would observe, that
she was brought up for a governess, and had to learn
many things, without really mastering any one; a statement more modest than true, because both for music
and sketching she had a very fine talent. She could
also read and speak English correctly enough, but not
write it.
    I used to go every morning, after post-time, and

read my newspaper in one of the two summer-houses, which stood on a little elevation at ten minutes' walk from the house. It commanded a beautiful view of the valley, with its winding river, the woody hills which hemmed it in, and the chain of the Alps behind. Well, one morning — it was the fifth since Mdlle. Maria's arrival — as I reached the spot, whom should I see but Mdlle. Maria installed in one of the summer-houses, and reading a letter! I was the more surprised to meet her there, that I had heard her repeatedly complain of the doctor's cruelty in tabooing the place for her, because of the little ascent. However, it was too late to withdraw, for the young lady had seen me; accordingly I went up to her and said jestingly, that I was afraid I was in duty bound to report to the doctor. She said she felt so much better this morning that indeed she could not withstand the temptation. The shower-baths were doing her a world of good.

"I am heartily glad of that," said I; "and I will reconsider my threat of turning informer. In the meantime, I will leave you to the perusal of your letter."

"I have read it twice over already," she said naïvely. "Your name figures in it."

"Does it indeed?"

"Yes, here it is;" and she pointed it out to me. I read, in fact, my name, at the end of a flattering phrase, expressive of a wish to make my acquaintance.

"You are not curious," resumed she after a pause, seeing that I asked no questions.

"I am only discreet," said I.

"I am sorry you are, because I want to prejudice you in favour of the writer. He comes to-morrow." (To-morrow was Sunday.)

"Who comes?" asked I.

"Adolphe."

"Is he a relation?"

"No . . . no relation."

"Something better, then?"

She blushed . . . "perhaps;" and Mdlle. Maria's little romance before long oozed out in driblets.

It was like most romances of most girls. She had known him from a child. He was the cleverest and best pupil of her father, who kept a school in a village, and the gentlest and kindest of play-fellows to her. When he left for town, at seventeen years of age, to enter as clerk in a commercial house, an attachment had already sprung up between them, known to and approved of by her father, who, however, put off all question of marriage to the time when Adolphe should earn money enough for himself and a wife to live decently. She was then scarcely fifteen, and studying to fit herself for a governess. The next three years proved the happiest of her life. Adolphe visited at her father's as often as business would allow; he advanced steadily in his profession, and her father was quite satisfied with him. At the end of the third year, the sky clouded at once. Evil reports — false, of course — of the youth's behaviour reached her father, who, unfortunately, believed them. This led to a succession of stormy scenes, the upshot of which was a rupture. During the long estrangement that followed, lasting nearly two other years, Adolphe had risen to the situation of head clerk in the business, and had plenty of advantageous offers of marriage, which, of course, he declined for her sake. Then her father had a stroke, and was not expected to revive; he did, however, and lingered on for months and months. And for months and months was Adolphe unremitting in his cares and attentions to the invalid — a son could have done no more. In short, the dying man's heart relented, and the grant of his daughter's hand was the seal of the reconciliation. He died shortly after. Adolphe and Maria were to be husband and wife at the expiration of her mourning.

This communication eased my mind wonderfully. That, after what I had heard of the selfishness and unconscientiousness of the relations on whom she depended, there should be an honest fellow ready to rescue her from thraldom, seemed nearly too good to be believed; and my sympathies, from this moment, were enlisted in favour of M. Adolphe. A love so constant, against wind and tide, spoke well for the man. I waited for his appearance with almost as much impatience as Mdlle. Maria.

The most impatient of the three, however, proved M. Adolphe, who burst like a bomb upon us on the evening of the same day, Saturday, just as we had done supper, and were cooling ourselves on the gallery. He had taken time by the forelock, he explained, and here he was. Judge of Mdlle. Maria's delighted surprise and beaming looks! I, for my part, was scarcely less pleased; I could have hugged him for his hurry. A lively blondin, with blue lustrous eyes, looking hardly his age, twenty-four, restless as a gutta-percha ball, full to the brim of talk, of fun, and exuberant spirits! He made himself quite at home, and was on terms of intimacy with everybody in no time. To me he was over-friendly. He shook me repeatedly by the hand, with a vigour that threatened my wrist with dislocation; and the warmth of his thanks was so disproportionate to the small service I had rendered Mdlle. Maria as positively to put me out of countenance. My horoscope of him was, altogether, very favourable. A warm-hearted creature who will make his partner an easy life, thought I; rather too boisterous and demonstrative for my taste — but what has my taste to do in the matter? She it is who marries him, and she likes him as he is. All right.

M. Adolphe was already discussing his toast and coffee, when I entered the breakfast-room next morning. I went up to him with outstretched hands, and lo! what could be the matter with him? The night had aged him by ten years! All the spirit and animation had gone out of his face and manner. He gave me the tips of his fingers, and stammered some broken words of greeting. He scarcely spoke during the meal, and always with some effort. Do what I would, I could not bring him to look me straight in the face. His eyes wandered restlessly right and left. A culprit who shuns observation — such was the appearance he presented.

I seized a favourable opportunity to ask of Mdlle. Maria, unheard by him, whether they had quarrelled. "Not in the least," said she; "what makes you ask?"

"Why, because M. Adolphe looks rather . . . thoughtful."

"He always does in the morning," said she "business weighs him down; only think, such a responsibility; all the concern on his hands, and he is so conscientious."

I accepted this explanation for what it was worth. Queer sense of responsibility that must be which makes

itself felt exclusively in the morning! Perhaps he was
only out of sorts, or ill. But he was always so, she
had said. I was more puzzled and vexed by this new
aspect of affairs than I dare say. Was this vessel I
thought so sound a damaged one, or was it only a false
alarm? I determined to watch M. Adolphe pretty
closely. I saw him go to church alone — so long a
walk was out of the question for Mdlle. Maria — and
return in her company; she had gone to meet him a
little way. He went in for no longer than five minutes,
and then came down and sat in the shade with the
company. His looks were improved, and so was his
manner; it had nothing in it of the buoyancy of the
previous evening, but the late constraint had passed
away from it; it was natural. He could now talk to
people, and look them full in the face.

The dinner did not work any appreciable change
in him, that I could see. We sat long after dinner
to watch the Sunday people coming — he seemed to
take very little interest in the sight, and spoke little.
At one time I heard him ask Mdlle. Maria if she had
not better go and have a little rest. Had she complained or not of being tired? That is more than I can
say. She complied, and he accompanied her into the
house. From that moment I lost sight of him for some
hours. The affluence of the Sunday visitors made it a
very hard task to follow the doings of an individual
among the crowd.

When I saw him next, he was sitting at a table in
the gallery with sundry acquaintances he had met,
Mdlle. Maria by his side. I noticed immediately a very
sensible rise in his spirits. He was growing talkative
and expansive. He would have me sit by him, drank

my health, and pelted me with protestations of friendship. My eyes were riveted all the while upon Mdlle. Maria, to spy the faintest indication of uneasiness in her face. None — there was nothing in her looks but pride, admiration, happiness. Need I say that by supper-time M. Adolphe had found again his youthful appearance, his brilliancy, his gift of the gab, his buoyancy of the previous evening? After supper we adjourned, as usual with us, to the dancing-room; the throng had cleared considerably by this time. Now it was that M. Adolphe shone in all his lustre, and won the heart of our ladies, whom he took almost all for partners, one after the other. Mdlle. Maria was forbidden to dance. M. Adolphe was a fine dancer, light and indefatigable withal; his occasional imitation of the ways of the peasants, including the great thump and the yell, were the *ne plus ultra* of comicality. How she laughed! I might have quarrelled with her for looking so pleased. How stupid women can be when they choose!

To me this merry exhibition proved anything but agreeable. There was no mistaking the source at which M. Adolphe drew his inspirations. What in the previous evening I had taken for granted to be, and might, strictly speaking, have been, exuberance of animal spirits, was simply the effect of drink. Was it an habitual or an occasional indulgence with him? That was the question on which Mdlle. Maria's future happiness hung, and the only desideratum by which it might be solved — time — failed me. M. Adolphe would be gone in the morning.

I could scarcely sleep for the harrowing thought that haunted me, and set out by break of day for a long expedition up the mountain. Locomotion and fresh air are my infallible medicine for the ailments of the mind, and did not fail me on this occasion. After a full two hours' ramble, I made up my mind to submit my observations to the doctor, and take counsel from his tried experience. I was, accordingly, wending my way towards home to have a hasty breakfast, and then proceed immediately to the village, when lo! at the turning of a path I overtook the doctor himself. He was returning from a hamlet up the mountain, to which he had been summoned in all haste during the night.

"I was just thinking of going to you," said I; and then and there I told him of my perplexity, and gave him an account of M. Adolphe's doings during the last twenty-four hours, with the accuracy and minuteness of a medical student reporting the symptoms of a patient confided to his care by his professor. The doctor at once pronounced the case one of confirmed drunkenness. What characterized it as such, he said, was the dejectedness of the young man in the morning; it was an infallible symptom, as he had been able to ascertain from alas! too frequent an experience. Habitual drunkards, previous to raising themselves up by a dose of stimulant, felt, and looked in fact, like culprits — to borrow, as he said, my graphic and felicitous simile.

The doctor's opinion coincided too well with my personal impression not to carry a decisive weight with it; yet it seemed hard — and I told him so — to convict a man, as it were, on one day's evidence, and act against him upon it.

"What do you mean by acting?" asked the doctor.

"Why," said I, "the young lady ought to be warned."

He laughed a dry laugh, and said, "I have warned against drunkards girls by the score, with no better result than losing them as patients. None so deaf, you know, as those who won't hear."

"I have not arrived at my time of life, dear doctor, without knowing what one ordinarily gets for one's pains in such occurrences, but there may be exceptions; and then, it is an affair of conscience. If I only could get some additional evidence."

"Is there no chance," asked the doctor, "of having this young man down at the baths for a few days?"

I said I feared there was none: business nailed him to town; he could only leave on Saturday evenings.

The doctor considered a moment; then said, "You shall have your bit of additional evidence, though. Here is how it shall be. Mdlle. Maria has begged me repeatedly for leave to go to the Rothen Flüe. Rothen Flüe is a high point on the mountain, easy accessible to carriages, and from whence there is a beautiful view. I shall grant her leave for Sunday next — she is well enough now to stand the exertion—but on condition that I shall be of the party, to make sure of her committing no imprudences. At the same time I shall mention you as willing to make the excursion; that will lead to your being invited. The trip will take us six hours at least. We'll see how M. Adolphe stands the trial."

The scheme succeeded beyond our wishes; I say beyond, because it had a tail, with which we could

have well dispensed. However, of this in its place.
Well, then, Mdlle. Maria brought me word in due time
that the doctor had at last consented to her going to
the Rothen Flüe next Sunday; that he was to be of
the party, and I too. M. Adolphe, on his side, when
told of the arrangement on the following Saturday, expressed his delight with all the flow of words and
spirits incident to the hour — nine o'clock in the
evening. But at five in the morning it was quite another story. We had the greatest difficulty in wrench-
ing him from his slumbers, and, when at last he made
his appearance, rather than the looks of a young lover
bent on a beautiful excursion with his betrothed, his
were those of a criminal called up for execution. I
may say, without exaggeration, that he sustained the
character throughout the expedition.

Not that he did not strive hard to shake himself
up, and look alive; but he lacked the stamina for it;
he had not a breath of life in him. Even blind Mdlle.
Maria noticed, and asked the reason of, his state of
collapse and intense look of *ennui*. He pleaded bad
headache; the sun was so hot, he said. We did our
best, the doctor and I, to entertain and interest her,
but in vain; where the finest view imaginable failed,
what could our efforts do? The mention of the bad
headache had taken all the sun out of her eyes. He
scarcely tasted the provisions we had taken with us,
and even refused the glass of wine, his allotted part
of the one small bottle in our possession. Our stay
at the Rothen Flüe was of the shortest; our drive
home dull and silent. We reached Schranksteinbad
at eleven, a full hour before our time. M. Adolphe
said he would go and lie down till dinner, when

he hoped — nay, made sure of being quite himself
again.

The dinner bell rang at twelve as usual, and . . .
here comes the tail. M. Adolphe had so well employed
the interval, that to see him, and say, *unâ voce*, "He is
tipsy," was, for the doctor and me, one and the same
thing. We learned afterwards from Jungfrau Madeleine that he had asked for and taken up to his room
a bottle of kirschwasser, under pretence of washing his
head with it. His bloodshot eyes, tottering gait, and
incipient thickness of utterance, intimated too clearly
that eagerness to make up for the long deprivation
of stimulant had betrayed him into taking an over-
dose.

M. Adolphe began by declaring that he would not
sit down at the low end of the table, so far from his
dear friends — the doctor, my guest for the day,
shared with me the presidential place — and actually
carried his and Mdlle. Maria's cover close to where we
sat, to the no small inconvenience of the whole company, who had to move down to make room for them.
He next called for champagne; and, on the waiter asking
how many champagne glasses he ought to bring, he an-
wered as many as there were people at table. Then
he began giving toasts and drinking them conscien-
tiously, rattling on all the while, and getting up at
every moment to go and hobnob with this and that
guest, who happened to be out of arm's length. Then
. . . but what is the use of dwelling on a scene as dis-
gusting as it is unfortunately familiar? Who has not
seen a man half-drunk bent on making himself completely so, with a zeal worthy of a better cause? All
that I could do, and that I did, in my capacity of

chairman, was to shorten the meal as much as could be decently done. The doctor and I, seemingly in jest, dragged reluctant M. Adolphe into the open air, and had him seated on a chair, from which, before long, he slipped to the ground in a state of coma, as the doctor scientifically termed it. So we had him carried to his room, and consigned to his bed.

How was Mdlle. Maria affected by this disgraceful episode? Well, believe it or not, Mdlle. Maria enjoyed the sport indoors very keenly; I daresay, in the poor young lady's eyes, M. Adolphe had no equal for wit, fun, and jollity. The catastrophe that followed in the open air took her quite by surprise. She looked alarmed and distressed, and kept repeating that surely it was the sun. The kind-hearted people around, to tranquillize her, agreed that it was the sun. I myself, when she appealed to me, laid it all at the door of the sun. Incredible the number of barefaced lies we tell with a good intention!

Nobody but Mdlle. Maria, who had probably little sleep, if any, that night, saw M. Adolphe next day. He was already gone when I went out for my early morning walk. I let two days slip by; and then availing myself of a moment of privacy, I threw out to her a dubitative hint or two. I did so with all the care and delicacy of touch of a mother dressing the bleeding wound of a dear babe. She stood up in arms, repelled the charge with scorn, flatly denied all the circumstances with which I supported it, made even a weapon of my admission that it was the sun — in a word, was as absurd as women always are in like circumstances. A similar attempt, made at my earnest instigation by the doctor, had a similar result. She

sent instantly word to her aunt to come and take her
away, and departed in high dudgeon. I wrote a long
letter to her: the letter was returned to me opened, but
without a word.

CHAPTER IV.

My Last Flirtation.

In spite of these and other disagreeable impressions, Schranksteinbad altogether left in me a longing
to revisit it — which I did the following summer; and
the more I saw of it, the more I grew in love with it;
so that I ended by being a constant visitor at the
establishment.

But what was it that so endeared this Schranksteinbad to you? I hear some one ask. I have told
you already. It was its plenty of air and verdure, its
fresh waters, its grand prospect of the Alps, its walks,
its fir-tree forests, its birds, its squirrels, and *vergiss-
meinnichts* — it was that, which might make it a temple
of Ennui to you, its comparative seclusion, its homely
feeling, its early hours, quiet old-fashioned habits, and
perfect emancipation from the tethers of conventional
life. Let me also mention, *en passant*, its very moderate charges. We live in an age, thank God, when
everybody is rich, or wishes to appear so, and I dis-
claim beforehand all invidious references, which may
be drawn from my having touched upon this ignoble
item; still, I beg to submit that cheap terms are a consideration.

Well, is this all? was there no other inducement to
your patronage of this spa? Since you press me so
hard, I will candidly admit that there was. Schranksteinbad had a peculiar feature of its own, which gave

it an additional charm in my eyes. It was never
entered by men under forty years of age. Open your
eyes as wide as you will, I don't bate a jot of what I
have put down. I don't mean, of course, that there
was any written statute forbidding the entrance of this
quiet haven to gentlemen under forty years of age. I
simply mention a fact, and that fact is, that not within
the memory of the oldest annual visitor had there ever
been (with one solitary exception) any gentleman under
forty staying as a boarder at Schranksteinbad. I say
staying as a boarder, for naturally there were plenty
of youngsters among the occasional visitors of the
Sunday.

It was several years before my time that this deplorable exception took place, — an exception, after
all, which only served to confirm the rule. The inter-
loper, a young man between twenty-six and twenty-
seven came with, and as a companion to, a gentleman
of the legal age, very infirm and nearly blind. I had
all these particulars from an eye-witness, a very amiable,
but terribly exclusive past-fortian. I still hear the ring
of indignation in his voice as the recollection came
vividly upon him. "Had the youngster been at least
indifferent-looking or vulgar-mannered!" growled my
informant; "but no — he was very prepossessing and
gentlemanly, and danced to perfection. I leave you,
Sir, to imagine the run he had with the young ladies;
they were quite unmanageable. The past-fortians had
a disastrous season of it, I can tell you. . . . Thank
God, it is a thing of the past now, and not likely to
occur again! For you must know that this young man
was reported to have died shortly after leaving — a
warning to those who might be tempted to imitate him

— and the report found credence at Schranksteinbad and forms part of the traditions of the place to this day. The fact is, that my young man was as alive as a young man can be, as I knew perfectly well, having met him at Geneva shortly after. It was his invalid friend who had died; but" — with a chuckle — "but I held my tongue."

To return. The stern sex being to the soft in about the proportion of one to five, Schranksteinbad had generally a floating account of from seven to eight gentlemen past the two scores, to an average number, let us say, of forty ladies, twelve or fifteen of them grown-up young ladies. Now, high-spirited, or, may be, soft-hearted young ladies do not spend a month or so at a spa without sporting and coquetting a wee bit, or perhaps indulging in a little sentimentality; in other words, without establishing a little current of often unconscious, always innocent flirtation, be it even with bachelors past forty. Bachelors on their part, for being past forty, are not the less men possessed of eyes and a heart too. . . . You perceive at a glance the charges, the benefits, and the dangers of the situation for this sprinkle of past-fortians, amid a bevy of young beauties.

Thrice happy the mammas and the little sisters and brothers! they had an easy life of it with us. How we spoiled the little ones, drove their hoops for them, and crammed them with bonbons! With what an assiduous care we watched for the comfort of the matrons; warned them of sun and draught, wrapped shawls round their shoulders, nay, petted their polysarcic poodles — nasty creatures! — when they had any. At what a double gallop we set off to fetch the gloves,

·the bonnet, the parasol, at the bidding of the young
ones! How many times have I not mangled my
fingers to pick sweetbriar for them, or compromised
the polish of my varnished pumps in some marshy
ditch, to get at a withered *vergissmeinnicht!* Sweet
toils, after all; and more than requited by the gift of a
small twig of the blue blossom, instantly treasured in
a pocket-book, or by the pressure of a lily hand holding prisoner the pricked finger, while the other, armed
with a needle, extracted the thorn from it.

Nor were these small ways of ingratiating ourselves with mammas and daughters the only string to
our bow. The preoccupation of the agreeable did not
make us forget the claims of the useful. One knows
one's Horace by heart at our time of life, and how to
mingle *utile dulci.* No little ailment or discomfort for
which we had not our little remedy — sticking-plaster,
eau des carmes, eau of orange-blossoms, sal volatile,
balsamic vinegar, creosotis Billiard, ammonia, benzine, etc. These two last articles, the two most in requisition, were an exclusive monopoly of mine — it
was only justice, because I had introduced them at
Schranksteinbad — and urgent must be the case, indeed, for recourse to be had to other methods of healing a wasp-sting, or a spot on a silk gown than my
ammonia or benzine. The respect for my privilege
was pushed so far on these two points, that a lady,
convicted of having taken a stain out of her gown with
her own benzine, was sentenced by her peers to have
the obnoxious phial sequestered during all her stay at
the Baths.

The dangers of this kind of intercourse, on our
side, are too obvious to need being pointed at; they

are all comprised in this one — the risk of sliding
from the slippery ground of flirtation into the slough of
earnest love-making. Only fancy a grave past-fortian,
with perhaps a bald pate, or a wig, playing the impas-
sioned for good and all with a luxuriantly-haired
blondine or brunette of seventeen or so! What could
come of it but heartache and ridicule?

I must say that, for my part, I never apprehended
a like result; and yet I courted danger, — I may say,
I played with fire. Impunity had made me reckless.
I felt so sure, so fire-proof . . . poor goose that I was!
But another word before I tell you of my narrow
escape; it is meant in exoneration of the fair young
ones.

On my first visit to Schranksteinbad, I found it to
have somehow transpired that I was an author; and on
my second season, I had the mixed satisfaction of
seeing two books of mine handed from bench to bench,
and from summer-house to summer-house, and now and
then forgotten there. My being an author, combined
with the ammonia and benzine I had just brought with
me, made me in some request. A man who can
manufacture lovely heiresses, and jet-haired lovers for
them, and marry them at will, is not like another man
in young ladies' eyes. They will lend him some of
the perfections and of the locks of his heroes. This
prestige — I beg pardon for the ambitious expression,
but I find no better — lasted generally from a week
to a fortnight. In cases of aggravated sentimentalism,
twenty days had been reached. I may just as well
remark, that this last limit of time was not overstepped
in the pass of arms to which I am going to advert. Including both those of her arrival and departure, Mdlle.

Emma's stay at the Baths amounted in all to nineteen days.

Yes, her name was Emma; I had heard her sister call her so. Mdlle. Emma was a lovely, kind-hearted, playful big child. That she was lovely, I had the irrefragable evidence of my own eyes; that she was kind-hearted, I knew from the fact of her having offered to go, and going every day, to dress an old lady, her next neighbour, and a perfect stranger to her, whose right hand was disabled by rheumatism. A little scene in which she had played the first part, and which I had witnessed at table, had given me the measure of her graceful playfulness. We had a lady-boarder noted for her greediness. One of her daily tricks at the dessert consisted in this: that she drew a dish of cakes near her, and cautiously slipped the contents, one by one, into her pocket.

It was to defeat the end of this manœuvre, that Mdlle. Emma applied herself on one of the first days of her arrival, and so quietly managed, and with the utmost politeness, as never to let the dish of cakes stop within reach of the rapacious hands.

I don't know how it came to pass, but, for the three or four first days of their stay, there was no communication whatever, save polite bows, between Mdlle. Emma and her company and me. The slow or quick growth of acquaintance between strangers at a spa depends pretty much on their respective situations at table, or on accident. Now, Mdlle. Emma's company and I sat at the two poles of the dinner table, and accident, as it seems, had done nothing to draw us together. But, whatever its cause, the longer this sort of distance lasts, the more difficult it becomes to break through it. I felt the truth of this one morning, when, on going as usual to my observatory to read the newspaper, I descried in one of the summer-houses Mdlle. Emma reading a book, and I could take upon myself to do no more than bow to her most respectfully — a politeness which she returned at compound interest, I suspect with a little caricature. If I am to speak candidly, both Mdlle. Emma and her sister — a married lady, and her senior by six or seven years — belonged to that set of queenly women I most admire at a distance. Tall commanding figures intimidate me.

However, it was written somewhere that we should become friends, and here is how it happened. I must premise that there ran against the wall of the house, on both sides of the flight of steps, a trellised verandah covered with Virginia creepers, which hung down in beautiful garlands, reaching to the ground, One day, towards dusk, I entered this cool recess to smoke a cigar. I was momentarily blinded by the match I had used, and, not to stumble against the rustic chairs or tables, I felt my way with my walking stick, "Are you going to cane me?" asked a saucy voice, so close, that I started; and out came a merry laugh, and Mdlle. Emma. I had instantly recognised her voice.

"God forbid that I should," I answered; "though I know somebody who would not be sorry if I did."

"Who is it?" asked she.

"Who, but your victim, Mdme. Lambin?" — (the monopolizer of the bonbons.)

Another merry laugh, and she said, "Are you going to stand up as Mdme. Lambin's champion?"

"Who knows?" said I; "perhaps I have an interest
in her trade: suppose I am a sharer in the spoil?"

"I am not sure you are not," said Mdlle. Emma,
and she called out to her sister to come and hear Mr.
So-and-So avow a tender interest in Madame Lambin.
This brought to the window not only Mdlle. Emma's
sister, but nearly all the boarders who had windows
in the front of the house, Mdme. Lambin included —
she was fortunately rather deaf — who asked who
wanted her. Mdlle. Emma answered forthwith that it
was I. I said it was I in fact who, yielding to Mdlle.
Emma's earnest request, had taken upon myself to
beg her, Mdme. Lambin, to give us, after supper, the
Rantz des Vaches she had sung so admirably some
nights before.

I observed during my harangue, that Mdlle. Emma
was preparing for an *éclat* of hilarity, and, wishing to
prevent that at any cost, for Mdme. Lambin was very
sharp and caustic, and having but one tongue in my
head, and that actually employed, I stole quietly close
to Mdlle. Emma, caught her by the wrist, and pressed
it rather tight. This diversion had the effect I looked
for — the young jester, in her unfeigned surprise,
dropped her threatened fit of merriment.

Madame Lambin declared that she was at the com-
mands of the society, but that she was never sure of
her voice after her meals — which did not hinder her
from giving us the "Rantz des Vaches" and all her
repertory after supper. We had much to do, her sister
and I, to keep petulant Mdlle. Emma within bounds
during this interminable performance. Mdme. Lambin's
natural over-graciousness to me, who had been the
means, in fact, of procuring her her present triumph,

was a ready-made theme of quizzing at my expense,
which Mdlle. Emma varied abundantly. I parried and
thrust with a will, but with indifferent success. I was
on disadvantageous ground, and, dear me, what a wit
she had!

I was more fortunate, or rather better armed, on
our first encounter next morning. We were, ten or
twelve of us, sitting *al fresco* as usual after breakfast,
when Mdlle. Emma joined us. An arch smile on her
lips as she turned to me to say good-day, warned me
of a fresh attack. "What a delicious evening we had
last night, thanks to you!" said the sly hypocrite.

"Thanks, rather, to you," said I. "It was at your
pressing request alone that Mdme. Lambin consented
to sing; I only acted as your mouth-piece."

"I was thinking," she went on, "and I could
scarcely sleep for thinking of it, how nice it would be
if you and Mdme. Lambin gave us duets."

"Let us do better and have trios," said I; "Mr.
Eisenschmidt has a very fine bass voice; use your influence with him to join us."

"What influence can I have with Mr. Eisenschmidt?
I know so very little of him."

"Not so little, perhaps, as you choose to say."

"How so?" asked Mdlle. Emma, rather puzzled.

"Deny, if you dare," said I, "that you make ap-
pointments with Mr. Eisenschmidt in the garden every
morning by break of day."

The charge, from its very absurdity, had a success
of hilarity, to which Mdlle. Emma herself richly contributed. Mr. Eisenschmidt, be it known, was a very
worthy and very accomplished past-fortian of . . . eighty-
three years of age, who could sleep but little, and was

always in the garden by sunrise, where I had seen him in slippers and flannel dressing-gown that very morning, *tête-à-tête* with Mdlle. Emma, herself an early riser.

Thus far the odd character of our first-spoken meeting determined the colour of our further intercourse. The key of the first notes was to remain the key of the sonata to the last. *Enfant terrible*, as I nicknamed her, and *Papa formidable*, as she nicknamed me, were for ever at daggers drawn, teasing, contradicting, finding fault with, saying disagreeable things to each other, and constantly seeking each other's company notwithstanding. No wonder, in a sportive, quick-witted thing of her age; rather less accountable, though, in a grave past-fortian like me. Well, all I can say in my defence is, that it all came of its own accord, without any the least pre-determination, or effort to humour her childish moods, on my part — far from it, I enjoyed the sport vastly.

We had a tiff, of course, the first time we went out for a walk together. We were a large company, a dozen at least, mostly ladies; her sister was with us, and her sister's husband, who came down occasionally, and their two little girls. Useless to say that I was on the best terms with all the family. Well, Mdlle. Emma, when out in the country, used to pick flowers for ever to make nosegays, which she made prettily indeed, and, as I watched her supple form sauntering right and left, and bending down gracefully, she reminded me of Dante's Matelda, in the twenty-eighth canto of the Purgatory — and, as I was thinking of Matelda, she called out to me to go and pick her some beautiful orchids, which grew on damp ground. My answer to this request was, that if the nosegay was

meant for me, as it ought to be in justice and reason,
I would; if not, I shouldn't slave for Mr. Eisenschmidt
or anybody else.

"What an ignoble selfish creature you are! obey,
and reckon upon my generosity."

"I might reckon without mine host if I did.
Promise first."

"Most vulgar sentiments most vulgarly expressed,"
quoth she. "I promise nothing, and I give you time:
one, two, thr . . ."

As I saw she was going to wet her feet, I went
first, and handed her the orchis, saying, "Allow at
least that I am the most chivalrous being in creation."

"The most conceited, you mean. Have you a penknife?"

"I have my stiletto," and I produced a charming
little penknife in the shape of a stiletto.

"I was sure you had," said she. "How many has
it helped you to kill?"

"I ought to consult my register of murders to
know."

"It is charming, though."

"Such as it is, it is at your command."

"I cannot deprive you of it; it is too necessary to
you."

"True — still, perhaps, by accepting of it, you may
save some lives."

"That is a consideration; out of Christian charity,
then, I will take it. Here is a penny to break the
evil charm. But don't hope to have bribed me into
giving you my nosegay. No such thing."

The nosegay, though, found its way somehow
(through one of her little nieces, as the child boasted

next day) to my table in the evening, carefully placed
in a tumbler of water; a graciousness which was acknowledged on the morrow by a speech to the effect
that I could not thank her for having done merely her
duty, but that I could congratulate her upon knowing
what her duty was. The nosegay, however, for being
a duty-offering, was not the less tended, and watered,
and exhibited upon my window. From that day I
became her constant purveyor of fresh wreaths, and
never once did she return from a walk in the forest in
my company, without a crown of honeysuckle, traveller's joy, or bright red cranberries on her hair or on her
bonnet, there deposited by my hands. Small presents ·
keep friendship alive.

She was good-humour itself; nothing could put her
out of her angelic patience with me — not even such
strictures on her weak points of beauty as few women
could have stood, be it only in jest, without wincing.
Once only did she feel slightly piqued and showed it.
The occasion of this little ebullition was this: We
were following a very narrow path in the forest, and
. . . but, to make it plain, I must briefly refer to a
previous occurrence. We had been playing at ball
with some apples that lay strewn under a tree. We
vied with each other as to who should throw the apple
highest for the other to catch. It so happened that
Mdlle. Emma miscalculated the parabola of one of my
most successful throws, and, instead of catching the
apple in her hand, received it upon her face, a little
under the left eye. For once, I dropped my jesting
mood, and went up to her in some alarm, it would
seem, for she laughed outright at my elongated face,
and said it was nothing. It was something, though —

the skin was bruised on a surface as broad as a half-penny, and there was a scarcely perceptible scratch in the centre of it. I said how sorry I was — it was so stupid of me to have thrown the apple so high. She begged me not to talk more nonsense; the fault was hers, she said; she was punished for her awkwardness, and would hear of no water, and of no plaster. Only think, a bit of sticking-plaster under her eye! it would spoil her beauty — no such thing; and she insisted on going on with her game.

She was a brave girl; this was not the last proof I had of her power of endurance. Who knows how many occasions of exercising it she had had already in her short experience of life, how many self-denials she had had to inflict upon herself, how many longings after a collar, or a gown, or a party of young companions, to check and leave unsatisfied!

Well then, to return. Half an hour after, perhaps, we were treading a very narrow footpath skirting the forest; she went foremost, and, as the skirts of her gown were ample and long, according to the fashion, I had had more than one narrow escape of stepping upon the hem of her garment. I told her so, adding, by way of jest, that, if I damaged her dress, I was not as sure of being pardoned as for having damaged her skin. She turned round, and said with a little frown of defiance, "Why so, pray?"

"Why, because women, as I hear, hold less to their skin than to their finery."

Her eye flashed. "And you believe me to be one of those absurd persons?"

"Possibly not," said I. "I spoke of women, and truly you are but a big child."

"Stuff and nonsense — a child at seventeen!"

"Everything is relative," said I; "you are one in my eyes, the eyes of *Papa formidable.*"

"I know of no worse coxcombs than men of a certain age. They would fain give themselves out for Methuselahs in order to benefit by the contrast."

"Shall I, to benefit by it, tell you my exact age?"

She put up both her hands to her ears, crying, "No such thing — if it is at all in proportion with your tiresomeness, it must be a fine old age, indeed," and away she ran.

The sky had quite cleared by the time I joined her; that is, three minutes afterwards. She bid me in her usual petulant way, help to pick oak leaves and ivy twigs, and look sharp. She herself, and all our party, and another party ours had met, were busy gathering oak leaves and ivy. And, in a wonderfully short time, nimble fingers turned those green materials into a variety of shapes — wreaths, garlands, collars, wristbands, scarfs, etc. — which were to serve for a general masquerade. Then, under Mdlle. Emma's direction, every one changed outer garments with every one — the gentlemen, three in number, showing off, of course, in the garb of ladies, and *vice versâ.* I had on, for my part, Mdlle. Emma's broad straw hat and blue caraco, and she my flapping grey hat and summer paletot turned inside out; that is, exhibiting red sleeves and yellow body, the colour of the lining; and besides my share of green in common with all the rest, I gloried in a quantity of moss and ivy twigs hanging down my face in the shape of ringlets. I was a sight indeed, and so we were all; we could not look at each other without laughing till we held our sides. In short, we had made ourselves such figures, that, when we entered two by two the precincts of the Baths, humming a lugubrious chant, people fled at our approach, and we were at some pains to have our identity acknowledged even by our fellow-boarders.

I must now mention an incident which well-nigh threw me off the rails of flirtation, and down the precipice of amorous infatuation. A few days after the masquerade just mentioned, a little before noon, I was sitting and reading my newspaper in a very odd place — the orchestra of the dancing-room. This orchestra was my refuge against the heat — it was always pleasantly cool there — and also my tent of Achilles when I chanced to be out of sorts. I was somewhat so on this morning. I am very particular, perhaps I ought to say fidgety, about my letters. Gentlemen past forty are apt to fidget about many things. Well then, I had a letter, which I wanted to go by the day's post — an end most easily secured by handing it to the letter-carrier, when he called about eleven A. M. As I could not do so myself this time, having ordered a bath which was ready, I begged Jungfrau Madeleine to see to it for me. Jungfrau Madeleine, to make assurance doubly sure, put my letter in her pocket, and . . . forgot it there. I must say, in fairness to her, that it was a washing-day, and poor Madeleine at her wits' end. When apprised of the mischance, after my bath, I grumbled a little — more, I am afraid, than necessary — but I would hear of no one being sent on purpose to the village — all hands were engrossed by the great wash — and withdrew moodily, paper in hand, to my elevated station in the dancing-room.

I had been there perhaps three-quarters of an hour,
when the door of the large hall, just in front of my
orchestra, was flung open, and there appeared on the
threshold a group of three ladies, two holding and
dragging in an apparently reluctant third one between
them. The prisoner was Mdlle. Emma.

"What is it? what new crime has the most terrible
of *enfants terribles* committed?" cried I, jumping down,
and striding towards the door.

"Come and see what a state she has put herself
in," said Mdlle. Emma's sister.

My blood gave a turn, as my eyes, following in the
direction of the elder sister's, rested on Mdlle. Emma's
shoulders. They were the colour of brick-dust, blistered
all over as if by a scald.

"How was it done?" I asked.

"By walking in the sun without a parasol," said
the sister; "did you ever hear of a piece of folly like
this?"

"Really it is too bad," I began; "a babe four years
old . . ."

"Don't scold," interrupted Mdlle. Emma.

The tone in which she said it was neither petulant,
as usual, nor propitiating; it sounded like a quiet
warning.

"You are right," said I; "we can do something
better than scold just now;" and I ran to the kitchen,
took hold of a paper bag full of flour, and scattered
handfuls of it on the poor neck, shoulders, lace tippet,
and all, ending by dabbing the tip of her nose, and
her left cheek, and this, and that, on which I pretended
to notice signs of an incipient sunburn. The upshot
was what might be expected — Mdlle. Emma snatched

with both hands the bag of flour, turned it topsy turvy,
and shook out the remaining contents over my head
and face. I had seen flour used with advantage, when
nothing better was at hand, as a sedative in cases of
slight scalds. If it did Mdlle. Emma only the tenth
part of the good which she professed it did, flour is a
wonderful specific for sunburns.

Enfant terrible showed admirable endurance, good-
humour, and cheerful wit throughout the day. She
made light of what she called her *bobo;* nay, joked
about it, parrying all the while with much skill every
hint aimed at drawing out from her the sort of errand
on which she had come by it. She had been taking a
walk, she said. I suggested the probability of her
having gone to the station, there to meet, by special
appointment, Mr. Eisenschmidt, who had left the day
before, and in the natural flutter of her spirits having
forgotten her parasol. She observed what wonderful
penetration novelists were gifted with, and gave me
leave to use the situation in my next tale.

I had occasion to go to the village early next morning, and met the letter-carrier on the road. I presume
he knew my fidgety ways, for he no sooner saw me
than he came up, and informed me that my letter of
the day before had been brought to the office in time
to start. Brought by whom? I asked. He said, by
the *tall young lady.*

Here was a discovery! A flask of the most generous Johannisberg, gulped at a draught, would have
left me cool in comparison. Mdlle. Emma braving the
noonday heat of the dog days, Mdlle. Emma getting
a sunstroke — in fact, nearly achieving martyrdom —
for my sake; what a rich premise to start inferences

from; I confess, to my shame, that I started some of
the wildest. The flesh is weak, you know, especially
at past forty. Thank God, the paroxysm was short.
A misgiving soon stole upon me, a misgiving that I
tenderly nursed and helped on, that I was making a
fool of·myself. A walk of four or five hours, my usual
medicine in cases of a conflict of feeling, being quite
out of the question in the present broiling weather, I
bethought myself of a substitute. I went home and
put myself under a cold shower-bath until my teeth
chattered; then I took my head between both my hands,
and read myself a good lecture in front of my looking-
glass. Thanks to this energetic treatment, I felt
sufficiently braced to go and meet my fair letter-carrier
not at too great a disadvantage.

Had I still wanted sobering, the sight of her would
have done so for me. There was so much of the
child in her looks; she had all the unconsciousness,
the trustfulness, the archness of one, as she said, shaking hands, —

"You have been keeping aloof in presentiment of
bad news in store for you."

"You alarm me," said I, with a look anything but
alarmed; "what can it be?"

"A most disastrous piece of news for you," she
said; "guess."

Her sister, from behind her, made me guess, by a
clever pantomime, that they were going away.

"Let me see," said I; "what can befall me so
tremendous, unless it be that you are going to stay
another week."

She turned sharply round towards her sister. "You
have told him already."

"How could I," said the latter, "when I have not seen him until now?"

"Well," wound up Mdlle. Emma, "we are going to start within three days."

"Three days!" I repeated, with as elongated a face as I could command at so short a notice, "it is a long way off; so we are in for seventy-two more hours of parched heat, and no hope of rain!"

"It will rain . . . tears enough when I am gone," said she.

"Maybe tears of . . . relief," said I.

Mdlle. Emma's stay at Schranksteinbad having coincided with a constant drought, I had, of course, ascribed the fact to some malignant influence of her presence, and pretended to sigh for her departure that the spell might cease.

The three days went off capitally. I had no momentary weakness to conquer, not even the least effort to make, in order to keep my resolution faithfully of letting Mdlle. Emma ignore my knowledge of her little secret. Withal our sporting warfare raged fiercer and more continuous than ever. My happiest hits are of that date. I kept cutting jokes to the last, in the very omnibus which was taking the family to the station, and to which I had craved admission on the plea that I must make sure that Mdlle. Emma was off — it was too good to be believed unless seen, and so on. I was positively astonished at my own self-possession.

It forsook me a little, though, when my turn came to shake hands with Mdlle. Emma. I don't know whether it was I who first pressed hers unwittingly very tight, or she mine, or both of one accord pressed simultaneously; whichever it was, the pressure had this

singular effect on both of us, that we did not find a
single word to say, and stood gazing at each other like
two geese. It was a very awkward moment. The
next she was leaning on the window of the carriage,
still gazing at me and I at her. She looked like a
picture — a beautiful picture — in a frame. A smile,
her would-be usual arch smile, was still lingering round
her mouth, but there was a quiver at one of its corners
. . . and her eyes were filling fast.

What was there extraordinary in the sight that it
should upset me so? I felt a shock in the very centre
of my heart. My eyes grew dim, and there rose to
my lips, trembling for utterance, the first person singular
of the first tense of a very hackneyed verb. . . .

Lucky that the train glided on, as if by stealth,
and, in less time than it takes to write it, Mdlle.
Emma was out of the reach of a whisper. Now, mine
being one of those bashful verbs, which can only be
whispered, I had no choice but to drop it, and give
out instead a loud and hearty "God bless you!"

The sense of the narrow escape I had had was so
strong upon me, that, unscathed though I came out of
it, if I did, I vowed then and there that this should be
my last flirtation.

CHAPTER V.

Herr Konrad.

THE season following that in which I had had a narrow escape of making a fool of myself with Miss Emma, did not open under the best auspices for Schranksteinbad. The weather was unusually cold (heat is a *sine qua non* condition for the success of all Spas), and the company assembled was yet scanty. But Herr Konrad was coming. Could things go otherwise than well when Herr Konrad was coming?

Who was Herr Konrad? you ask.

Herr Konrad was a man, whose face had not been seen in those parts for thirteen years, but whose name still lived in every heart of the populous parish.

What had he done? you ask again.

Just this. He had conferred a far greater and more lasting benefit on the inhabitants of Schrankstein, than if he had discovered a golden placer in each of the spurs of the Jura, against which that village leans. Herr Konrad had . . .

But I must tell the story in my own way, or I shall have no chance of interesting you in it.

On a sultry summer afternoon of the year 183—, a young traveller, staff in hand, and a slender knapsack on his shoulders, was plodding ankle-deep in dust along the road which skirts the Jura, in the direction of Schrankstein. He looked hot and tired, but not weary, not at least with that weariness which blunts

all interest in the landscape. On the contrary, he
seemed thoroughly alive to the beauty of the scene
through which he was passing, as was testified by the
frequent halts he made to take in and leisurely enjoy
such and such of its details as most vividly struck his
eye and fancy. It was now a gentle curve of the river
on his left, or an effect of light on a patch of pasture,
hanging like an emerald on the mountain side, the
brighter for the black pines behind; now a far-spreading
oak, or the majestic soaring of a bird of prey across
the liquid azure of the sky. But what most engrossed
his attention, what most fascinated him, what he could
scarcely detach his eyes from, and to which, if momentarily diverted, they invariably returned, was the chain
of Alps — the Alps towering in all their glory, all
their immense contours, sharp, defined, clear. The
sight was manifestly new to the wayfarer, and he could
not gaze enough on them. His delight was intense —
to the point of forcing from him, alone as he was, short
ejaculations of admiration.

The young wayfarer, as we said, looked flushed
and tired, and had for some time been seeking for a
place sheltered from the sun, where he might lie down
and rest. A cluster of saplings faintly waving in the
breeze on a knoll almost above his head, seemed to
beckon him to their shade. He accepted the invitation,
struck into the rugged zigzag path which led thither,
and threw himself down on the soft moss, drew out a
cotton bandana, wiped the sweat from his brow, and
leaning his chin on his upraised palms, remained absorbed in an ecstasy of admiration.

Presently, up the same rugged zigzags that the
traveller had climbed, came a peasant boy in shirt-

sleeves, with a bundle of books and copy-books strapped together. At sight of a stranger, whom he must pass if he went on, the boy stopped short.

"Where dost thou come from?" asked the man.

"From school," replied the boy.

"From school, where?"

"At Schrankstein."

"Is Schrankstein a large place?"

"O yes."

"How many inhabitants?"

"I don't know."

"Ah! but thou shouldst know, or what is the use of thy going to school?"

"I was never told, — how can I know?" said the boy, whose face was intelligent enough.

"So far thou art right, but somebody is wrong. Canst thou tell me what those white mountains in front are called?"

"The Bernese Oberland," said the boy, brightening up; "that biggest one is the Jungfrau."

"And that white sugar-loaf in the far far distance, dost thou know its name!"

"That is Mont Blanc."

"Is it in Switzerland?"

"Yes."

"No, it is in Savoy. Hast thou ever been told about Savoy?"

"No."

"Nor about the cardinal points?"

"No."

"Dost thou know where the sun rises?"

"There," said the boy quickly, "in the east."

"And where is the west?"

"There."

"Is France to the east or to the west?"

"I don't know."

"And Germany?"

"I don't know."

"Hast thou ever heard of the Rhine?"

"No."

"Or about ancient Greece and Rome?"

"No."

"Who discovered America?"

"I don't know."

"Who invented printing?"

"I don't know."

"Thy ignorance is past belief. Then what do they teach thee at school?"

"To read, to write, and to cast up."

"How dost thou write Helvetia?"

The boy began, H E L, hesitated, stammered, and stopped.

"How much is six times seven?"

"I don't know."

"Come now, think, how much 19 and 23 make."

"I don't know."

"But thou oughtest to know all these things, and many more. How old art thou?"

"Eleven."

"It is a shame that thou art so ignorant — a shame not for thee, poor lad, but for those whose bounden duty it was to teach thee; for what is the benefit of being born free?" wound up the speaker with an angry jerk of both hands, which would have made the boy take to his heels, had he dared. "What is the benefit

of being born in a free country, if you choose to remain the slave of ignorance."

"Bravo!" cried a voice behind the indignant orator;
"I wish all Schrankstein could hear you, and be put
to shame!"

The voice belonged to the M. D. of Schrankstein,
the same, only minus 25 years, whom we had the
pleasure of introducing to the reader in the first part
of these authentic memoirs. He had been paying a
visit at a cottage close by, from whence a short cut to
the village lay by the zigzag path, on the shady knoll,
at the top of which lay resting the dusty pedestrian.
The sound of an unfamiliar voice had first brought the
doctor to a stand-still, and listening; what he heard —
call it dialogue or soliloquy, which you will — had so
much interested him, that he had remained its attentive
auditor to the end.

This doctor was anything but a common village
doctor. He had studied and taken his degree at Bonn;
had travelled not a little, had walked the hospitals of
Vienna, Berlin, and Paris, and had carried back to
his native place, besides a stock of professional science,
a largeness of ideas, a love of progress, and a devotion
to knowledge, which could not but be often wounded
by the narrow-mindedness and ignorance, coupled with
self-complacency, in those around him. The deplorable
state of instruction, or rather its absolute deficiency,
in his parish, had been for years, and was still, a
never-ending source of vexation to him. Even in
Switzerland, a model country in matter of public instruction, there were gaps in it, especially thirty years
ago, and none, perhaps, more deep than at Schrankstein. This village had but a primary school of the

weakest sort, and no secondary one at all. All the
doctor's efforts to have the first improved, and the
second established, had failed through the general
apathy. The utterance of sentiments chiming in so
well with his own, had immediately won his heart.

An acquaintance originating in a warm sympathy
of feeling grows fast into intimacy, especially between
young people. They had not walked together more
than half-an-hour before they knew everything about
each other; and by the time they reached the village,
they were so mutually well pleased, that an offer of
hospitality was as cordially made by the one as accepted by the other.

The name of the wayfarer was Konrad. Politics
had set him at variance with the Government of his
country, and to escape arrest, he had expatriated himself. He had read law in the University of Heidel-
berg, but with neither zest nor perseverance; the bent
of his mind was towards pedagogy, and all that concerned education had an irresistible attraction for him.
Theories of instruction, considerations of how best to
promote the diffusion of knowledge, had gradually become his paramount interest and occupation, or, as he
said himself, his hobby-horse. He held ignorance to
be the root of all evil, that to instruct was to moralize,
and that every generation owed in that respect to the
one about to follow a duty as binding as that a father
owes to a son. Hence his indignation at the discovery
of the crass ignorance of the peasant boy.

At the end of the third day Konrad spoke of going
away. The doctor would not hear of such a thing.
"Going; and pray where? You said you had no en-
gagements."

"Ah! but I have one though," retorted Konrad; "an engagement with myself to earn my bread, and which I hope to be able to fulfil at Geneva."

"And why not here?" asked the doctor. "We have several manufactories of watches here; and if you object to manual work, we might find you a situation as accountant in one or other of them."

"I don't object to manual labour," replied Konrad, "but I do, on more grounds than one, to life in a village or small town; and, in fact, nothing could reconcile me with the disagreeables of such a residence, but the conviction of being really useful to my fellow-creatures, or, in less ambitious phrase, the freedom to ride my hobby."

"Of that I see no chance here. You might preach till doomsday without converting our people to your views."

"I should not despair of that if I could but first convert you!"

"Convert me!" cried the doctor; "as if I were not sufficiently alive to the disgrace of the system of darkness which prevails here; as if I had not deplored it for years and years!"

"Agreed!" said Konrad; "you are converted to the belief of the existence of the evil, and of the desirability of its removal, but not to the belief of your power to remove it, and it is to that faith I would convert you."

"I have Horace by heart, my dear friend; I know *quid valeant humeri, quid ferre recusent.*"

"I beg your pardon; you don't know your own strength. A man of your attainments, a physician, a

town-councillor, and member of the Great Council to
boot, ought only to will to succeed."

"I tell you that no power of will could get the
Town-Council of Schrankstein to vote funds for a
school such as you mean; and no penny no pater-
noster."

"And I bet you a wager that I'll bring them to
vote the funds for such a school, if you will promise to
stand by me, and support me in real earnest."

"That I will with all my heart," said the doctor,
half convinced by his new friend's sanguine confidence,
and pricked also by an incipient misgiving whether
indeed he had done all that he might have practically
done towards the accomplishment of an object which
he certainly had had most sincerely at heart. And if
you ask how I came at so minute a knowledge of
what passed in the doctor's mind, my answer is, that I
had these particulars from the doctor himself, who did
not spare himself whenever his own disparagement re-
dounded to the greater glorification of his friend.

Herr Konrad set to work immediately, and drew
up a clear, concise, and practical memorial to be laid
before the head of the department of public instruction
for the Canton. The doctor took charge of the document, to which he added a strong recommendation from
himself. Lucidity and practical sense were Herr Konrad's distinguishing attributes; he had a horror of all
that was vague and indefinite; his suggestions were
always cast in a precise and matter-of-fact mould; and
whenever he required anything to be done away with,
he considered himself bound to suggest a substitute.
The gentleman who received the memorial chanced to
be a liberal, and a clever man — one capable of ap-

preciating the species of talent displayed by the me-
morialist; he was indeed so favourably impressed by
what he read, that he resolved to make acquaintance
with the writer, and, with golden republican simplicity,
drove in his *char-à-banc* the very next Sunday to
Schrankstein. It· was at these very baths from which
I write, or rather at the small and modest Wirthschaft,
out of which the present establishment was to spring,
that he had a long and pleasant talk with Herr Konrad
and the doctor over a bottle of markgräfler. The
result of the interview was, that in so far as the Central Government was concerned, Herr Konrad's views
were approved, and he himself was empowered to put
in action his programme of a secondary school; — a
decision the more honourable to the liberality of the
Government from which it emanated, that the Canton
in which Schrankstein is situated, is a strictly Catholic one, and the new professor appointed was Pro-
téstant.

This nomination meant, at the same time, much
and nothing; much, in so far as, to be legally entitled
to teach throughout the breadth and length of the
Canton, the sanction of the central executive was indispensable; nothing, in so much as it lay in the power
of the Town-council to refuse its exequatur. In other
words, it might frustrate the nomination by declining
to grant the funds necessary to give it practical effect.
The great point then was, to lay siege to, and to can-
vass each and all of the members of the Town-council,
so as to secure a majority to confirm the decision of
the Cantonal Government. Here it was that the struggle
began in right earnest. Whether he reasoned, argued,
cajoled, tickled their self-love, or stung them with

7*

ridicule, Herr Konrad made but little impression, and the motion had to be postponed from week to week in order to avoid certain defeat.

Besides being a Protestant, and dealing in an article without value in their eyes, Herr Konrad lay under a third disadvantage of which he never dreamt, until it was revealed to him by the doctor. Herr Konrad was a poor wine-drinker, nay, drank only water. "And," added the doctor, "so long as you cannot stand a couple of bottles or so without flinching, so long you need never hope to exercise any ascendency over these fellows. They recognise no other standard of manliness than the quantity of liquor you can imbibe."

"So be it," said Herr Konrad with a merry laugh. "Those who choose to associate with wolves must learn to howl like them. I have not been a student for nothing; and it is not so long ago since, either out of bravado or for a wager, I used to gulp down more wine or beer than was good for me. Surely, what I could do in a bad, I may manage in a good cause. A little practice will soon put me up to their mark." And so it proved. Konrad's was one of those iron constitutions which can accomplish any task set to it; he had steel nerves, the stomach of an ostrich, and a head to match the one and the other. In an incredibly short time he felt himself a match for the hardest drinker the Town-council could boast of, and abided the occasion to prove it. Some contemptuous remark as to water-drinkers afforded the opportunity. Herr Konrad replied to the bully who had uttered the sneer, that it was never safe to take for granted that a preference for water indicated incapability of carrying a *quantum suff.* of wine; he was himself an instance in point. The assertion was met with ridicule, expressed by word and grimace. Konrad continued his provocation; a challenge ensued — a challenge as to which would drink most wine. The bully was defeated, signally floored.

This feat won for Herr Konrad a degree of consideration which ten years of a useful and blameless life would probably have failed to do. Henceforth, his arguments were listened to with due respect, and his taunts about the valley of darkness, and so on, no longer missed their mark, but were bitterly repulsed and resented. Briefly, Herr Konrad and his scheme gained ground every day, and, to make a long story short, one memorable morning the Council, in a fit of generosity, allotted, out of the funds of the parish, a sum for the salary of the new schoolmaster, a sum not enough to live upon, just enough not to die upon.

You mistake if you believe that his difficulties were now at an end — no such thing. He had the scissors, as the phrase goes, but the cloth to operate upon was wanting. To be more explicit, the school was opened, the schoolmaster at his post, but no scholars were forthcoming. The curé and his assistant, foreboding no end of evils if the Catholic children were confided to the teaching of a Protestant master, had tabooed the school. The women, as always happens in such cases, agreed fully and emphatically with the opinion held by their spiritual advisers, and saw to their being obeyed. The men, as always happens in such cases, stood aloof from fear of their wives, and let them have their way. Here was a pretty mess!

Herr Konrad's coolness and composure in this critical situation were truly admirable. He had but four pupils, two orphans sent by the Town-council, the son of the mayor, an *esprit fort*, and that same boy, the son of a widower, whom he had questioned on the shady knoll some months back. Had these four pupils been a hundred, Herr Konrad could not have been more earnest, more assiduous, more indefatigable in his exertions to instruct without tiring them. After the first week they adored their master, and preferred lessons to play. It is possible, nay probable, that the force of example, acting on the principle of the drop of water boring the stone, might have sooner or later got the better of prejudice and opposition; nay, there were already faint indications of a change in that direction, when it so happened that two unforeseen and notable additions to the scanty group of Herr Konrad's scholars, came in rapid succession to give an irresistible impulse to the hitherto slack-going wheels of the educational coach.

The first accession was that of a young peasant some twenty years of age, who lived in a village hidden in the folds of the Jura, distant at least two good hours' walk from Schrankstein. This youth, born, as it seems, with a natural thirst for knowledge, which he had never yet had an opportunity of slaking, no sooner heard of the new school within his reach, than he determined to attend it. Every one can easily imagine the sensation produced by the presence of a full-grown man in a class of children, coupled also with the fact of his obstinately coming every day from so far off. People began to suspect that what was bestowed at the school must be worth having, if it repaid such continued personal inconvenience.

But the accession of a single peasant youth was as

nothing to that which followed close upon its heels. It
must be known that Schrankstein marks the limits of
the canton of which it forms part, and that the next
village to it belongs to another canton, which is Protestant. Now, whether the schoolmaster of the neighbouring village was disabled by illness, or that he did
not give satisfaction, I cannot say, but the fact is, his
pupils, more than a score in number, having first asked
and obtained leave, came over *en masse*, and enrolled
themselves as Herr Konrad's pupils. This was the
coup de grâce to the curé, his assistant, and their party.
Heads of families acquired now the conviction that
what they had scorned at first, had some value in it,
and the argument that Schrankstein did not pay a
schoolmaster merely for strangers, was rife on every
tongue. The upshot is not difficult to divine — every
urchin, who could, by the most liberal construction, be
considered fit for the new school, was sent to it.

The vessel was now fairly launched, and with a
man at its helm of Herr Konrad's zeal and ability, no
doubt of its reaching a good port. In fact, at the
end of the first scholastic year, the report he sent
in to the corporation was one that gave fair hopes
of success for the future; hopes that were fully confirmed the ensuing season. This last memorial concluded with the petition, that "whereas the present
schoolroom was insufficient for the accommodation of
so many scholars, unwholesome from the want of ven-
tilation, dark and damp, in short, in a state of general
dilapidation, and in all respects ill-becoming alike the
dignity of its purpose, and of a large and flourishing
community: and whereas the premises where the rising
generation were to be instructed, disciplined, and trained

to become useful citizens, ought to be, next to the place of worship, the noblest building in the parish, so the Town-council was prayed to see to the erection of a new and appropriate schoolhouse, worthy its destination, and the thriving and enlightened community of Schrankstein," etc., etc.

The *Patres Patriæ* returned thanks for the able report; but as to the concluding recommendation, they shrugged their shoulders, and there was an end of the matter . . . till the following year, when an identical petition being presented, instead of shrugging their shoulders, they bestowed a larger room on the school. Nevertheless, and in spite of this concession, the petition was reiterated a third time, and the project was discussed in council, and lost by a great majority. By way of consolation for these continued failures, the position of the disappointed suitor was bettered, and his stipend slightly increased. This sop to Cerberus, however, did not prevent his urging his point year after year, until, at length, on the eighth or ninth application, I am not sure which, Herr Konrad gained the victory, and a vote was passed, almost by unanimous consent, for the erection of a schoolhouse. A rising ground was chosen for its site, and two years later was completed that lofty schoolhouse for which Schrankstein is famous — a schoolhouse which it would be difficult to match throughout Switzerland.

A proud and happy day it was for our schoolmaster, which saw the inauguration of that building — emblem of a thorough mental revolution in the parish, a revolution brought about by the perseverance and intelligence of one man. Schrankstein was, by this time, fully converted to a belief in the blessings of education; and to show their sense of this, as well as their gratitude to him who had opened their eyes, the greatest honour in their power was bestowed on Herr Konrad, that is, they granted him an act of naturalization.

The commotions of 1848 re-opened for him the gates of his native land, and, though sincerely attached to the country which had adopted him, he was unable to resist the spell of the old fatherland. Accompanied by universal regrets, good wishes, and blessings, he left Schrankstein. It was a cruel wrench on both sides, but to Herr Konrad the bitterness of parting was tempered by the faith he entertained, that the good work he had begun would not perish because he went. He had, in truth, more than once contemplated the possibility of his having to leave, and, with a view to meet such a contingency, he had singled out a certain number of his more promising pupils, and trained them so as to qualify them to take his place and continue his labours in an undertaking which had succeeded beyond his hopes.

Herr Konrad threw himself, heart and soul, into the politics of his native country, and when adverse circumstances cut him off from that field of activity, he resumed his favourite studies and avocations with much composure. To enlighten and instruct was, after all, the best and shortest road to the attainment of those objects which Germany had just failed to realize. He had an absolute faith, which bordered on fatalism, in the future unity of his country; hence the equanimity, almost indifference, with which he bore shortcomings and failures, which might retard, but could not prevent, according to him, the goal from being eventually

reached. He filled places of trust in several of the
best educational institutions in Germany, and published
a work on education, which created a sensation throughout the land, and which ultimately led to his being
offered the Portfolio of Public Instruction in the cabinet
of the not inconsiderable principality of which he was
a native. This offer occasioned a great conflict of
feeling in our friend's mind. The administration which
he was invited to join was liberal, and as national as
it could be in such a parcelled-out country as Germany. The men composing it all possessed his respect
and sympathy — one among them was his esteemed
friend. The proposed office opened for him a wider field
for doing good than he had ever dreamed of. But all
these advantages were more than counterbalanced by
by his innate horror of all official shackles and empty
ceremonies. The rude simplicity of republican ways
and manners, in the midst of which he had passed the
best years of his life, had left a tinge upon him. It
was therefore more in obedience to the argument of his
friend, that no man had a right to let his individual
idiosyncrasies stand between him and the good he might
do, than from any choice of his own, that Herr Konrad consented to become a minister of state, a post
which he has continued to hold to this day.

Such was the man for whom, not quite a fortnight
after I had been installed in the quiet nook, Schrankstein was raising triumphal arches, for whom Schranksteinbad was trimming its hedges, rolling its gravel
walks, and decking its great hall with German and
Swiss flags.

CHAPTER VI.

"See tho Conquering Hero comos."

HERR KONRAD'S arrival gave rise to a trifling difficulty, the speedy solution of which, while testifying to
his presence of mind, gave me one more proof, had
that been wanted, of the facility with which men allow
themselves to be ruled by words.

Thinking it not unlikely that his fellow-citizens of
Schrankstein would wish to pay him some public honour,
Herr Konrad, with that considerateness which distin-
guished him, sent word that he had arranged so as to
arrive on a Sunday, the only day in the week which
gives the hard-tasked labourer leisure to indulge in a
demonstration.   But Herr Konrad could not, and did
not guess that his friends and former pupils had set
their hearts on treating him to a Fackelzug, or pro-
menade by torchlight, and to a display of fireworks,
and had taken it for granted, the wish being father to
the thought, that he would come by the train, which
reaches Schrankstein at a quarter-past eight in the
evening.   Instead of which . . . but everything at its
place.

Just at half-past eleven A.M. of the Sunday in question, I happened to be at the doctor's. I was there by
his request to witness the trial of a new machine for
pulverizing water, which he had commissioned me to
bring him from Paris, and from which, if it answered
as well in practice as in theory, he anticipated the most

beneficial effects in the treatment of diseases of the
larynx and of the chest. Well, we were literally enveloped in a cloud of water-dust, when the doctor suddenly gave a bound as if he had been stung by a
wasp, and, in shirt-sleeves as he was, shot through the
garden, and across the road, which only separated his
house from the railway station opposite, ran up to a
gentleman on the platform (Herr Konrad, of course,
thought I), and after heartily shaking him by the hand,
took the arm of the new-comer, and hurried him over
the road, and through the garden into the house. The
doctor was rattling away all the while, evidently im-
parting some news to his friend. Something *mal à
propos* rather than evil, as I guessed, partly from certain little bursts of laughter with which he interspersed
his tale, and partly from the twist full of humour
which the information gave to the features of the
listener.

All this had not taken more than a couple of
minutes, but a couple of minutes had sufficed for the
respectable sprinkle of local gentry, who had witnessed
Herr Konrad's arrival and his immediate disappearance,
to recover their wits, and to feel desirous of ascertain-
ing what had become of him. The surest way was to
follow in his track, that is, cross the road, and enter
the doctor's garden — this they did, advancing in a
body towards the open window, before which stood
conspicuous the tall figure of Herr Konrad. A recogni-
tion seemed inevitable.

The doctor first glanced piteously at the approaching group, and then at Herr Konrad, as much as to
say "What shall we do?" Herr Konrad whispered to
him. The doctor put his head out of the window, and

waving his hand significantly to the intruders not to come farther, repeated in a loud voice the short formula which Herr Konrad had whispered to him. The party first came to a stand-still, and then without so much as interchanging a look, wheeled round, and retraced their steps.

What shibboleth, what magic spell, had the doctor used? Merely the two syllables *incog.* Informed by the doctor of the great preparations for the evening, not even yet completed, and desirous of extricating his friends of Schrankstein from the dilemma of either giving him a welcome inadequate to their feelings, or of seeming to neglect him for hours, — a dilemma into which he had unwittingly thrown them by his premature arrival, Herr Konrad had bethought himself of having it announced that he had come incog., and that such being the case, nobody was to take notice of him, nor he take notice of anybody until eight o'clock that evening — a contrivance which succeeded far beyond his expectation, as the contriver himself, to whose courtesy I am indebted for the preceding explanation given in most excellent French, assured me between one jolt and another, of the anything but well hung omnibus which was taking us to Schranksteinbad.

Here also the word *incog.* produced a reaction, for no sooner had Herr Konrad dropped it with much mock gravity, than the flow of pleasurable excitement, which his presence had put in motion, stopped short, and Madely and Frantz and all the rest felt awkward and chilled, without knowing exactly why. I use the identical words employed by Madeleine as she told me her impressions. Even the score or so of bathers who sat down to dinner with Herr Konrad, and most of whom had previously professed themselves anxious and proud to make his acquaintance, caught the infection and grew shy; and none of them had the courage to go beyond the commonplace inquiries about his journey, and the weather, save, however, my right hand neigbour, Mdlle. Jacottet, who made an honourable exception to the rule.

This lady, in whose immediate vicinity I had the privilege of taking my meals, was a tall, lean, shrivelled spinster of seventy or thereabouts, more generally known as Boa Constrictor — a nickname for which she was indebted to a constant rotatory motion of the head, which, combined with a long neck and a wide gaping mouth, might to a certain degree call up the image of a serpent coiling itself previous to darting on its prey. Mdlle. Jacottet was not the least remarkable of a pleiad of oddities which graced the upper part of the table, where it was my fortune to sit. To mention only some — my two neighbours on the left were a brother and sister, well-to-do country people, both so desperately deaf, that they had given up any attempt at communicating, not only with strangers, but even with each other. When they had something particular to discuss, they went to some out-of-the-way field or hill, and roared out their business in each other's ear. Beyond them, that is, at the head of the table (the order of arrival was most strictly adhered to in the allotment of places), sat the first arrived, a very old Rector of a not distant parish, who had not a single tooth left, and for whom consequently the process of dining was a continual terrible struggle, and accompanied by a display of grimaces and sounds more original than agreeable to behold or hear. He was a

"Baigneur Sérieux," — nay, the recognised leader of the so-called party, and not for the world would he have sat down to his mid-day meal without having first imbibed his thirty-four glasses of curative water.

The "Baigneurs Sérieux" were one of the three groups, into which some unknown Linnæus had classed the visitors at our spa previous to my discovery of it, and I had ample opportunities to test and acknowledge the justness and felicity of the classification. The first group, then, comprised all those inmates of Schranksteinbad, who came solely for sanitary purposes, who had an implicit faith in the curative virtue of the waters, and whose all-absorbing occupation was to follow the régime prescribed by the doctor. You met them at all times, and in all sorts of weather, hanging about the springs (of these there were two, one ferruginous, the other alkaline), each armed with a glass and a bottle, some exposing the water to the sun to take off the chill, according to orders, some walking leisurely, some going at a quicker pace, and some running as if for a wager, between one draught and the other — all consulting their watches at every moment. If not a gay sight, it was a curious one.

The eclectic bathers constituted the second group; to it belonged all the able-bodied, those who came solely for the sake of change from the routine of business or town-life, and who had no other desire than to spend their time as merrily and agreeably as they could. To these may be added a sprinkle of delicate people of both sexes, who neither absolutely believing nor disbelieving in the healing power of the waters, used them in great moderation, chiefly relying on rest, fresh air, pure milk, and the bracing emanations of

the pine forests encircling the Baths, for their restoration
to health.

The third, and not the least numerous group of the
three, bore the generic appellation of the "Menagerie."
It consisted of those boarders who, heedless alike of
water, country air, and lovely nature, had but one
thought, one care, one aim — that of eating and
drinking their full at the smallest possible cost. Whenever the last bell for any of the meals was five minutes behind time, the members of the "Menagerie"
mustered in force in the passage leading to the kitchen,
and roared like wild beasts for their food. Hence the
name of this group.

To return to our pleiad of oddities, and, through
them, to the brightest of all, Mdlle. Jacottet. To complete the sketch of the old Rector, the president of the
table, I must add that he was deaf as a post, and resolute not to confess he was so; very irascible, and fond
of talking — a propensity this last which, considering
ne had the brother and sister on his left, who for all
purposes of communication were as good as dumb, he
could only hope to indulge with his neighbour on the
right. Now this happened to be an old professor, as
deaf, as irascible, as fond of talking as our president
himself. I leave you to imagine what could come of
it — nothing but grunts and snorts, and metaphorical
daggers-drawing. My ears still ring with the dis-
paraging asides with which they pelted one another.
"When one has such an infirmity, one ought to give
up trying to converse," muttered the Rector. "He is
as deaf as a stone, I declare," grumbled the professor.
I still hear the angry protest of the one old gentleman
whenever the other happened to raise his voice to a

louder pitch. "You needn't bellow so, I am not deaf."
Really, sometimes there was wherewithal to make one's
sides ache with laughter. `

Mdlle. Jacottet had, to put the case mildly, a
screw or two loose somewhere, and her line of thought
and action gave sad evidence of the defect. They
were about as consistent as the gait of a drunken person, or the course of a rudderless vessel. The fact
of her having felt the necessity, or more probably of
some friend or relation having seen the necessity of
securing for her the services of a pilot to guide her
through the world, militates strongly in favour of the
last of the above similes. The pilot or companion was
a resolute and not unhandsome-looking young woman,
who sat opposite to me, never opening her mouth but
to eat, to answer Mdlle. Jacottet, or remonstrate with
her. Mademoiselle's crotchets and delusions varied *ad
infinitum;* but there were three of more frequent re-
currence than the others, and according to the one of
these paramount for the moment, she would assume
and act either the part of some great personage, or
that of an old wretch afflicted with every imaginable
disease, or else of a young girl of eighteen; and thus
be by turns courtly and patronizing, querulous and
whining, naïve and bewitching. Fancy how this last
assumption became a poor creature who was less like
a woman than a roll of old parchment.

It was not the personation of juvenility she chose
for this occasion. She mounted instead her high stilts,
dropped Herr Konrad a most dignified courtesy, and
begged him to be seated, and to partake of such
hospitality as she could offer. It was very amiable of
him to have come to pay her a visit. She hoped he

had had a pleasant journey. And what sort of weather
had he met in the Bay of Biscay? And how was the
Princess, his wife; and how were the young Dukes?
And how had he left the Emperor Soulouque? Was it
true that H. M. was going to abdicate in favour of the
Duke of Wellington? Had His Highness brought over
with him his grand crosses, orders, and medals? She
made the inquiry because she intended to give a State
Ball, and should like him to wear all his decorations
on that occasion. By the bye, did he prefer fried or
mashed potatoes? The cook must be informed which.
She was afraid he would find her present residence
and the company assembled there dull, the more so as
he had just left the brilliant Court of St. James's.
Most of the people about her were low-born, it was
true, but they were obliging and good-natured. Had
she said good-natured? Deuce take her if they were.
They were nothing better than a pack of heartless
jackanapes, and the twopenny doctor at the head of
them, who coolly watched a poor old woman dying by
inches of a polypus in the corner of her stomach, and
would do nothing to save her — nothing! nothing!
nothing! For God's sake, would he have mercy on
her and keep her from dying; from dying — dying!

If I had cause to admire Herr Konrad for his quick
perception of the real state of the case, and for the
presence of mind which enabled him to repress all
surprise at being thus strangely addressed, I had still
more cause to love him for the gentle, and I may say,
chivalrous care he took to abstain in his replies from
any, the least word or look, or even inflection of voice,
which might convey the impression to any of those
present, that he was aware he was speaking to a lunatic.

And this was the more kind, considerate, and meritorious, as he was a man superlatively alive to fun and humour. Indeed, his behaviour was so natural throughout the scene, that some doubted whether he really was conscious of the abnormal condition of Mdlle. Jacottet's mind. And thus he succeeded in checking, or rather in keeping within certain bounds, the mirth which her stately airs and queer expressions could not but excite.

And when the unfortunate lady fairly broke out into lamentations and pitiful calls for help against an imaginary foe, far from contradicting, or even arguing the point with her, he admitted it at once, only observing that stomach-complaints were no longer the bugbear they had been hitherto. Science had progressed, specifics had been found, and many were the sufferers he had seen recover perfectly through them, and live to a good old age. He was himself a martyr to cramps of the stomach, and never travelled without a flask or two of a certain elixir, which did him a world of good. Would she try a few drops of it in a glass of champagne? Miss Jacottet did try the elixir, and felt wonderfully revived.

When dinner was over, Herr Konrad disappeared — I suppose he went to rest after a jumbling of twenty-four hours in a railway carriage — and I did not see him again until the evening, at half-past seven or so, when the doctor came to fetch him, and invited me to accompany them. Leaving the more frequented thoroughfare, we struck into by-paths and lanes, to avoid putting in jeopardy the incog. of our companion. Of this, however, there was little fear, considering that Schrankstein had entered so fully into the concealment

8*

scheme, that, I verily believe, they would have kept
up the farce against Herr Konrad himself, and denied,
if necessary, his identity to his very face. They had
pushed their scruples on this head so far, said the
doctor, that they had refrained from going to the baths,
their usual Sunday lounge. It was by a long circuitous
way that we reached the rear of the railway station,
and, concealing ourselves behind the wall of an adjoining shed, used as a storehouse, we waited for the
arrival of the eight o'clock train, which took place
within a few minutes, and then we made for the platform, intending to mix with the crowds of passengers
alighting, or getting in.

But, whether we had started a second too late, or
whether the train had no passengers, or very few to
disgorge or swallow up, or both, certain it is, that
when we arrived in front of the station the platform
was clear, and there we stood conspicuous *coram populo*,
who began immediately to wave their hats and cheer
lustily, while the band, which was one of Herr Konrad's creations, struck up "Heil Vaterland," I am sorry
to say sadly out of tune, but that's of no consequence.
Herr Konrad took off his hat and flourished it to the
crowd, which now choked the station, and every approach to it. All Schrankstein was present. The
doctor took off his hat, and flourished it to the crowd;
and what else could I do but follow his example? It
was anything but agreeable for me, I assure you, to
stand there confronting that sea of heads, all surging
towards us; to feel that the group of which I was one,
was the focus to which converged the stare of all those
eyes. I vowed to myself that it should not be long
before I escaped from a post of honour so little suited

to my taste, to resume the more modest place assigned me by fate, that of an observer from the pit, and not from the dress circles. But, for the nonce, there was nothing for it but to follow in the wake of the bigger and the lesser luminary shining before me.

The Mayor, the Town-council, and most of Herr Konrad's particular friends, who had come to meet him within the station, instantly pounced upon him, and amidst greetings, congratulations, and unlimited shaking of hands — of which last I came in for a good share — led him, or, I may say, led us, for I was one of a group of twenty persons at least, and to all practical ends and purposes as free as a state prisoner. Well, they led us from off the platform into the road, along which we had to parade, greeted and greeting for some five minutes, until we reached an arch of foliage erected for the occasion, and there we came to a stand-still. The object of the halt was to offer Herr Konrad what is called in those parts the *wine of honour*. The good Swiss folk seem to think with an Italian poet — Redi, if I am not mistaken — that

> " Chi ben comincia ha la metà dell' opra,
> Nè si comincia ben se non dal bere."

For my part, I had every reason to thank this practice, for the confusion inherent to it afforded me the longed-for opportunity for taking French leave of my official surroundings, and finding refuge among the common ranks. In order to enjoy yourself, and to be your own master, there's nothing like being nobody.

While the cup of honour was being drained, the cortege which lined the road, along which we had passed, began to form in procession four abreast, filing

off amidst loud vivats before the hero of the fête and
the group assembled under the triumphal arch. The
band headed the procession, playing to the best of its
powers; after it came a good number of torch-bearers,
then six gentlemen on horseback, then the boys' and
girls' schools, with their respective masters and mis-
tresses; then more torch-bearers, and carriers of lighted
lamps stuck on a pole. After these last, Herr Konrad
and his friends fell into the ranks, and were followed
by the bulk of the population. The six mounted gentlemen were considered, and justly so, the great gun
of the pageant; every one gazed at them with pride,
and they looked not a little proud of themselves. All
six had been Herr Konrad's pupils, who had since
made their way in the world. None of them were at
present living in Schrankstein; they had come from a
good distance to do honour to their former master, and
to have celebrated his arrival in their absence would
have been a positive cruelty to them, and a bitter disappointment to their fellow-villagers.

Night was closing in when Schranksteinbad was
reached. A kind of estrade had been raised on the
balcony, which ran outside the whole length of the
great hall and the dancing-room, both already more
than once alluded to. Upon this estrade Herr Konrad
and his escort of magnates took their seats, he, of
course, being in the centre. He had the Mayor on
his left, and a sort of giant on his right, who, said I
to myself, must be a personage indeed, to occupy the
post he has. He was a stranger to me, who knew
every living soul in the village. I had remarked this
tall individual at the station, and I had been struck
by the particular warmth and effusion of the greeting

he had given to, and received from Herr Konrad. Demonstrativeness is not the besetting sin of the brave German Swiss; they may be likened to matches kept in some damp hole, and which require a deal of friction to make them ignite. My stranger wore a black coat, but a glance sufficed to show that he felt ill at ease in it. His shirt-collars were extraordinarily high and stiff as boards, and insinuated themselves under his ears so as to raise them in quite an alarming manner. The expression of his countenance was good, but every separate feature gave you the idea of its having been cut by some third-rate carver in wood, and stuck on the face at hap-hazard.

The estrade afforded space enough for all the bathers, who had reserved seats in it, and for many of the casual visitors, who, it being Sunday, you re-collect, had come from the environs to dance, and who, for novelty's sake, had deserted the ball-room. The procession drew up on the ground below the bal-cony, at a sufficient distance to allow of seeing and being seen; torch and lamp-bearers in front, torch and lamp-bearers in the rear, the gentlemen on horseback, the band, and the schools in the intervening space. Hemming in the cortege, and indeed as far as the eye could reach, was wave upon wave of human forms, looking in the twilight like shadows. The scene was impressive enough, as all large gatherings of people out of doors are, particularly when dimly illuminated, and that only by fits and starts, as was the case here. From serene the weather had changed into fitful, and intermittent gusts of hot wind had begun to blow, owing to which most of the torches had been ex-tinguished, and the few that remained alive were

madly quivering and flickering in the blast, shooting
long flashes of flame right and left, and producing
thereby the most fantastic effects. It was well that
considerate Frantz had bethought himself of stopping
the jets d'eau of the two artificial pieces of water, in
order that the splashing and trickling might not interfere with the hearing of the speeches that were to be
delivered, or more than one Schranksteiner would in
all probability have had the benefit of a shower-bath,
improvised for him by the rattling breeze, without
paying for it.

As soon as every one had subsided into his proper
place, and the band had finished playing, a young
man with a long black beard, and a very intelligent
set of features, came forth from the ranks of the
schools, and, fronting the balcony, began to recite an
oration, of which all I know is, that I found it rather
too long for the occasion. The public evidently did
not share my opinion, for there were no signs of impatience; on the contrary, repeated cheers and applause.
The orator was the head-master, a former pupil and
favourite of Herr Konrad. When he had ended, Herr
Konrad rose, and with him all the persons in the gallery, and he addressed the crowd. A dead silence
prevailed, alone interrupted, at long intervals, by the
moaning of the wind in the trees. He spoke plainly
and distinctly — not a word was lost. As he spoke
in German, I understood about as much of his speech
as I had done of the one preceding it; but I was much
struck with the difference of his accent from the head-
master's; that of the latter was sharp as vinegar, that
of the former as smooth as oil. Herr Konrad had
scarcely spoken five minutes, when his audience were

like soft wax in his hands: he made them laugh or look grave, say *yes* or *no* at his will. Every one of his sentences was cheered, and, as if to win my heart completely, he had the good taste to be short. His resumption of his seat was the signal for a burst of applause, which lasted for several minutes.

The band struck up again, and when the music ceased, the fireworks began. They were of the most common sort, giving not the less pleasure for that, as was attested by the shouts of admiration they elicited. Being few in number, they were soon at an end, and with them concluded the out-of-door part of the entertainment, and the in-door gala began.

CHAPTER VII.

Vilo doubts dispelled with a Vengeance.

THE large hall to which the company repaired presented a sight worth seeing. All the spaces between
the windows were decorated with trophies festooned
with garlands of leaves, tastefully arranged and interspersed with German flags, gold, red and black, and
the canton flags red and yellow. Every table, — there
were three rows of them stretching from end to end of
the hall, — every table at regular intervals showed a
large bouquet and a young fir-tree, the branches of
which were studded with diminutive German and Swiss
flags, and rosettes and flowing ribbons of flaming
colours. It would be difficult to conceive anything
more gay than these simple decorations, flooded as
they were with light from the enormous centre chan-
delier, only lighted on extraordinary occasions, and
from hundreds of sconces on the walls, and lamps on
the tables. It was a blaze of light such as reminded
one of our Italian *illuminazioni a giorno*.

Seen from the entrance door, whence the eye could
take in the whole scene at a glance, the flowers, the
lights, the triple range of tables with their variegated
green, surrounded by beaming faces, with an occasional
glimpse of forms floating vision-like in the furthermost
background, — substantial and thick-shoed realities
though, waltzing and polking in the ballroom; — seen
from the door, I say, the *coup d'œil* was enchanting.

The boarders enjoyed it from a gallery above the door, where chairs had been provided for them. All our ladies were there, Mdlle. Jacottet most conspicuous in a low white dress, and flowers in her hair. She appeared much excited.

The hall contained seats for four hundred persons, and not one was unoccupied. In the centre of the middle table sat Herr Konrad and his self-constituted staff. I observed that its number had been augmented: it now included the six horsemen, the head-master (the spokesman of the address), and several under-masters. It did not take the guests long to dispose of the eatables before them, and then the cup that cheers *and* inebriates began to circulate freely. If it be good to begin by drinking, why should it not be good to end by it also? Speeches were made, healths drunk, toasts given, and the clinking of glass against glass was almost incessant. Old and young, gentle and simple, issued from the remotest corners to hobnob with the hero of the fête. Before the bottle, all Swiss are equal. The only distinction I remarked was in the quality of the wine imbibed. While aristocratic champagne flowed plentifully at the privileged table, where sat Herr Konrad, the common herd had to rest satisfied with ordinary wine. The unceasing exertions of Frantz and Madely, backed by a numerous staff of supplementary waiters and waitresses, scarcely sufficed to make the supply keep pace with the demand. The rows of empty bottles on the table grew in no time appalling.

By and by my giant friend of the extraordinary shirt-collars rose, and, in a voice quite in accordance with the bull-like thorax from which it issued, gave forth the first notes of the national anthem, "Rufst du, mein Vaterland?" In an instant all the company were on their feet; and all, including the dancers, who at the first note had ceased their whirling, joined in the song. A very impressive one it is, as every Englishman knows who has ever heard "God save the Queen" — and what Englishman has not sung "God save the Queen" with all his soul? The Swiss and English national anthems are, in fact, identical, so far as the music is concerned. The singing, in the present instance, was nothing wonderful, unless for the number of voices united. What did render the performance more striking and effective than I can express, was the new spirit which it had awakened in the assembly: it was the earnestness with which all raised their voices; it was the thrill of intense feeling with which all rested upon the grand and holy oft-recurring words "Vaterland" and "Helvetia." You felt that that dear vaterland, which every tongue hailed and blessed, was a real living thing that filled every heart. It was this which imparted to the gigantic chorus a truly solemn, almost religious character.

The elevated state of feeling into which I had been thrown was sadly jarred by the drinking bouts and bacchanal songs which closely succeeded the anthem. The heat too was tremendous, and I thirsted after a breath of fresh air. So out I went, and happening to meet in the passage my nymph Egeria bending under a tray full of bottles (Madely not being deep in profane history, rather objected to my calling her Egeria, probably out of fear that the nymph of that name might be no better than she should be), — well then, happening to meet Madely, I stopped her to ask who

that big fellow in black was, who was sitting on the right
of Herr Konrad. "Why, who should he be but Michael
of the mountain?" cried Madely; "Michael who came
from so far away to attend Herr Konrad's first class,
and did not mind sitting on the same bench with little
fellows, a grown man of twenty as he was. I wonder
you did not guess at once;" and on she hurried with
her bottles.

She might indeed well wonder — how stupid I
had been not to have perceived what was so obvious!
The truth is, my imagination had endowed Michael
with a set of features more in accordance with his
aspirations, than those bestowed on him by Dame Nature. Michael's elevation to knowledge, be it said in
a parenthesis, had brought him more substantial re-
wards than it does in general to the votaries of learning. He was by this time a well-to-do farmer, a happy
husband and father, mayor, attorney, schoolmaster; in
one word, the first man of the mountainous little
hamlet in which he was born.

The night was not inviting, the hot wind had entirely subsided, not a leaf stirred; the air was heavy,
and charged with electricity. The few stars which
pierced the veil of vapour whitening the sky, twinkled
faintly, like lamps needing oil. Masses of black clouds
of the most fantastic shapes were rising slowly, one
after the other, from behind a particular cleft in the
Jura to the west, the quarter from which came storms
and rain. I loitered in the grounds barely long enough
to smoke a cigar, and then returned to take another
survey of the banqueting hall. There was nothing
there to detain me, quite the contrary; for signs of
maudlin stupidity and tipsy drowsiness met my eye

from more sides than one. And then it was fifteen minutes after eleven, a quarter of an hour later than my usual hour for going to bed, and, like the methodical bachelor turned forty that I profess to be, nay, that I boast of being, not even for Herr Konrad would I further break a rule of life, which I consider to be as rational as wholesome.

So to my room I went, and to my bed; and while waiting for the touch of Morpheus's magic wand, I recapitulated to myself the various incidents of the day. I found in them much that was gratifying to mind and heart. Yes, the day had been good for me, one to be signed *albo lapillo*. If an honest man struggling with adversity is a sight pleasing to the gods, why should not he who shows himself superior to prosperity be entitled to the same honour? At any rate a man, who, having risen in the world, courts the people and seeks the haunts associated with his former humbler state; and a whole population, who preserve so fresh the memory of benefits conferred, are phenomena of the best kind, which do not often offer themselves to our observation. And I felt truly thankful that it should have fallen to my lot to witness them.

But no Sybarite's couch is without its rumpled roseleaf; the one in my present couch was a certain impression, or semi-impression, I might say, so faint was it, left on me by my last visit to the hall; an impression scarcely noticed at the time I received it, but which, as if it had needed only solitude and darkness for its nurture, was now occupying my whole mind — just as the small cloud on the horizon grows and grows till it overspreads the whole sky. Lying in my bed,

I recalled that Herr Konrad — how shall I word it?
— that Herr Konrad, in the last glimpse I got of him,
was looking more flushed than I should have wished
to see him. Mark that I don't say he was, but he
looked so; for my impression, the result of a fugitive
glance, rested on no other foundation than the deep
red of his cheeks and the sparkle of his eyes, both of
which, I must hasten to add, might be easily accounted
for by the high temperature of the room, without the
agency of any other stimulant. I repeated to myself,
that in all probability this was the cause, and the only
cause, of the signs I had observed; and yet I could
not banish a doubt, to get rid of which I would have
given something handsome. I verily believe that the
certainty of the worst, extenuated as it would be by
the inducements of the occasion, would have been less
painful to me, than the uncertainty, fraught as it was
with the suspicion that I might be doing an injustice
to a person I was so inclined to respect. This feeling,
akin to remorse, became at one moment so harassing,
that I debated with myself whether I would not go
back to the hall, and confront the reality, let it prove
what it might. But before I had settled the point,
sleep stole on me.

I was startled from my slumbers by a tremendous
crash. Mercy on me! what can it be? cried I aloud,
as I woke sitting bolt upright in my bed. Had there
been a powder-mill in the neighbourhood, I should not
have doubted an instant that it had exploded. There
being no powder-mill, the only conjecture I could form
was, that the new wing of the establishment, which
many said was weak, had fallen down. I lighted my
candle, and looked at my watch. Half-past one in

the morning. I heard casement after casement open,
and hurried questions and answers interchanged.

I opened my window, and in my turn inquired
what had happened. "Donner" (thunder), reiterated
several voices. I made sure that the house had been
struck by lightning. I snatched at my clothes, hud-
dled them on in two seconds, thrust my money and
my pocket-book in my pocket, and hurried downstairs
to the little parlour, which was Frantz and Madely's
private sitting room. It was almost full. There were,
besides Frantz and Madely, Herr Konrad, most of the
house-servants and farm-labourers, all the horsemen
but one, who had departed after supper, a good half
of the boarders, the great majority of them ladies in
various stages of *déshabille*, and some disposed to be
hysterical. As I was making my way in, Mdlle. Jacottet rushed past me, and crying in a frenzy of terror,
"Save me, save me!" threw herself into Herr Konrad's
arms.

Exclamations, questions without answers, and answers without questions, mingled at cross purposes in
utter confusion. Frantz and Madeleine turned from
one person to another with incoherent words. All had
at least half lost their wits, except Herr Konrad, who
stood there calm and collected, and as fresh as if he
had risen from a ten hours' sleep.

"A loud and near clap of thunder, that is all,"
said he, addressing the excited group of ladies in his
quiet manly voice, and gently disengaging himself
from the grasp of Mdlle. Jacottet. "I have myself
ascertained that both in the front and back of the
house, all is wrapt in the most satisfactory darkness,
and Frantz has seen that nothing has befallen the barn.

In all probability the storm has exhausted itself, and its remains are rolling away. So, ladies, you may dismiss all alarm, and retire once more to your rest."

"Oh! ne-ver, ne-ver!" sobbed Mdlle. Jacottet, weeping hysterically on the bosom of her companion.

Another feminine voice objected, "How do we know that the lightning may not have made its way in at one of the windows, and is not smouldering within the house at this very moment?"

"We will soon ascertain that," said Herr Konrad good-humouredly; "Frantz and I will examine the upper storey and the loft. This gentleman," turning to me, who happened to be near him, "will go with Jungfrau Madeleine through the ground and first floors; and you, Michael," laying his hand on the shoulder of that high-collared individual, "have the goodness to accompany the woman of the Baths into her own realms, and see how things stand there." And he led the way with a quiet smile, and a light composed step. How I hated myself for my vile doubts and conjectures! I could have dropped on my knees before him, and begged his pardon!

Meanwhile, my allotted companion had begun in her bewilderment, to apologize for the disturbance I had suffered, as if it had in some way been her fault. Madeleine was the mistress of the ceremonies of the establishment, and on her devolved exclusively — Frantz being a man of few words, and shy and awkward — the duty of doing the agreeable to the boarders: a most important task at all baths. It had thus become a habit with her to be polite and flattering in and out of season. I interrupted her with a joke, and then asked at what hour the feasting party had broken up.

She said it was past one when they left, and Herr
Konrad had not been in his room more than a quarter
of an hour when that terrible crash came. As for her
and Frantz, they had anticipated a storm, and sat up
in consequence, as they always did on such occasions,
because, as she observed philosophically, who can tell
where the fire of heaven may or may not fall? This,
in fact, is the practice in many Swiss households. In
no country is lightning so much dreaded; and indeed
in none does it so much harm.

Well, after a careful survey of the ground and first
floors, we returned, Madely and I, to the parlour,
where Herr Konrad and Michael had already preceded
us, and a satisfactory account was just being given in
on all sides (to the effect that all was perfectly right
and safe), when suddenly the clang of the fire-bell in
the village fell upon our ear; that awful sound, which
never fails to blanch the cheek of the stoutest-hearted
among the dwellers in wooden houses, and not unfrequently under thatched roofs.

A moment of dead silence ensued, presently broken
by fresh wailings and lamentations from the ladies.
At the same instant Frantz, the servants, the horsemen,
rushed to the door.

"Wait a moment," said Herr Konrad quietly.
"Herr Frantz, I think that your presence is indispensable here; it will reassure the ladies. You may
be of use down there, by sending us without delay a
cartload of spades, pickaxes, ladders, and pails from
the Baths. Michael will lend you a hand, and see
that the whole reaches its destination as soon as possible."

Michael, who watched Herr Konrad as a sheep-dog does the shepherd, instantly went off with Frantz in the direction of the farm.

"And now for it," resumed Herr Konrad, leading the way, and we all followed. We had scarcely set foot out of the house, when a deluge of rain began to pour down straight upon our heads, drenching us to the skin in a moment. "Not pleasant, but useful," said our leader, "the buckets of heaven come to our aid against the fire."

"Fortunately there's no wind," observed somebody.

"Fortunately not," answered Herr Konrad; "but in this sort of weather who can tell what the next moment may or may not bring?" He had scarcely done speaking when the rain ceased as suddenly as it had begun.

Shortly after we met a man at a half run, des-patched by the doctor to convey the tidings. The house struck was Peter Schleuz's. The fire had spread from thence to Hans the butcher's, just where the buildings were thickest. The inmates of the two burn-ing houses had escaped with difficulty, so rapid was the progress of the flames. The cattle too had been saved, excepting a poor goat which would not leave the stable. One of the engines was beginning to work, the other was found out of repair. A telegram was being sent to town for the engines.

"Utterly useless," said Herr Konrad, "the telegraph office in town is always shut up at night. Far better that one of you, gentlemen," turning to the horsemen, "should gallop over at once for the engines."

One of the five horsemen directly volunteered to

run back for his horse, and be off with the message. The news-bearer was desired to continue his way to the Baths, and we continued ours. The night was pitch dark, save where a reddish tinge illuminated a space above the horizon. Schranksteinbad lies in a flat hollow on the same level, or thereabouts, with the village, but the one cannot be seen from the other, because of some intervening rising ground. As with every step up hill we gained a more extensive view of the horizon, so the reddish glare widened and became more vivid, until at last it mingled with a fiery column of smoke, and sparks, and flames, the lower part of which, however, was still hidden from sight by the interposed mass of the school building. Here we all, moved as it were by one impulse, set off at a run, and thus arrived on the scene of the conflagration more like a troop of schoolboys bent on fun, than like a body of sober men actuated by a will to afford help.

Whether it be raging over stately piles, the honour and pride of a world-famous city, or only destroying a few huts in a poor hamlet, a fire of any considerable size is always a spectacle full of grandeur. I suppose there is in the display of a power all but uncontrollable a peculiar spell which compels admiration. Such, at least, was the effect it produced on me. Two cottages were already in a blaze, and on a third the work of destruction was beginning by the thatched roof. A thick hail of burning fragments was falling in every direction. A motley crowd of men, women, and children, were hurrying to and fro in front of the blaze, like moths in a sunbeam, many of them with no other apparent object but that of venting in some way their distracted feelings. Others were helping to remove furniture and other articles out of danger; some looked on without moving, as if spell-bound. My attention was attracted by a group which would have been a godsend to a painter. Some half dozen men were hanging on to the horns and tail of a cow rendered unmanageable by terror — the infuriated beast shook them right and left like so many bundles of rags, they still holding on most tenaciously. "Blind her!" cried Herr Konrad, "throw something over her head;" which being done the animal became shortly quiet.

A multifarious noise filled the air — hoarse cries and whistling of men calling to each other, screams of women, wailings of infants, barking of dogs, the lowing of cattle, the grunting of pigs, the hissing and crackling of wood and trees, and, above all other sounds, the rumbling of the flames, which might easily have been mistaken for the roaring of distant thunder. The intense purple glow in which everybody and everything within the circle of the conflagration was steeped, helped to give the whole scene a weird and unearthly character, somewhat suggestive of Dantesque bolgias.

The chain to convey water had just been formed when we arrived, and the engine was beginning to work with a meagre supply. We found the doctor, the head-master, the mayor, and most of the councilmen on the spot actively assisting, and to their exertions it was due if the inmates, and the cattle, and most of the furniture of the premises on fire, had been saved. But acting, as they did, independently of each other, every one according to his individual views or impulses of the moment, they could not but often paralyse each other's efforts, and bewilder the people about them with contradictory orders. To say nothing

of the numerous volunteers, who, in their distracted
zeal to be useful, impeded without helping, and were
in everybody's way. It was unity of action that was
wanted, and Herr Konrad's presence supplied the
desideratum. Each and all recognised him instantly
as their natural leader, entitled to command and to be
obeyed, and came to him for directions. This ascendency
of his enabled him to put, as if by magic, some order
into the confusion that prevailed.

First of all he commanded that all the houses in
the immediate radius of the focus, two on one side,
five on the other, should be instantly evacuated, beginning by the two detached buildings, which stood
quite alone to the left. To carry out this measure he
formed three squads of volunteers — there were plenty
of them — one to see to the safety of persons, the
second to that of cattle, the third to the removal of
property. To each of these squads he appointed a
resolute and intelligent leader; the doctor to the first,
the head-master to the second, and one of the horsemen
to the third. He went himself with Michael, who had
long since arrived with the cartful of implements, to
superintend the reinforcing of the chain drawing water,
so that a larger and more continuous supply might be
obtained. Confidence was revived, and every one
worked with a will. And when word was brought him
that the two houses on the left had been emptied, he
had the engine removed from the corner, whence it
was made to enfilade the whole of the burning block,
and thus protect, to some extent, the two cottages in
question; and, leaving these to chance, he had the
fire-engine placed in front of, and its whole effect concentrated upon, the one burning house that projected

on the opposite side, and beyond which was a thick row of buildings. But one engine, well managed and well supplied with water as it was, could do but little execution against so intense a focus of conflagration. Shortly a fourth house, in fact, caught fire. Was there no means of seconding the efforts of the engine?

Herr Konrad thought there was. He had noticed a heap of sand lying close by, for building purposes; he knew that wet sand had been successfully employed before to extinguish fire, and he determined to try the experiment. His idea he communicated to Michael, who took it up with enthusiasm, and set to work forthwith. Our friend the giant was on the spot in no time, at the head of a willing band, and then and there improvised a chain to convey sand with the pails of the baths, which stretched to the back of a house close behind, and looking down upon the two burning ones, on which the engine was playing with more zeal than fruit. Ladders were placed against the one to which the chain of pails abutted. Michael and half-a-dozen stalwart youths climbed up, took their stand on the roof, and from thence hurled down pails of sand on the very heart of the fire, as fast as they were handed to them. A good twenty minutes of this sandy hail produced the best results. The flames were partly subdued. The play of the engine, on its side, thanks to this unexpected auxiliary, grew far more effective.

This contrivance, however, even had it lasted longer than it did, owing to the scantiness of the material employed: this contrivance, we say, could not be expected to arrest, but only helped to retard, the progress of the foe; and to retarding it was limited the ambition of the contriver, who knew that every minute that passed brought nearer and nearer the chance, nay, the certainty, of succour, not from the town yet, but from a neighbouring village, the firemen of which took great pride in their skill, and made a point of being first with their engine at all such dangerous meetings as the present. Nor was his confidence deluded; five minutes more, and the longed-for help made its triumphant entry on the field of action, to the repeated acclamations of the crowd.

But along with this friend a fresh enemy entered the lists — one Herr Konrad had been in dread of all the time — we mean the wind, a sudden gust of which swept over the glowing furnace, fanning it anew into flames, and whirling a shower of sparks and firebrands along the road eastward. After all, was this wind an enemy or a friend?

True, that blowing from the west, it put in imminent jeopardy the two detached cottages to leeward; but then did it not remove all fear of a catastrophe in the opposite direction, where a cluster of buildings and a continuous row of houses offered easy and uninterrupted fuel to the devouring element?

"Provided the wind does not veer round!" I heard Herr Konrad mutter repeatedly to himself, and a cloud for the first time fell on his countenance.

"The school! the school!" shouted suddenly a voice, and on all eyes turning to the well-known spot where it stood, lo! a lively jet of flame issuing apparently from the roof. A general clamour arose, and away ran to the rescue all present to a man, save those engaged in some special task; fortunately the alarm was a false one. A stray firebrand had, it was

supposed, fallen upon some shavings accidentally lying
on the roof, and hence a blaze almost as soon ex-
tinguished as seen.   The roof of the school-house was
of zinc, and fireproof.   This escape from a luckily
imaginary danger, was probably suggestive to many
of the obvious thought that, great as was the calamity
befalling the village, it might be still greater.   Only
fancy the model school, the pride of Schrankstein,
falling a prey to fire!

And now the gusts of wind growing more and
more frequent, and the flames under their lash bound-
ing forwards as if bent on attack, all the efforts of the
defence were brought to bear on the two detached
houses.   The two engines crossed their waters over
the projecting fiery column, and checked it successfully, so long as a new and stronger blast of wind did
not force it irresistibly on.   An extemporized fire
brigade, composed of the most active young men, and
led by one of the horsemen, whose ubiquity I had
more than once remarked and admired, got on the
roofs, both unhappily thatched.   Electrified by the
example of their leader, who would have put a squirrel
to the blush, the men climbed, and crept, and leapt
at the peril of their lives, in vigorous contest with the
enemy.   They soaked the thatch with buckets of water,
pulled up by ropes; spread wet blankets on the roofs,
so as to deaden the effect of the fiery missiles; in
short, disputed the ground inch by inch, and only
gave way when the intolerable heat of the flames,
whipped on by the now continuous gale, began actually
to scorch their hands and singe the clothes on their
backs.   Nay, their leader, who left the last, and when

the roof was actually taking fire, had a narrow escape
of being burnt to death.

When the town engines arrived, which they did
shortly after — day had just broken — they were too
late to save any of the six houses which the conflagration had seized. The first four which had caught
fire were burnt to the ground, and the two last were
enveloped in flames. The engines were still of use in
extinguishing these, and laying that rain of sparks
and burning embers which, scattered far and wide by
the wind, might produce more mischief. But even
this modest honour was not individually theirs; for, as
if in mockery, the engines had no sooner begun playing, than the tempest abated, and all the cataracts of
heaven poured down upon the village. The firemen
persevered, however, and by four in the morning the
only trace of the fire left was a thick column of
smoke rising from the ruins of what had been six
homes.

There was no loss of life, thank God! save that of
the obstinate goat. The only bodily sufferer, was that
one of the horsemen, to whose zeal and cat-like agility
I have just had occasion to render justice. His right
foot, just as he was about to leave the roof, slipped
through a crevice, and in the effort to get it out, was
sprained, and he lay disabled. His comrades, who
had already descended, happily became aware of this
in time, and rushed back to rescue him. The doctor
bandaged the ankle at once, and looked upon the hurt
as very slight. A carriage was fetched from the Baths
to remove the patient thither; and our presence at the
village being of no further use, we followed on foot,

not a little in want of refreshment and rest after all our emotions and fatigue.

We had scarcely reached the Baths when we noticed that the wind had veered to the east. Lucky, indeed, it had not done so sooner!

CHAPTER VIII.

Discoveries.

THREE days later, I went after breakfast, according
to custom, book in hand, to enjoy the fresh breeze of morning in an open rustic rotunda which stood in the middle
of the garden. The Schranksteinbad grounds teemed far
and near with similar shady recesses, where you might,
if so disposed, listen undisturbed to the thousand whis-
pers of nature, and inhale the reviving influences of
earth and sky without molestation from the sun. Some
of these retreats had their particular tenant or tenants,
who held them in right of long occupation, a right
which was acknowledged and respected by everybody;
so much so, that most of these bowers went by the
name of the person or persons who habitually haunted
them, just as if they had been their special property.
There was one in particular, to the rear of the
house, most beautifully situated on a little *mamelon*,
overshadowed by Italian pines; and which, from being
the favourite resort of a deaf professor already mentioned in the catalogue of our oddities, was called the
professor's cage, or more generally the blackbird's cage
— a most appropriate appellation this last, for to look
at the old gentleman's black figure against the trellis-
work, and not think of a blackbird in a cage, was next
to impossible. 1 myself had the honour of having a
small hermitage called after me, and which, for all
practical use and purpose, was as much my own as if

I had built it at my own expense. It was one of the
two summer-houses already spoken of, which were at
the opposite ends of a little raised terrace, not more
than ten minutes' walk from the house. Mine was that
on the left: it had taken my fancy from the very first,
on account of its magnificent view of the chain of Alps.
Habit had little by little endeared and made it a sweet
necessity for me. There comes a period in life, when
sameness is as indispensable a condition of enjoyment
as variety during youth. But on this particular morning I found my verdant observatory occupied by new
arrivals, who as yet knew not what was what; and so
I had to take temporary refuge in this rotunda, which
was near at hand, being situated midway between the
house and my usurped seat. An enviable *pis-aller*
after all, full of sweet scents and sounds. Bees hum-
med about among the syringa and the clematis which
nestled and climbed against its sides, birds sang in the
acacias which shaded it, and the soft gurgling of a little
silver thread of water running close by invited reverie.

I had with me a volume of Leopardi: his works are
an especial item of my travelling paraphernalia. I
chose for my morning's reading his paper in 'Praise of
Birds.' Leopardi, though little known elsewhere, is
one of the contemporary glories of Italy. He died in
1837 at the age of thirty-nine. He has written little,
but that little is stamped by a power and originality of
thought, sufficient alone to make his name immortal,
even had that thought not been cast in a mould of
such perfection, that to find a parallel for it we must
go back to the best times of Greece and Rome. More
than once, when I have been asked by some English

Italian scholar to point out some Italian book besides
the everlasting *Promessi Sposi* and *Le mie Prigioni* (remark that the epithet 'everlasting' is not mine but the
querist's), more than once have I had it on the tip of
my tongue to say 'read Leopardi.' But then, I have
always refrained, from a fear that he might perchance
not suit English taste, especially the unformed taste of
very young people, on account of the morbidly despond-
ent, nay gloomy, view he took of life, a view which
runs like a black thread throughout all his writings,
even to the little masterpiece of graceful sentiment and
delicate observation, which he has consecrated to the
feathered citizens of the air, the blithest and most
fascinating of the animal creation. For this let us
pity, and not condemn him.

One of the best men I ever knew, whenever he
happened to hear of a capital sentence passed on a fellow-creature, used to thank God on his knees for having so ordered his birth as to place him out of the way
of the temptations which lead to the gallows; — a
very wise and Christian sentiment, to my mind, for
who does not know what terrible inducements to evil
there may be in the mere accident of beginning life in
certain quarters, and under certain circumstances? I
confess to a like feeling whenever I meet or hear of a
misanthropist. I would also fain thank God on my
knees that I have been spared the trials which can
lead to so sorry an issue; for, believing as I do that it
is natural in man to love his fellow-creatures, I cannot
but take it for granted that one must be dragged by
the hair, so to say, in vulgar phraseology, to be brought
to a conclusion so contrary to nature.

Poor Leopardi was born an invalid, almost a

cripple, and bodily suffering was his attendant throughout his life. His eyes were always very weak, occasionally sore, and forced him to abandon for months together — once for a whole year, his only solace and consolation — study. His boyhood was lonely and sad: he met with no sympathy from his own contemporaries, who either shrank from his companionship, or, worse, made him bitterly feel his physical inferiority. One who knew him well, the late Gioberti, has often told me that young Leopardi found little compensation in his home for the coolness and slights which were his portion abroad. Manhood had in store for him still crueler trials. He loved with the passionate love of a rich heart crushed from infancy — a love not altogether unrequited, as we may gather from many a passage in his writings. Well, that woman died, and left him desolate. His fellow-townsmen eyed him with distrust and scorn; the grounds of his superiority escaping their obtuse intellects, they resented his keeping aloof from them and their ways as an intentional offence. They filed against him the everlasting indictment of the caterpillar against the butterfly. Why was he unlike them? Why did he not creep as they did? We must bear in mind that Recanati, Leopardi's birthplace, is a small town in the Pontifical States, and was at the time I allude to a priest-ridden nursery of ignorance and superstition. To go from the church to the public-house, and *vice versa*, to discuss in the same breath the last miracle and the price of corn with the intention of taking one another in, was the circle of pursuits and occupations in which the community revolved. No wonder that Leopardi had no sympathy with such. Very probably he did not choose to dissemble his disgust

now and then, and for that he was made to suffer
cruelly. Picture to yourself the shy sensitive misshapen
child of genius limping along through a crowd of these
stalwart boors, a target for their quizzing and practical
jokes. Angels ought to have wept at the sight. The
degraded condition of his country also weighed down
his proud spirit with the weight of a personal disgrace.
Add to all this the perpetual gnawing of physical pain,
and perhaps you will not consider it extraordinary that
the moral retina of the man so situated should reflect
rather the shady than the sunny side of life. His existence certainly was a most unhappy one; it would
have indeed proved an unbearable burden, but for the
affection of one of his sisters, Pauline, and of that of
a true and enthusiastic friend, Antonio Ranieri, who
stood by him to the last, and after his death, superin-
tended with jealous eye the publication of his works.

Now, then, I was reading Leopardi's charming
sketch in praise of birds, and I had only to look up
now and then from my book to certify the truth to
nature of the descriptions therein given. Birds of various sizes and hues were hovering round my little
specula, indulging in that continual and graceful motion of theirs, turning to the right, to the left, bending,
fluttering, hopping with an indescribable elasticity. One
among others, a chaffinch, for whom I seemed an object of anxious observation, particularly attracted my
attention. He began by eyeing me sideways, shaking
his head at me, but from a respectful distance. After
a little, growing bolder, he ventured nearer, and still
nearer, until he perched on a branch which hung over
the front of my rotunda; but no sooner had he alighted
on it than, as if seized by a sudden panic, he withdrew

in great haste. He repeated the same evolution from
another and another point of the compass, as though
he were planning how to turn my position. I was
evidently in his way, though I could not guess why or
wherefore. For if his nest was anywhere near, and
he was desirous of carrying food to his young ones,
which I knew was the case from something pendant
from his beak, how did I prevent him? Unless indeed
his nest was inside my temporary shelter; but of that,
after a close inspection, I could find no sign.

Presently the first chaffinch was joined by a second, the latter also with something hanging from the
beak. Number one took number two aside, and from
the sharpness of the first one's accent, and the eagerness with which the second scanned me at all possible
tangents, I had not the slightest doubt but that number
one was apprising number two of the situation of
affairs, and denouncing me as an intolerable nuisance.
They sat awhile together in anxious consultation, and
finally, I conjectured, hit upon a line of operations, in
pursuance of which, they made straight for the rotunda,
as though resolved to force their way into it. But
their hearts failed them in the decisive moment, for,
after hovering for a second in front of my citadel, they
turned their tails, and beat a precipitate and rather
ignominious retreat.

The flapping of the parental wings, momentary as
it had been, was sufficient, it seems, to awaken from
their nap, a very young, innocent, and probably hungry
family of fledgelings, who gave a responsive series of
feeble twitters from above my head. I immediately
climbed up on the round table which occupied the
middle of my present retreat, and by dint of straining

my eyes in the direction from whence the twitterings
had proceeded, I ended by discovering, to my dismay,
in a dark recess formed by the junction of a beam
with the thatch of the roof, a collection of ugly mouths
lined with red, and prodigiously distended.

I say to my dismay, because by the time I had
made this discovery, I was no longer alone, and my
companion was no less a personage than a huge and
very sociable tom-cat, who after purring and rubbing
his back against my knees in token of sympathy, had
coiled himself up on the round table, and was sleeping
the sleep of the just, which however did not prevent
his noticing the calls of the babies above, as I knew
beyond a doubt by a nervous twitching of his ears
and tail, and from the ominous play of his tongue
about the corners of his mouth, as if the sound were
suggestive of some sweet gastronomic recollection. Between his place of repose and the nest there intervened
no more space than what a cat of ordinary agility
might clear at a spring, and a shudder came over me
as I contemplated the possible consequences. Really
fathers and mothers must have lost their wits when
they expose their progeny to such awful risks. Was
there anything to be done which might avert a terrible
catastrophe? I could devise nothing, unless it were
to remove the nest to some spot out of the reach of a
feline leap. But inside the rotunda that was impossible,
and to choose any place outside was fraught with a
greater danger still than that I was bent on warding
off; for I had always heard that nests interfered with
are in ninety-nine cases out of a hundred deserted by
the parents. However, as I could do no good, it was
time to cease doing evil. I must put an end to my

long intrusion, and to the anxiety of the bewildered
father and mother, who kept fluttering in the vicinity
and eyeing me most piteously. I therefore took up
pussy coiled as he was, and deposited him most carefully on the ground at a distance out of sight of the
rotunda. That done I returned to fetch my book, and
was again sallying forth, when I beheld a sight which
for a while set at nought my benevolent intentions.

Through the foliage, myself concealed by it, I saw
Madeleine passing through the garden gate. · She was
carrying a chair and cushion under her right arm, and
supporting with the other the young horseman, who
had sprained his foot on the night of the fire at the
village. He had been confined to his bed ever since,
and this was his first attempt at walking out. He
looked pale, and moved with difficulty; his right arm
was round Madely's shoulders, and he leant his whole
body against her. What was there in this sight to
arrest my progress, you will ask? It was this, that
Madely was transformed: her looks had that in them
which I had never noted before, a transparency, a
glow, a halo, the reflex as it were of a new light within
her; and, taken in connexion with her present occupation, this sudden illumination pointed out its source as
unmistakably to my eyes as the midday glare indicates
the sun from which it emanates. Pity had begotten a
tenderer sentiment, and while in attendance on the
wounded swain, my Nymph Egeria had in her turn
received a wound. As she moved complacently along,
entwined with her charge, not a muscle of her countenance, not a glance of her eyes, not an inflection of
her voice, not a bend of her form, or fold of her dress
I was going to say, but had a tongue of its own which

10*

proclaimed her secret. Now you understand what kept
me from showing myself — it was a sense of honour
akin to that which makes you turn your eyes from an
open letter not intended for your inspection, or that
prompts you to whistle or to shuffle your feet when
you find yourself in the vicinity of persons who are
exchanging confidences not meant for your ears.

They were coming along the main gravelled walk
leading to my rotunda, and I thought I could not es-
.cape, when happily pussy came across their path, and
created a diversion in my favour. Pussy was a great
favourite of Madeleine, and to see him and not to
speak to him was out of the question. Pussy on his
side was so full of acknowledgments for her attention
that his caresses effectually impeded her progress, and
she had to put the chair down under the shade of a
tree, and beg her companion to sit down there. She
then placed herself on the ground by his side with
pussy on her lap. They were talking merrily, and I
did not lose a syllable of their conversation; only, as
it was in German, there was no occasion for my shuf-
fling my feet or clearing my throat.

While watching the movements of my wingless
pair, I had naturally overlooked those of the winged
one, yet not so entirely as not to have caught a glimpse
of a desperate rush in and out of the nest by one of
the parents. Had the daring feat been achieved by
the father or by the mother? This was more than I
could tell, for such had been. the lightning rapidity of
the movement as to give me no time to identify the
adventurer. Of course, I took it for granted, nay, laid
a wager with myself, that it was the mother. For,
now that the ice was broken, I had not the least doubt

but that the attempt would be repeated, and so it was; and that not once, but twice, thrice, nay, ten times and more, and always by the same bird; and, I am sorry to say, not by the mother. You say, how could I be sure of its not being the mother? My answer is that hen birds never attain to the size or the splendid plumage of the cocks, and that the bird which made its way to the nest was the larger and more richly-coloured of the two — *ergo*, it must be the father.

Nor is superior beauty in the male the portion of birds alone. Nature has ordained it as a rule throughout the ranks of inferior animal creation, that the male should far excel the female in beauty and nobility of form and colour. That this is so, you must acknowledge at once if you compare the lion with the lioness, the peacock with the peahen. It is only at the top of the scale that this rule is reversed, and that all sorts of excellencies, as everybody knows, are combined in woman to mark her natural superiority over man.

I hoped to the last that the brave husband might inspire the cold-blooded mother with some of his pluck, but no; not once did she venture farther than the acacia bough which hung against the rotunda. She left all the work and the peril to him. I confess I was much disappointed in her, nay, incensed against her, and put her down in my book as an arrant coward — a harsh and hasty judgment, which not very long after I had to cancel. Had I looked into the matter with a little less passion and a little more philosophy, I should have discovered that, let appearances be what they may, a mother cannot be a coward when her offspring is concerned. That she should

have less coolness and courage in difficulties of an
ordinary character than her less finely organized mate,
was but in keeping with her more nervous impressible
nature; but let an occasion arise worth the display of
extraordinary energies, and you will see if she is not
equal to it. Feminine heroism for its fell development
needs the lash of powerful excitement. . . . But I am
growing declamatory.

When I said that the hen chaffinch left all the
work and peril to the cock, I was not quite just to
her. In fact, she was far from idle or passive — she
contributed largely towards the feeding of the fledgelings, indefatigably seeking, collecting, and conveying
it to the bold father, who, taking it from her beak,
carried it in his to the nest. And what do you think
was the dainty nourishment provided by parental solicitude for their brood? I give you twenty, nay, a
hundred guesses, and I bet you what you like, you
don't guess right. It was neither less nor more than
the panting bodies of decapitated honey-bees. I could
never have believed it, had I not actually picked up
one of the mutilated corpses, which the father let drop
in his haste. Only fancy the poor unoffending industrious little creatures going out to their daily task with
no other thought but that of a rich booty from the
flowers, and finding themselves suddenly pounced upon,
and made minus of their heads by one dexterous blow
from the beak of one of the loving parents, and served
hot to a young and hungry family by the other! A
summary proceeding, which must have cruelly shocked
the moral feeling of the eaten individuals, had they
had time to reflect on it, which I hope and believe
they had not, their execution being carried on with a

precision and a rapidity bespeaking long practice and worthy of all praise. I believe I could point out some highly-respected and respectable fathers and mothers without feathers, who bring up their children on the same principle, that of fattening them on their neighbours.

While making these reflections, I saw a party of ladies and children coming along the gravelled walk. They stopped, as I expected, to exchange greetings with Madely and her companion, and I improved the occasion to emerge from my hiding-place, and slip by the group with only a passing salutation. The moment she saw me, Madeleine grew as red as a cherry, and made no attempt to stop me. Poor thing! she had already the self-consciousness that a newly-awakened and all-absorbing sentiment gives. I could, for my part, have wished that its object had not been the hero of the sprained ankle, Mr. Telliker. This wish was prompted by no lack of good-will towards that gentleman; on the contrary, from the first his person and manners had greatly prepossessed me in his favour, and his conduct at the fire had inspired me with the greatest respect for him. My objection to him was on the ground of his age. He was not yet twenty-six, and did not even look so old. He was too young for Madely. I shall not commit the indiscretion of putting down her age in round numbers, though I could if I chose, she having herself told me in days of yore the day and the year of her birth. But Madeleine was in the full ripeness of womanhood when I first knew her, and some years had elapsed since then, and I do not think I should be very far from the mark, if I stated that she must have been, at least, five years Mr. Tel-

liker's senior — too wide a gulf, in my opinion, to be
leaped without danger. She was still very handsome,
still blooming if you will, but it was a bloom on the
wane. Now you understand why I wished that she had
fallen in love with a man of an age less disproportioned
to her own.

But all my wishes and misgivings could change in
no wise the fact. Madely was smitten to the very
core, and could not help showing the wound. On that
same day, for the first time since his accident, Herr
Telliker dined with us, and was, as a matter of course,
the object of a little ovation. Everybody insisted on
shaking hands with the convalescent, everybody complimented him on his prowess, everybody congratulated
him on his recovery. Madely, who waited at table,
was literally swimming in a sea of bliss. She could
not take her eyes off him. She was uneasy lest sitting
so long upright might injure his foot, or that such and
such a dish might disagree with him, or that he might
be overfatigued by so much talking; in short, her
secret oozed out in those thousand little ways in which
such secrets do.

Immediately after dinner I was obliged to set out
for the town on some personal business, and did not
return till half-past ten at night. I went straight to a
storeroom fronting the kitchen, where the bather's
candles were kept. The lamp which lighted the little
room was at its last gasp, and reminded me of the
poet's humorous description —

> "Un lumicin che parea spento
> Sì facea lume a stento."

As I groped my way to the table, a well-known
voice, calling me by name, asked, "Is it you?"

"Your humble servant," I replied. "What are you doing here in the dark, Madely?"

"I was waiting to wish you good-night," said she, rising and lighting the candle for me.

"Very kind of you, Madeleine; good-night and pleasant dreams."

"Do you know," she went on, holding back the candle as a hostage, "do you know that you have not so much as said one word to me this whole day?"

"Haven't I? Well, I have not thought the less about you for all that." And this was quite true.

"And pray, may I inquire what were your thoughts? I am curious to know," said she.

"Would you really like me to tell you?"

"Yes — indeed."

"Well, then, I thought that you were in a fair way to jilt me without ceremony one of these fine days." To make clear what this silly sally meant, you must know that there existed between Madely and me a jocular agreement of long standing, to the effect that when she sold the establishment, and realized a million of francs for her share, she would come and settle in Paris, and make a marriage *de raison* with a certain bachelor past forty of her acquaintance.

Madely laughed merrily, and answered, "It is I who am jilted. When such beauties as we know of come all the way from Zurich on purpose to bid for you, what can a poor old maid like me do but withdraw, and retire from the consest?"

"You hypocritical little wretch," said I in my turn,

laughing, and, snatching the candle from her, I left
her with a good-night. Madeleine's allusion to the
beauties come to seek me will be made plain by and
by.

My first step before breakfast next morning was
bent to the rotunda — the nest was safe, no cat was
prowling near, none was in sight. I returned thither
an unlimited number of times during the day, and
always found things *in statu quo.* I repeated my visits
the next day, and the next after that, with a similar
happy result, and I then came to the conclusion that
if, according to the saying in France, there is a
providence for drunkards, so is there one also
for fledgelings most wantonly exposed by imprudent
parents.

CHAPTER IX.

More Discoveries.

MEANWHILE, I had become very intimate with Herr Konrad, who begged me one morning at breakfast to accompany him to the school, where certain examinations were to take place in the French language, and I readily agreed to his wish. This was on the fourth day since my discovery of the nest, and after my usual early inspection as to its safety. So, with a mind at rest, I went to the school, and heard a good deal of French more or less murdered; and that done, Herr Konrad took me through the village, until we came to a little path with a wooden fence on both sides breast-high. This led to a very nice cottage with a large garden in front. It was a very picture of a house, a very picture of a garden; so clean, so trim, so coquettish, the former, surrounded by verandahs of ivy and eglantine; so nicely trimmed, and so rich in all sorts of flowers and plants, the second. My conductor halted in front of the small gate, and, without speaking, pointed out to me a woman squatting on her heels at the other end of the garden. She had a sort of dibble in her hand, with which she was making little holes in the earth at equal intervals. That done, she took from a basket by her side, bulb after bulb, planted one in each hole, and carefully filled up and smoothed the earth round each bulb, so as only to allow its pale green shoot to peep out. She wore a very wide-brimmed straw hat, and as she worked sang in a low very sweet voice.

"The woman you see gardening with such nicety, and who manages to make a livelihood by her garden, is blind," whispered Herr Konrad to me.

"Then it is Martha, the singer," said I.

Martha, the blind woman, was celebrated for her singing, and I had often heard her name mentioned with pride at the Baths and in the village.

"Now follow me, but walk very gently," said my companion, opening the gate loudly, and going towards Martha with a heavy tread.

"Is that you, Baptiste?" called out Martha without moving. Then as we drew nearer she stood up suddenly, and confronting us, cried, "Bless me, it is Herr Konrad; I know his step."

"I was sure of it," shouted Herr Konrad with childlike glee, as he took her by both hands, and kissed her on both cheeks. Martha, though evidently not a little proud of her guess, modestly protested that she might not have recognised his step had she not been aware that he was in Schrankstein, and also had she not been expecting a visit from her old and good friend. "But you are not alone," she added; "I do not know the step of the person with you." Hereupon Herr Konrad introduced me by name, which she had no sooner heard than I found, to my surprise, she knew all about me, at least all that was known of me in Schrankstein.

Frau Martha was a stout woman, something above forty, not handsome, but with a very pleasing expression of countenance. Her voice was exceedingly sweet, what we Italians call *simpatica*. There was nothing

in her eyes to indicate that she was blind, save a certain fixity of look. She had lost her sight when
already upwards of twenty. Her serenity and good-
humour were proverbial, and her company much sought
for on that account. She carried on a small trade in
plants and seeds, and in prunes, that more than sufficed for her few wants. She could do almost everything for herself, even to the lighting of her fire and
cooking her meals. For what she could not manage,
she found plenty of ready volunteers among neighbours and friends. Hers was altogether a happy and
easy life.

Frau Martha did the honours of her cottage and
garden as effectively as if she had had her sight, pointing out to our notice those flowers and plants in which
she took a particular pride, such as a very fine collection of roses, another of various mosses, a pomegranate
in full blossom, and so on. She insisted on our resting
ourselves in her best parlour, brought glasses, and a
bottle of wine out of a cupboard, drew the cork, and
filled the glasses herself, doing everything with as sure
a hand and step as if she had seen as well as we did.
In return for our drinking her health, she gave us a
graceful German ballad sung to perfection. We took
a cordial leave of the good soul, charmed with her
voice, her courtesy, and her cheerfulness.

Why are blind people always more cheerful than
those who are deaf? Nature would seem to point to
quite a contrary conclusion, for, give a hundred persons the hypothetical option whether they would lose
their sight or their hearing, and I am satisfied ninety-
nine out of the hundred would choose deafness rather
than blindness. As we took our way homeward, Herr

Konrad and I tried to account for this contradiction between the actual fact and the apparent prompting of nature, and even ventured upon some ingenious speculations, according to which blindness might, after all, be the lesser evil of the two; though we wound up with a declaration that practically, and as far as we were ourselves concerned, we should each of us prefer to be deaf rather than blind. From such an alternative God preserve us!

We were a quarter of an hour late for dinner when we reached the Baths, and trout was being served when we took our seats. I remarked that the conversation was more general and brisk than usual, but I was too busy in making up for lost time to stop and investigate the cause. The deaf rector at the head of the table, and the deaf professor on his right, were exchanging some shots preliminary to one of their customary pitched battles.

"Have I heard?" shouted the irritable rector; "heard what?"

"I didn't say 'heard,' I said 'bird,'" retorted, at the top of his voice, the not less irritable professor. "I asked you if you had seen the bird."

"The bird!" repeated the chafed chairman, "I should think I have, and plenty too. What do I care for birds?" — and here followed a muttered volley of apartes, which set the whole table into roars of laughter.

"By the by," said Miss Jacottet, turning to me, "have you seen the chaffinch?"

I had so entirely dismissed the subject from my thoughts ever since breakfast, that I was startled at its being suddenly mentioned.

"Yes," I replied; "that is to say, I saw the little ones early this morning in the nest. How did you come to make the discovery?"

"I made no discovery of any nest," replied Mdlle. Jacottet, who seemed to be in one of her lucid intervals. "I am talking of a full-grown bird; the professor says it is a chaffinch, which, curiously enough, has been chasing the cat the whole morning. I have seen *passim* cats hunt birds, but birds hunting cats I had never beheld."

I felt more alarmed than I chose to show. I scented in the air some foul deed of blood. "I beg your pardon," said I; "I don't quite understand you. You say that a chaffinch was chasing the cat. In what way? what did it do? was it angry?"

"Angry!" said Mdlle. Jacottet, "why, it was downright furious. What did it do? it did everything a bird could do: it positively shrieked, flew at the cat, pecked at him, did everything but actually beat pussy."

"Then it is my chaffinch," exclaimed I; and leaving the trout on my plate untouched, I darted out of the room and rushed into the rotunda; and oh, what a sight I saw! it is beyond description. Fragments of the nest, torn, shattered, mangled, were flung about on the table, on the bench, on the ground — scattered here and there lay feathers from the wing of a full-fledged chaffinch, easily to be recognised, from their gay colours, as those of the unlucky father of the family. Three large drops of blood, on the edge of that part of the table just below the nest, marked the spot where he had been murdered. In all likelihood, it was there the frail fabric, with its tender contents,

had fallen. I could rehearse to myself the whole scene
of horror — the fatal spring of the fiend, the scream of
the little ones for help, the crash, the desperate rush to
the rescue of the maddened parent, and the wholesale
butchery that had followed!

The only point which remained obscure to me, was
what had become of the mother during the tragedy.
Was she a looker-on, or not? If not, how could she
identify and pursue the criminal, as she had been
doing? If she had been there, how had she escaped
the cruel fate of her whole family? This is a mystery
I cannot solve. That hers was a stout heart enough to
struggle and die in defence of those dear to her, no
one who witnessed the recklessness with which she
afterwards courted danger can gainsay — I, least of all,
who had so unjustly set her down as a coward.

I religiously gathered together the mournful relics
(they stand on my mantelpiece to this day, and many
a repetition of the sad story have they entailed on
me), and returned with them to the dining room; and
then and there imparted, to as many as chose to listen,
the story of the awful catastrophe. I did so with an
emotion, which proved catching — eliciting from all
breasts a responsive feeling of pity for the innocent
victims, and of undisguised horror for the murderer.

From all breasts save one! Madely, I am sorry
to say, treated the matter lightly, nay, even jeered
at the importance I gave it. Madely, we must recollect,
had been brought up in the country, that is to say,
among oft-recurring scenes of carnage of a similar
description; and, besides that, in her capacity of head-
cook, she had had to wring or cut off the heads of
thousands of unhappy pigeons, fowls, ducks, and geese.

No wonder, then, that the habit had blunted her sen-
sibilities in so far as the winged tribe were concerned.
By a curious contrast, she was very fond of, and even
tender, to all sorts of four-footed domestic animals —
horses, cows, dogs, and cats — tending them in their
ailments as though they were infants. The guilty cat
in particular was a great favourite of hers, and it might
have been with the aim of extenuating the awful responsibility weighing on him and sheltering him from
the consequences, that she expressed so lenient an
opinion of his trespass. "It was not his fault," was the
conclusion of her harangue, "that he was fond of birds
and mice, was it?" And truth to say, there was no
answering that query.

We went all of us after dinner, and sat out of
doors before the house, waiting, not without some
trepidation, for a repetition of the extraordinary passage
of arms, of which we had been told. We waited to no
purpose. Pussy, contrary to custom, for he was a very
sociable animal, and rarely missed taking his afternoon
siesta in company; pussy was nowhere to be seen; and
no pussy, no chaffinch. Messengers were sent to find
pussy; all his usual haunts were searched. Madely,
vainly protesting from her stand on the threshold of
the house door, that she knew nothing about him, was
summarily required to produce him alive or dead; and
still not a sight of pussy to be had. An hour and a
half went by in a useless watching. Some sceptics of
the party were beginning to sneer, and hint that it was
all a hoax and a humbug, when lo! and behold, pussy
was seen looming in the distance, slowly making his
way towards us. A general hum of satisfaction rose

from the ranks of the assembly, such as that which in
a theatre welcomes the entrance upon the stage of a
longed-for actor. Simultaneously with this murmur the
shrill treble of a bird issued from one of the poplars of
the avenue, "Tchwing, tchwing, tchwing!" and a slender
little creature fluttered through the foliage to perch on
a lower bough: "Tchwing, tchwing, tchwing!" three
times three. The unexpected sound sent a thrill through
my whole body. Had it said in so many words, "Here
I am," the chaffinch could not have given a clearer
meaning to its note.

Pussy meanwhile strode on leisurely, closely watched
and followed by the bird, who kept step with him,
hopping forwards from branch to branch, but now quite
mute. Pussy's step and bearing were alike exempt
from swagger as from humility; it was the step and
bearing of one who owes nothing to anybody, and
without pluming himself too much upon the fact, knows
it. He reached us in due time, went his rounds, paying
compliments and asking for caresses; and then as if
hurt by the want of cordiality shown him, withdrew a
little to one side, and choosing a spot in the sun between a table and a chair, coiled himself up, and went
to sleep.

He had no sooner done so, than the chaffinch,
which had eyed all the movements of the enemy from
a forward low branch, began the attack. "Tchwing,
tchwing, tchwing," thou shalt not sleep, and down she
was on the table; "Tchwing, tchwing, tchwing," and
now she perched on the chair just above him; "Tchwing,
tchwing, tchwing," and suddenly she was by his side,
almost touching him. Her cries gradually increased,

and grew more and more passionate, until they reached
a paroxysm of fury. "Coward, murderer, monster!
cursed, cursed, cursed!" — and as she screamed this
— I am sure that was her meaning, her throat swelled
prodigiously, her feathers stood on end, and all her
little body quivered with rage. Now at the cat's head,
now at his tail, now on his left, now on his right, she
seemed to take delight in cursing him from every point
of the compass. Oh that her strength had only been
equal to her passion, how she would have pounded
him, and been avenged!

Pussy stood the attack with the superb indifference
of might confronted by impotent right. He did not
deign even quite to open his eyes to identify the im-
portunate creature interfering with his slumbers, but
only winked at her. Scarcely did an incipient twitch
of his tail now and then testify to his annoyance. Only
once did he stand up with some resentment, and that
was when she trod on his tail; however, upon second
thoughts, he contented himself with a yawn and a
stretch, and then coiled himself up again.

Presently the chaffinch flew away, and we lost sight
of her among the thick foliage. Had she given up
the unequal contest? We thought, we hoped so; but
no. What we had taken for the end was merely a
pause. Probably the little thing was exhausted, and
wanted breathing-time; perhaps — such is the misery
of flesh — she wanted food to recruit her failing strength.
She reappeared in a few minutes, and made a more
desperate and close onset than ever. She repeatedly
pecked the cat, and at last goaded him out of his in-
sulting equanimity. He made a snap at her two or

three times in good earnest, and very narrow escapes
she had of joining her family in his stomach. The
sight grew positively agonizing, and we had to interfere and keep her away from him and from certain
death. Madely was loudly called for, and entreated
to take pussy away with her, and keep him a prisoner
for some little time. She promised to do this, and
walked off with the cat in her arms, and thus there
was an end for the day to this most extraordinary and
most painful exhibition.

But Madeleine could not be expected long to continue the jailer of her favourite cat, and accordingly
next morning he recovered his liberty, and at dawn
was roaming abroad. The chaffinch was as early a
riser, and so the two enemies met, and the implacable
"Tchwing, tchwing, tchwing!" resounded far and wide.
Some of the occupants of the front rooms were roused
from their sleep by the cries, and opened their case-
ments to remonstrate. Those whose more sound slumbers
had been proof against the angry notes of the chaffinch
had been awakened by the creaking of neighbouring
windows and the grumbling of the complainants. In
short, by five in the morning, all Schranksteinbad was
astir, and angry — angry with the cat, the chaffinch,
particularly angry with Frantz, and more particularly
angry with Madeleine, on whom the responsibility for
everything that went wrong devolved.

The annoyance, temporarily put a stop to somehow or other, recommenced later in the day, then again
later in the evening, to the great exasperation of the
public. What had for a moment served as a pabulum
for curiosity, had by this time become a downright

bore, nuisance, nightmare, which destroyed the peace
and comfort of all of us. Frantz and Madely were at
their wits' end. "But what can we do?" cried each of
them in turn. "Hang your cat!" was the angry retort
in chorus, "and let us have done with it." Now
Madely, I believe, would far rather have faced martyrdom than harmed a hair of her favourite's beautiful
fur. Herr Telliker, who naturally sympathized with
her, suggested a *mezzo termine*. "Suppose you take
pussy to the village to your sister, and leave him with
her" — "And charge your sister not to let him out,"
added somebody. Madely immediately acted upon this
advice. She went to her sanctum, and after a while
reappeared with a basket on her arm — a basket of
which she lifted the lid as she carried it round to the
company, so that every one might see with their own
eyes that pussy was in it. This ceremony accomplished, she departed.

For my part, I was not very sanguine as to the
ultimate success of this expedient. I too well recollected
poor Suldi's return from banishment; and as I thought
of Suldi, I looked about me to see if there were among
the present party, any of the boarders of the first year
of my discovery of the quiet nook. There was not one.
Suldi, truth to say, had the intelligence, the strength,
and the courage of twenty such as pussy, but then he
had had to find his way back from the Oberland, a
long way off; while pussy was only separated from his
habitual haunts by a quarter of an hour's walk on an
excellent road. The only flattering unction I dared lay
to my soul was, that pussy's absence might perhaps
last as long as the life of the poor childless widowed

bird; for I did not expect, nor indeed wish her, to survive many more days. But it was fated otherwise.

Late in the afternoon of the morrow, it might be four o'clock, a few of us were sitting, not as usual in front of the house (the excessive heat of the day had chased us from thence), but in the shade of the trellised verandah already described as spreading right and left of the entrance of the house. The luxuriant Virginian creepers, which hung down curtain-like, shut out the sun, and kept the recess comparatively cool, even in the hottest weather. Two small windows, belonging to a storeroom for fruit, opened into the verandah. Well, I and some others had sought refuge there on this very hot afternoon. There was Mdlle. Jacottet and her companion, another middle-aged lady, the deaf professor, Herr Konrad, and myself. Herr Konrad was reading the French paper aloud to us. To have more light on his paper he sat facing the windows, while we were seated with our back to them, looking towards the garden. All of a sudden the reader stopped, and exclaimed, "Confound him, there he is again!" We all turned round, and saw the cat issuing with serpent-like flexibility from between the bars of one of the windows. Mdlle. Jacottet began to scream, and the rest of us to shout for Madeleine. Pussy looked at us with the most perfect indifference, did not seem to approve of the dim light of the verandah, and went forth into the sun. "Tchwing, tchwing, tchwing — here I am!" cried the accuser, and down on the ground lighted the chaffinch, confronting the murderer. At this sight Mdlle. Jacottet went into hysterics. Madely quite out of breath had just arrived. "Madely, just go into the verandah," cried Frantz's voice from above. She had scarcely done so, when we heard the report of a gun, and the poor little chaffinch lay dead on her back. At the very same instant, Mdlle. Jacottet bounded up from her chair and fell flat on the ground. A universal shout of horror, and we all rushed towards her.

CHAPTER X.

After the Tragedy, the Farce.

IN the first bewilderment of the moment the impression of all present was, that the same shot which had for ever silenced the poor chaffinch, had wounded, if not killed, mademoiselle. One moment's reflection would have sufficed to show that the thing was physically impossible, but nobody had time for reflection. That, at least, she was not killed, was proved beyond all doubts, by her incessant groans of pain while we raised her as gently as possible, and tried to place her in a chair.

"What is it? where is it?" chorussed all our anxious voices.

"My leg is shot, broken, shattered!" moaned Mademoiselle Jacottet.

Her companion immediately knelt down, and, while we stood with averted faces examining the ceiling of the verandah, proceeded to a rapid inspection of both the nether limbs of her mistress, which, to the relief of all present, she pronounced to be sound and whole. This intelligence, however, had a very different effect upon the old lady herself.

"Of course they are!" cried she in the tone of the bitterest irony; "of course I don't feel the smart of the wound; of course I don't feel the blood trickling down — everybody knows better than me. I am mad! ain't I? Haven't I got a keeper? No pity, no help, for

an old wretch — let her die like a dog — like a dog
— like a dog!" and she fell to crying bitterly.

"Every one here wishes you to live and be merry,"
said Herr Konrad gently. "We are all at your service,
dear madam. Will you allow us to carry you up-stairs
to your own room? and then we will send for the doctor to dress your wounds."

"Yes, do," said the poor creature amidst her sobs.
"Bless you for your charity, prince. Is it prince or
duke? I am so distraught with pain that I can't recollect which." And on she went, rattling in this incoherent strain all the while two farm-servants were
carrying her in a chair up-stairs. "Don't forsake me,
prince — all of you come up with me, pray; you won't
be too many for my enemies. Their name is legion.
Where is the little Italian who sits next to me at table?
he never spoke an unkind word to me, though he is
not of noble birth. Birth is everything. Ah! there
you are, signor. I used to speak Italian once. Oh,
what a quantity of blood I am losing! You must have
the stairs washed, Jungfrau Madeleine. I wonder if
my assassin has been arrested. His name is Fieschi.
Fetch the doctor, the doctor, the twopenny doctor!
Tell him to be gentle with me, I am only a woman.
I mean I was once a woman, now I am a chaffinch
— tchwing, tchwing, tchwing — that is why they
shot me; tchwing, tchwing, tchwing — poor chaffinch!"

We accompanied the poor lady thus raving, and
nodding, and gesticulating, and what not, to the door
of her room on the second floor, distant only two doors
from mine, and there we men left her to the care of

those of her own sex, of whom there were at least six or seven present.

This new episode had taken me so by surprise, and had so entirely engrossed my attention, that I had not once thought of the poor chaffinch lying dead outside the verandah, until Miss Jacottet's exclamation of "poor chaffinch" reminded me of the bird. I rushed down to the scene of the catastrophe with the charitable intention of rescuing the corpse from insult, and of giving it decent burial. But to my great disappointment, strain my eyes ever so, I could discover no corpse to be buried. What could have become of it? had any child chanced to see it, and picked it up? As I was looking round in search of information, I espied the cat under a table not far off, and a horrible suspicion entered my mind — a suspicion which, alas! grew to a certainty (too horrible for utterance), the moment I noticed the lusty zest with which puss licked, and licked again, his lips and moustache. My heart rose at the sight. If ever there was a case the reverse of all poetical justice, that case was thine, oh ill-fated chaffinch, martyred even after death!

Frantz obtained but a scanty meed of approval for his pains, and a liberal one of blame — the fate of all cutters of gordian knots. The approval he received with modesty; and as to the censure, he merely shrugged his shoulders at it, in which I think he was right.

The doctor went and saw the patient, humoured her by putting mock splints on her leg, and left her much relieved in mind. He told us he had seen many analogous instances of delusion, and always found contradiction useless, if not injurious. As for Mdlle. Jacottet's late unwonted agitation, he attributed it

partly to the extreme heat, partly to the excitement
caused by the chaffinch's strange exhibition of revenge.
Doctors, as a rule, are cleverer in explaining than in
healing.

The next event worthy of notice was the departure
of Mr. Telliker, which took place on the morrow. He
was not yet quite recovered, and still limped a good
deal; but he said that his business most imperatively
required his presence. What his business was I could
never precisely ascertain. The little I gathered about
it from Madely led me to believe that he was a com-
mission agent to dealers in general goods. A very
safe, extensive, and profitable employment, asserted
she — an assertion that was met by the deaf rector
present when she made it, with many a dubious shake
of the head, and many ominous ohs and ahs; and the
rector was a very shrewd old man.

Whatever else it was, Mr. Telliker's business was
undoubtedly a profitable one, judging from the expenses
in which he indulged; less, it is only justice to say,
on his own account than on that of everybody about
him. A more open-handed, generous, obliging young
fellow I never chanced to meet. He had real pleasure
in giving for the sake of giving. He insisted on treating us all to champagne almost every day, besides
providing the smokers of the company with excellent
cigars — quite impossible to refuse, so earnestly and
graciously were they pressed upon us. On one very
hot day, I recollect, a lady happening to say what a
treat ice would be! he immediately ordered the chaise,
and sent a messenger to town to fetch ices. Indeed,
no one ever went to town without a list of articles to
buy for him — cigar-cases, work-boxes, pocket-books,

keepsakes of every description, and bonbons; all of
which were no sooner received than dispensed right
and left. He was very fond of children, and liked to
play with them, which made him still more popular
with the little ones than his various gifts. In short,
there was no instance on record of any person having
ever succeeded in becoming such a general favourite
in so short a time; nor was there an instance of any
other at his departure inspiring such universal and
affectionate regrets. The intensity of those of Madeleine may be easily imagined. She stood the trial
bravely, however, so long as she was in company;
whether she succeeded as well when out of sight, I
have my doubts — doubts founded on the red condition of her eyes, when I next saw her. Fortunately
for her, the house was rapidly filling, and she had not
one moment to herself.

And so Herr Telliker was gone. Let me see what
was the next novelty. I can recollect none worthy of
note until the 7th of July, a date which brings me to
an episode of my reminiscences, which I would willingly omit, could I do so with a clear conscience. But
my present performance, if I am not mistaken, has
many a point in common with a limited autobiography,
and I am of opinion that an autobiographer is no more
justified in withdrawing at will from the public such
and such facts as may perhaps not exactly tell in his
favour, than a painter is justified in suppressing in his
self-painted portrait such and such features as may not
exactly enhance the beauty of the original. "Fair
play" is my motto, and *fais ce que dois* — you know
the rest.

Well then, on the morning of the 7th of July, as

I was putting on — I beg pardon — my right patent leather shoe.... Indeed, I don't know why I ought to apologise for naming an article which, both as to material and workmanship, would not have been out of place in any one of the great exhibitions. I always was very particular and a little coquettish about my shoes; and I owe it to a happy chance that I have been able to satisfy to the full this innocent hobby of mine, — to a happy chance, I say, which a few years ago brought me in contact with a German shoemaker, every inch of him an artist. I judged him to be such, I cannot say at first sight, but at first hearing. I entered his shop to ask my way. My hero was in the act of showing a pair of boots to a gentleman.

"What is the price?" asked the intending purchaser.

"Forty francs," replied the artist.

"Far too dear," said the gentleman.

"Too dear!" repeated the artist; "Parisians are not worthy of wearing my boots;" — and having pronounced this fiat, he hastily withdrew them, as if he would not have them longer profaned by undiscerning eyes. The action and the sentiment expressed reminded me of Ronchetti, and of an authentic fact in the life of that famous countryman of mine. Ronchetti was a man of genius at the head of the shoemaking trade in Milan, towards the end of the last century. The conqueror of Lodi sent for him, and ordered a pair of boots. Could he make them at all similar to the Parisian ones the general-in-chief had on? Ronchetti replied that he thought he could. The general muttered something like "more easily said than done." Ronchetti was cut to the quick, but made no answer.

He returned some days after with *a* boot. The future
emperor, who was a good judge of most things, examined it, and was evidently struck by the excellence
of the workmanship. "And where is the other?" asked
the General. The reply was, "You may send to Paris
for it."

I am growing, I feel it, really intolerable with my
digressions. I humbly beg pardon. I will do so no
more. If my younger readers could only guess what
almost irresistible charm these memories of the past
have for bachelors past forty, I am sure they would
not grudge me a step or two out of the straight road.
Add to this the instinctive feeling which prompts all of
us to put off as long as possible disclosing what is but
little agreeable. However, not further to aggravate
my offences, I will to the point without any more
preambles.

On this particular morning, then, of the 7th July,
I was drawing on my right pump, when I all at once
became sensible of some obstruction. I took off my
shoe, turned it upside down, gave it a good shake . . .
out dropped at my feet a sealed note. For a moment
I stood aghast, without courage to pick the thing up.
It was narrow and oblong, clumsily folded; it had
fallen direction downwards, so I could see that it was
fastened with a glazed blue wafer, on which was em-
bossed a white dove holding a letter in its beak. I
hoped for an instant that there was some mistake: I
mean that it was a missive destined for some other
shoe in the vicinity, and which had found its way into
mine, owing to the flurry of the depositor; but I recollected that my two nearest neighbours on the left were
the deaf brother and sister; and those on my right, the

deaf professor and Mademoiselle Jacottet, not one of whom were persons likely to receive clandestine epistles with amorous devices. Then I bethought me that perchance it was a letter which the post had brought me; and that Madeleine, aware of how particular I was about receiving my correspondence quickly, had placed this one in my shoe, that I might have it the moment I took in my shoes. But this conjecture was based on no precedents. Madely, had there been anything for me by the post, would have knocked at my door to let me know; and besides, it was only eight o'clock, and the post never arrived before eleven.

The quickest way out of all doubt, here observes the impatient reader, were to take up the letter, look at the superscription, and, if for me, read the contents. Ay, to be sure, but the quickest way is not the most natural in cases where a disagreeable discovery is anticipated, and I had a presentiment that what was awaiting me would bring me no good. Quiet bachelors past forty are, as a rule, apt to take alarm at any, the smallest, incident threatening a deviation from the ordinary routine of their life.

After a minute or two, however, of suspense (my idle suppositions had occupied no more time), I lifted the letter and examined the address. No doubt was possible, for my Christian and family name were very distinctly written, and perfectly spelt. The handwriting was large, old-fashioned, and very clear; the paper was not scented. I tore open the envelope, and the first thing I saw was a small bunch of dry forget-me-nots neatly arranged, and tied with red silk. The contents were in French, and consisted of five lines, each beginning with a capital letter, arranged so as to look like

verses, very probably meant as such, though there was
no attempt at rhyme or metre, except at the close,
where "*étranger*" was made to answer "*aimer*." Here
is a literal translation:

> " What my lips dare not articulate ,
>   What my eyes lack power to express ,
>   This forget-me-not comes to say for me.
>   Who can see you, handsome stranger ;
>   Who can see you, and not love you ?
>   JULIA."

This point-blank declaration produced on me the
stunning effect of a blow on the head. I staggered
under it. Robinson Crusoe's consternation when he
lighted on a strange footmark in his uninhabited island,
was not greater than mine at that moment. You
think I exaggerate — indeed I do not; and you will
agree with me that I had good cause for alarm, when
I tell you that I had had some precedents to go by,
which allowed me to guess the quarter from whence this
missive came, and it was a quarter than which none
could be more dangerous to the peace of an old bachelor. Such plain speaking seemed really inconceivable;
and yet the more I thought it over, the more I told
myself that my conjecture was unnatural, absurd, and
impossible, well, the more I could not help confirming
myself in the belief that my correspondent could not
be other than — she.

What she? Wait a moment and I will tell you all
about it. I did not know her Christian name, her
family name I don't choose to give, and that is why I
designated her — she; let us call her for the time
being Mademoiselle Leblond. She was a blonde —
uncommonly so, as blonde as a woman can well be

without being an Albino. She had blue eyes, cherry
lips, and a white-rose complexion. This combination
of tints may sound insipid, and yet the result was a
beauty full of originality and distinction — a beauty
which may please more or less, but can neither be
overlooked nor contested. She had a way of wearing
her hair thrown back from her forehead, and hanging
in heavy masses on her shoulders, which reminded you
of the head of the sphinx. For my part, I thought her
beautiful; and certain it is that she created quite a sensation on her first arrival, which took place a day or
two before that of Herr Konrad. No wonder, for
hitherto we had had, truth to say, but a collection of
uglinesses to choose from.

Mademoiselle Leblond brought with her either a
lady friend or a companion — I never discovered
which. The two ladies were seldom apart, were very
retired in their habits, seldom seen, and bathing and
drinking of the water assiduously enough to be classed
among the *baigneurs sérieux*. It was to Mdlle. Leblond
that Madeleine had alluded when joking me, as you
may remember, about beauties coming all the way from
Zurich to bid for me, as she phrased it. It seems that
Mdlle. Leblond had asked Madely after me with some
show of interest, and had added that but for having
heard of my being at Schrankstein, she should have
gone to some other baths, which she named, nearer her
home. This statement, and the previous inquiries,
Madely had reported to me, drawing from one and the
other conclusions utterly absurd. Madeleine was of a
sportive nature, and nothing loth to exercise her live-
liness at my expense. The only effect of these com-
munications had been to make me very shy of Mdlle.

Leblond, and extremely guarded in my behaviour and
speech whenever chance threw me into her company.
In fact, I rather avoided her, and we had not exchanged twenty words during the whole of the time we
had passed under the same roof. My passage of arms
with Miss Emma had taught me my weakness, and the
wound I had then received was scarcely yet scarred
over. So I held aloof from beauties.

For all that, I could not help perceiving that I
was the object of the not unfrequent and not unfriendly
observation of the blue-eyed one. More than once had
I been sensible during meal-times that her eyes were
on me; rapidly averted with a blush the moment I
glanced towards her; and once especially, as I was
relating at table the catastrophe of the chaffinch's
nest — relating it certainly with unfeigned emotion
— so marked was the sympathy expressed in her looks,
that I was slightly embarrassed. But I had satisfactorily accounted to myself for all this by ascribing
it to the interest which one who is a professed story-
teller always excites in the breasts of the young, until
the present complication came to force on me a different
explanation.

I strove to be calm, not to rush to any hasty conclusion. I counted upon my fingers all the lady
boarders. The number was not many; the gentlemen,
as an exception to the rule, mustering this year in
great force. There were eight ladies, exclusive of
Mdlle. Leblond and her friend, and of some new
arrivals, as yet perfect strangers to me. I told off each
of the ladies, and subjected each to a severe scrutiny.
Mdlle. Jacottet and her companion, the deaf farmeress,
a grandmother with a bevy of grandchildren, an elderly

valetudinarian, and a very infirm sexagenarian, were
all, I argued, out of the question. There remained
three. It could not be the stiff spinster of a certain
age, who was so good as to profess a cordial antipathy
for my poor self and for all Italians; it could not be
the jolly widow, between whom and me, her ignorance
of French, and mine of German, had raised a Chinese
wall; lastly, it could not be that sweet-faced young
lady, betrothed to the young man who came to see her
every Sunday, and whom evidently she dearly loved.
And so, by dint of eliminations, I returned to the point
from which I had started. It could only be — she.

After all, what was the use of thus racking my
brains? Had I not an infallible means of identifying
the writer of the note? All that was needed, to make
assurance doubly sure, was to ascertain that "Julia"
was Mdlle. Leblond's name. My first impulse was to
go and inquire of Madeleine. But the host of inferences which Madeleine would draw from my query,
deterred me. I was not enough of a diplomatist to
have any chance of success in any attempt to pump
the name from her unawares. So I had to bethink
myself of some other method by which to get the information I wanted.

Not long ago I had occasion to mention a little
parlour to the left of the entrance passage, where
Frantz and Madeleine were used to sit when free from
household cares. In a corner of this parlour there
stood a writing-desk opening atop, and in this desk
Frantz kept his account-book, in which the names of
the boarders were entered. It was not an unusual
case that this ledger should be lying upon the desk.
If I could only find it there now! I peeped into the

12*

Venus's bird was the bearer of a profusion of pansies
of every hue, and of four lines, of which I subjoin the
translation. The verses were legitimate verses this
time.

> "Gentle shepherd! to you, as to their centre,
> Come all my pensées, what'er their hue.
> Oh that only one of yours, gentle shepherd!
> Would come in return to her who loves you.
> JULIA."

My annoyance knew no bounds. I could have
cried with vexation. I, who have a horror of agitation, whose beau-idéal is repose, here was I, for three
times four-and-twenty hours, haunted by one image,
become the sport of one fixed idea, made restless,
miserable, and about what? It was high time that
this kind of persecution should cease, and I vowed
to myself that it should be so this very day, or that
the next should no longer find me at Schranksteinbad.

The ground at the rear of the house had the form
of an oval, at the apex of which were the springs,
opposite to one another, each covered in by an urn,
and shaded by a nice grove, and with wooden benches
all around. Along the outside of this oval on both
sides ran two wide walks edged with fruit-trees, and
abutting on the springs. These walks were broken
here and there by small lateral paths leading up the
hills, which overhung right and left this cosy little
valley. About eleven A.M., I took up a position on a
bench in the least frequented of the walks just mentioned, and waited. I knew that Mdlle. Leblond was
in the habit of going to the springs after her bath,
sometimes alone, oftener with her friend or companion,
to fill a bottle with the ferruginous water for her use

at dinner. In fact, at half-past eleven, I perceived her
coming up the walk facing mine. She was alone.
After having filled her bottle, she began to retrace her
steps, stopped, stood irresolute for a moment, consulted
her watch, and then diverged into the nearest path
leading to the hill. Seeing this, I struck into a parallel
path, doing my best not to lose sight of her through
the trees. According to my reckoning, I could not
fail to come across her on the road to the village, to
which both our paths led, and which, moreover, was
her shortest way home. But the road, when I got to
it, was, as far as eye could see, solitary. I hastened
on in a state of distraction, when, as I was hurrying
past a cottage, lo and behold! there she was on the
threshold of a door, under the shelter of the projecting
eaves of the house. I had been so beside myself that
I had not discovered that it was raining. I at once
opened my umbrella (*N.B.* — I never walk out without one) and went up to her.

The moment she saw me she became as red as a
poppy, and I fancy that I must have matched her by
looking like a full-blown peony. I stammered forth
something about being so fortunate — for the life of
me I cannot recall the exact words — in being able to
offer her my umbrella. She faltered something in
reply about it not being likely the rain would last,
and about her wish not to shorten my walk. I counter-
replied that . . . but I should make my story too long
if I were to repeat all the preliminaries. Suffice it to
say, that after a little demur she accepted my umbrella, not my arm, for the simple reason that I had
not the courage to offer it, and we proceeded for some
time side by side in silence. She was pale, her hands

trembled, and her bosom heaved. Had I entertained any doubts, which I did not, as to her being my mysterious correspondent, her extreme confusion would have dispelled them. I ransacked my brains in search of a subject of conversation, and found nothing more to the purpose, than to request she would allow me to carry her bottle of water for her; but she of course refused. As I naturally looked at her while making this request, I saw some freshly-gathered sprigs of forget-me-not stuck in her waist-ribbon. So said I, with *malice prépense*, "I see you have not been idle in your walk — what lovely forget-me-nots you have got!"

The reply was, "I never can pass without gathering some. I am very fond of them — are not you?"

"Yes, indeed."

She blushed and said, "These are not quite fresh, but such as they are will you accept them?"

"With great pleasure," quoth I, as she held out the little bunch to me; "I shall put them with the others," added I pointedly.

I expected anything but the look of unfeigned surprise with which her calm limpid blue eye met mine. She paused a few seconds as if seeking to understand, then uttered the little ah! of one who has found what he sought. "Of course," she said, "you must receive quantities of flowers, and souvenirs of all sorts."

"Who should send them?" I asked.

"Why, your numerous admirers and well-wishers."

I smiled and said, "Of well-wishers I hope I have

some; as for admirers, I am past all pretensions to
having any."

"I am acquainted with one person, at all events,
who is a most enthusiastic admirer of yours."

"Are you, indeed? I should like to know who that
can be, if only for the singularity of the case."

"You have seen her often."

"It is a lady, then?"

"Yes, and I have a message from her to you."

"To me?"

"Yes, to you."

A message from a lady to me, thought I. Is she
going to make a clean breast of it under the mask of
an imaginary friend? She went on: "Yes, I bring you
a message from a dear friend of mine. She has not
forgotten you, though perhaps you may have forgotten
her. She was in mourning for her father, when you
met her in a railroad carriage."

"Ah! now I understand; you are speaking of
Mdlle. Maria," said I. "She made some stay at these
Baths long long ago, when I first came to them. She
was engaged to be married to a young man called" . . .

"Adolphe," suggested Mdlle. Leblond, "and against
whom you vainly warned her."

"Alas! yes," I replied; "and what of him and
her?"

"Would to God she had listened to you! She
would have spared herself and her two children much
misery. As to him, he lost his situation in less than a
year after his marriage: he drank all his wife's little
fortune, and then deserted her. No great misfortune
that; and she is reduced, poor soul, to gain her own

and her children's daily bread by needle-work, and a
sore struggle it is."

"I am very, very sorry for her."

"Often and often has she spoken of you, and of
your great kindness to her; and often and often has
she said with bitter tears, "Had I only listened to him,
how different my life might have been!" It was she
who put it into my head to come to Schranksteinbad.
She was aware that you were a regular frequenter of
these Baths, and she wished me to make your acquaintance, and to tell you from her of her repentance and
of her affectionate remembrance of you."

"Pray," said I, "if the inquiry is not indiscreet,
why did you delay so long in giving me your friend's
message?"

"It was very childish of me to put it off from day
to day, but you must forgive me, I am so stupidly
shy, and somehow your grave look and manner awed
me."

"I hope neither will do so any more," said I. We
had reached the flight of entrance steps. I bowed, and
leaving her, I hurried to my own room. The scales
had fallen from my eyes. I had now the moral certainty that Mdlle. Leblond and my mysterious correspondent were two and not one. Who then could
the author of these poetic effusions be? As I was
meditating on this mystery, there was a scarcely audible
knock at my door, which I had left ajar. "Come in,"
said I; and in walked Mdlle. Jacottet's companion. A
thought flashed across my mind at the sight of this
most unexpected visitor. By Jove, could she be the
writer of the letters? She was rather handsome, and

still young; under thirty, I should say; certainly not yet of an age to be impervious to Cupid's shafts.

The lady was manifestly greatly discomposed. She began, "I beg your pardon for thus intruding, but I much wish to ask you a question."

"As many as you please, mademoiselle."

"I wish to know — excuse my boldness — if you have received — what shall I call it? — something meant as a love-token — perhaps a letter."

"Supposing I have," returned I gallantly, "the person who sent it may rely upon the most inviolable secrecy; only I would beg her to send no more to the same address."

"I was sure of it," said the lady with a burst of impatience; "and pray, was the handwriting of the note you received at all like this?" And she placed before me a crumpled paper, on which was the scrawl of the letter I had received that very morning. I said that the writing was identical to that now shown to me.

"And — a thousand pardons — how did the letter reach you?"

I could not repress a smile as I answered that I had found it in one of my shoes.

"How cunning!" she exclaimed. "Excuse her, and don't expose her to ridicule — she is not answerable for what she does, you know."

"Do you mean to say that the person who did me the honour to correspond with me was Mdlle. Jacottet?"

"Certainly — who else could it be?" answered she naïvely.

Served right, old fellow! said I to myself; here is

poetical justice for you with a vengeance. Then I added aloud that I had believed Mdlle. Jacottet to be, or at least to think herself to be, incapable of walking.

"She does walk though, especially at night. I guessed that something of this kind would happen from the day you sent her a French book to read. She talked a good deal of nonsense about it and about you. I saw her copy some verses out of a book, and I watched to see what she would do with them, but she managed to elude my vigilance." (The second bell for dinner was ringing.) "I must go, thank you very much; and I may rely, may I not, on your absolute silence as to her folly?"

"Set your heart at rest on that score. I have more interest than you or any one else in keeping the story from transpiring: if it did, the laugh would not be with me, but at me."

After the companion was gone, and while I was completing my ablutions, I could not help soliloquizing aloud to myself — "And so my fair correspondent was Mdlle. Jacottet, *alias* Boa Constrictor! *Vanitas vanitatum, et omnia vanitas!* Provided only that the melancholy fact does not get wind, I shall recover the shock," and down I went to the dining-room. Most of the company were already at table, some few laggards like myself were taking their chairs. I went straight to my accustomed seat, and I was in the act of sitting down, when — (even now at the recollection my hair stands on end) — when an universal shout of laughter welcomed my appearance, and I found every eye riveted on me. My guilty conscience could suggest only one explanation for this extraordinary reception. No doubt, my secret was already the sport of the public. But how? who could have told? Mdlle. Jacottet's companion had betrayed me and it. I felt myself growing all the colours of the rainbow, and drops of cold perspiration rose on my forehead. Had the floor beneath me opened and swallowed up my chair and me, I should have been thankful. This terrible suspense lasted only a few seconds, but they were seconds of exquisite agony.

Herr Konrad, rising from his place, purple with convulsive laughter, took me by the arm, and forcing me also to rise, led me in front of a mirror. No sooner did I catch sight of myself than I joined in the homeric hilarity shaking the very windows in the room. Impossible to do justice to the figure I was. All the lower part of my face, including the tip of my nose, was one mass of black. How had it happened? The explanation was this. I am an inveterate smoker, as the reader is aware, but I make it a point that nobody, especially my neighbours at table, above all if such were ladies, should suffer from this my habit; and so, besides washing before dinner, as all good Christians do, it is my custom to pour a little eau de cologne into the palm of my hand, and pass it over my moustache and chin. This operation I used to perform at Schranksteinbad almost in the dark, for the door of the cupboard in which I kept my eau de cologne opened against the window, of which the blinds, as a rule, were down. Now, the eau de cologne bottle was not the only one in the cupboard. There were several others, and in the number was a bottle of ink; and this, in my to-day's bewilderment, I had used instead of the eau de cologne, thus unwittingly qualifying myself for

Othello's part. It took a good week to efface from
my skin all trace of the ink.

The moral of my tale is so short, that I venture on
giving it: Never trust to circumstantial evidence, however conclusive it may appear. Let jurymen reflect
on this!

CHAPTER XI.

A Peep behind the Scenes.

AND now to pass from personal to matters of general interest, I said some pages back that the establishment was filling apace; I can now aver that it was chokeful. Flaming accounts of the fête given in honour of Herr Konrad, of the fire which had followed, and of the conspicuous part he had played on that occasion, had appeared in all the local newspapers; and having been copied into all the Swiss and most of the foreign Journals, had spread the fame of Schranksteinbad and its doings far and wide. The natural consequence was that people flocked to the Baths thus made celebrated, not only from the different Swiss Cantons, but also from many parts of Germany. Not the most uninhabitable chamber, including stores and lumber rooms, but found its tenant or tenants — there was not an available hole left, and still the tide of visitors kept flowing in. Some of the new-comers accommodated themselves in the village as best they could, many more had to go away disappointed. Schranksteinbad was at the zenith of its glory.

Madely and Frantz did something to meet the exigencies created by this extraordinary affluence. First of all, they overtasked themselves, and were half killed in consequence. Secondly, and what was more to the point, they hired a female cook, a butler and under-butler, and strengthened the staff of general servants,

But this was not enough. To wait at all effectively
upon a hundred persons or so, the actual number of
servants should have been at least trebled, and this was
far from being the case.

The inefficiency of the service began very quickly
to be the great subject of conversation and of universal
complaint. Frau So-and-so had not had her room done
at three in the afternoon. Herr So-and-so had pulled
his bell thirteen times without eliciting a sign of life —
one had lost his boots, another had been disappointed
of a bath ordered the previous evening: there was a
chorus of lamentations.

I cannot say that, for my part, I suffered much
from this state of things, for in truth I am not exacting, and prefer in most cases waiting on myself; still
there was a grievance which I shared in common with
my messmates; one to which I could not be blind;
and this was the inordinate length of the dinner — a
length wholly arising from the disproportion between
the waiters and the guests. I thought I might as well
say a word or two on this *sore* point to Madely. I say
sore point, because the inconvenience arising from
want of sufficient hands had made itself felt more or
less, but always felt during previous years, more especially in the height of the season; and complaints and
appeals had often been made on this score to Madely
and Frantz, but all in vain. The increase of domestics
was a topic on which neither brother nor sister would
listen to reason. So, one evening after supper, happening to meet Madeleine limping sorely, while searching
the garden for her favourite cat, I advised her to let
that monster take care of himself for the nonce, and
to come and sit down by me, and have a talk. Nymph

Egeria complied, and this is the dialogue that followed: —

"Your feet are swelled and ache with long standing; you are killing yourself, my poor Madeleine, and nevertheless contenting no one."

"I never expected I should."

"You ought though, for your own interest, to try to do so. The boarders complain, and with cause. The time we have to sit at table is intolerable — take a friend's advice, my dear girl, get more servants."

"Ah! yes — get more servants; fine profits would be ours if we did."

"Let your profits be a little less, and the satisfaction you give a little more."

"What if the question with us is not of gaining more or less, but of not losing?"

"But that is impossible."

"So far it is from impossible, that the net balance of our profits last year was — Zero! I see you don't believe me, but I am telling you the plain truth — Frantz will show you the accounts if you like."

"But then what makes you hold to a losing concern?"

"I can't tell — force of habit, I suppose — just what makes our old mare Many jog on when harnessed."

"I fall from the clouds — and what has caused this deplorable state of things?"

"Our low charges. The value of every article of consumption has doubled during the last twenty years, and the terms of our establishment have remained unchanged."

"Raise your prices."

"Easier said than done. We have repeatedly tried to do so, and failed. Do you recollect the year you first came here and found the house empty? It was in consequence of our having raised the terms for board half a franc a day. We had immediately to re-issue a circular naming the old prices."

"In fact, I remember being struck with the extreme moderateness of your terms."

"A cheap establishment like this," went on Madeleine, "could not be made to pay, even in old times, except by a numerous family who could do all the work themselves. And that was once our case. So long as my grandmother was strong, my father alive, and my sister, who has married, and a younger brother, since dead, were all at the wheel, everything went smoothly with us, and though less frequented than now, Schranksteinbad gave us good returns, and we were able to buy a good deal of the land surrounding it. But all is changed now there is only Frantz and me. From the moment you are obliged to hire underlings, farewell to gain. That is why Frantz and I have been often thinking of selling the establishment. It is not so much the wages of the servants that is ruinous — it is their waste. The cook, for instance, who has not been here three weeks, has already by her neglect allowed fifty francs' worth of meat to spoil. The gardener, instead of doing his work, sells our best vegetables, flowers, and seeds underhand. The butlers, not content with drinking themselves stupid whenever they go to the cellar, hide away bottles of wine, which they drink with the maids at night. The maids help themselves to the best they can find in the kitchen to bestow on their sweethearts. The cowman

keeps back a part of the milk, and either sells or
gives it away. A general pillage is going on."

"And not to be tolerated," said I; "make a clean
sweep of them all, by Jove."

"And where are we at once to find substitutes for
them in the height of the season? Cooks, butlers,
waiters, are all at a premium just now. And then,
what would be the good of changing? Those who
came would be just as bad as those who went. It is
a hopeless business."

And as far as I could judge, so it was. Madely
did not stop at this point. After the servants, came
the turn of the boarders, and I was initiated into the
mysteries of the meanness and shabbiness of many
among them. It would require a chapter to do these
mysteries anything like justice, and I should not grudge
them time and space, were shabbiness and meanness
not the weary, stale, unprofitable things that they are.
So we'll let them fester unseen and undisturbed, and
rest content with the peep we have had behind the
scenes.

On the morrow, it was a Friday — I recollect it
well from the coincidence of Mdlle. Jacottet resuming
her seat at table next to me, not without some emotion
on my part of a mixed character — on the morrow,
the number of waiters at dinner was augmented by
four persons, two men and two women from the village.
It were presumptuous in me to say that this novelty
was the result of my last evening's conversation with
Madely, but perhaps it may have had something to do
with it. Whatever be the cause, this timely concession
to public opinion on the head and front of offence had

the best effect, and disposed the company to be more
accommodating on many other minor points. Complaints there continued to be, of course, and of criti-
cism not a little; hints also of real or imaginary deficiencies, and suggestions as to how they were to be
remedied. Suggestions cost nothing, and, as a rule,
mankind is generous of them. The ladies, for instance,
wanted riding donkeys for their excursions, and sadly
missed goat's milk — an item indispensable in Switzerland, and in general easily to be had. Why could not
Frantz write and order a dozen or more donkeys, and
a herd of goats to be sent from Appenzell? The gentlemen grumbled at having neither reading nor billiard
room. Frantz listened to everybody, said *yes* to all
proposals, and put off the realization of them to . . .
next season.

The present one, at all events, had gone off with
unprecedented brilliancy. Every evening there was
dancing; almost every day there were picnics and excursions, besides concerts, theatricals, lotteries, and
what not, for the sufferers by the fire. The originator
and promoter of all these charitable undertakings was
Herr Konrad, who succeeded even at our Spa, where,
judging from precedents, failure seemed inevitable —
I mean in raising subscriptions. True it is that he
had a method of his own for arriving at that desirable
result — a method which I had not seen put in practice before; and that was first to put down his name
at the top of the list for a good large sum, and then
himself to present the list so headed to each and all
of the boarders, afterwards in person collecting all the
sums set against each name. So that those who perhaps were not disposed to give out of charity, gave

from vanity, or regard for the collector; and thus a good deal of money was realized.

And the Sundays — what crowds arrived! It happened more than once that we sat down three hundred to dinner. The grounds in the afternoon looked like a fair. The bottles of wine sold on those occasions were reckoned by thousands. Though I was slightly annoyed by the confusion and noise inevitable where numbers are gathered together, I submitted to it all willingly for the sake of my kind hosts. I knew from some of Madely's further revelations, that, of all days in the week, Sunday was the one which yielded them some clear gain. Herr Telliker, faithful to his promise, never failed to come on Sundays; and Madely would forget her fatigue, and find leisure to indulge in her favourite amusement of dancing, doubly delightful when he was her partner. Herr Telliker was always much coveted as a cavalier, being reckoned a capital waltzer. That he was an indefatigable one, I can bear witness to.

Towards the end of the first week in August, the company began to decrease. One of the first to go was Mdlle. Leblond. We parted excellent friends, as indeed we had been ever since the day of our walk in the wet; and many and sincere were the kind messages I sent through her to her unhappy friend. The next who left us were Mdlle. Jacottet and her companion — a departure hard to bring about, and towards which I had to lend a helping hand. Here is the how and the why.

Mdlle. Jacottet, who professed to be weary of her stay at the Baths, had fixed a certain day and hour for leaving; but when the moment arrived, and the

omnibus was at the door, she flatly refused to move,
giving no other definite reason than that to go would
be certain death. Arguments, entreaties, remonstrances,
persuasions, coaxing, were all in vain. The same scene
was enacted three days running. Her companion was
in despair. Great as was the discomfort of having to
go on from day to day, with everything packed up, it
was as nothing to the awkwardness and absurdity of
the situation. In short, she at last applied to me with
an entreaty that I would help her out of the dilemma.
She was sure, so she said, that if I would volunteer
to accompany them to the station, Mdlle. Jacottet would
no longer object to start. Unpalatable as the proposal
was, I accepted it. I am not at all sure I would
have done so, had I had any conception into what a
wasp's nest my obligingness was to precipitate me.

On the morning of the day fixed on for this notable
event (we were to set out after dinner), I asked Mdlle.
Jacottet, as the companion had arranged I should do,
to allow me to avail myself of the omnibus which was
to take her to the station. Mdlle. Jacottet immediately
mounted on her high horse, and granted my request
with as much condescension as if, instead of a public
conveyance, her own carriage and four had been concerned. The three previous failures had created the
greatest excitement as to what would be the result of
this fourth attempt at departure, and the omnibus was
surrounded on all sides by eager spectators when I
walked forth with my fair charge. I handed her into
the vehicle amid the undisguised merriment of the
company. Apart this little episode, all went smooth
as oil till we reached the station; but there came the
rub. Nothing would induce Mdlle. Jacottet to enter

one of the railway carriages, unless I got in first; and
to put an end to a scene as ludicrous as disagreeable,
I had to comply. A fresh effort for my liberty at the
terminus of the nearest town proved as unavailing as
the first. Mdlle. Jacottet would not hear of my leaving,
and in a state of dreadful excitement actually held me
by the flaps of my coat. There was nothing for it but
to go on to the next station, and then to the next; and
I have no doubt I should have been obliged to go the
whole length of the way to Mdlle. Jacottet's destination,
if some kind souls in our carriage, a priest among
others, for whom my gratitude will be everlasting, had
not taken compassion on me, and so effectually diverted
her attention at a given moment, that I was able to
slip out of the carriage unperceived. On my arrival
at the Baths late in the evening, many were the ironical compliments and jokes I had to stand about my
good fortune and the elopement. Some witty ladies
even tried to fix on me the soubriquet of Mdlle. Jacottet's knight, but it did not take.

The next to say farewell was Herr Konrad: he left
on the 21st of August, and we may say that with that
day the most memorable season in the annals of Schranksteinbad virtually closed, for a general break-up followed
shortly after. As he made his way to the station, ac-
claimed and blessed by all the village, he had the
satisfaction of seeing where the old cottages had been
destroyed the walls of new ones fast rising, the result
of his indefatigable exertions. It is superfluous to say
that the exit from the scene of the friend in whom my
interest had principally centred, damped my spirits,
and left a void in my existence. I call him my friend,
because such he became before we parted, and such he

continues to be, thank God! to this very day. His sympathy with my country, and her efforts to help herself, served in a great measure to render him dear to me. Herr Konrad was the first and only German liberal I ever met, who, consistent with logic, admitted the claims of Italian nationality without restriction; that is, Venice included. I have known men more brilliantly gifted, but none whose qualities of mind and heart were more happily balanced. Simple as a child and tender as a woman, he was nevertheless possessed of a wonderful insight into men and their motives, and had an iron will when necessary.

In proportion as he took the realities of power in earnest, insomuch as conducive to good, so did his excessive horror of what he termed the foppery of power lose somewhat of its intensity. "Who wills the end must will the means," he used to say; for all that, I am not sure that, even at this day, after years of office, he has ordered the official costume indispensable at court on gala days.

CHAPTER XII.

Capulets and Montagues.

THE first sight that met my eyes on entering the
grounds of Schranksteinbad the following summer, was
a flock of goats spotting the meadow which skirts the
so often mentioned avenue of tall poplars. Twelve
superb animals, with long silken hair; eleven of them
as white as snow, and one, the ram, as black as jet.
A few were browsing lazily, others dosing in picturesque
attitudes, the greater number reclining on the soft
turf, enjoying a *dolce far niente*. A comely woman
past thirty, the shepherdess, and a boy of ten or so,
the shepherd, both in the costume of Appenzell, sat
close by, weaving osier baskets and singing. It was a
truly Swiss picture, one of which Rosa Bonheur would
make a *chef-d'œuvre*. Several small children stood by
admiring, while others, older or bolder, were making
free with the goats, stroking their silky sides, or
coaxing them to take bread out of their hands.

This is Frantz's doing, thought I; and as soon as
the first welcomes were over, I complimented him on
such a stroke of policy. "A capital idea, is it not?
and a most successful hit," said Frantz; "goat's milk
is at a premium at Schranksteinbad."

"I hope, at all events, there will be some left for
me," I replied.

"I can't promise, there's such a demand for it."

I knew not what to make of Frantz's answer, nor

why Madelcine nudged me. Frantz was the last man in the world to be sarcastic: it was not in his nature; and yet there was that in his tones which sounded like bitter irony.

My room was free, of course, though I came unusually late, and my installation in it was the affair of five minutes. When Madelcine presently came in with water and towels, I asked, "Why did you nudge me just now? what is the mystery about the goats?"

"Mystery there's none; this is what it is: Frantz is out of sorts about the goats, and cannot bear to hear them mentioned. He went all the way to Appenzell himself to choose the best that could be had, and now that they are here, and give plenty of milk, no one will have a drop. You recollect what a clamour there was during the last season, especially among the ladies, for goat's milk and whey."

"Perfectly; and so Frantz has taken the matter to heart."

"Dreadfully! It is not so much the loss, for naturally loss there must be; it is the mortification which makes him smart so. And besides, this is not the only source of vexation to Frantz."

"What else?"

"It is a long story: I will tell it you by-and-by. How long you have been coming! we began to be afraid you were ill, and had almost given up the hope of seeing you. Everybody has been asking about you."

"Is the house pretty full? — any of my old acquaintances?"

"Not many — ah, yes, one, Mdme. Collet; she asks for you every day."

"A tall handsome lady from Neuchatel?"

"Yes, Mdlle. Emma's eldest sister." (I don't know why I felt myself blush at the mention of the last name.)

"Is Mdlle. Emma here also?"

"I knew that would be your first question. Alas, no! Mdlle. Emma is somewhere in Germany." I drew a sigh of relief at what, according to Madeleine, must have disappointed me deeply. How often mistaken are the judgments of those who fancy they know us best!

"And what of Herr Telliker?" asked I, carrying the war into the enemy's camp. It was Madeleine's turn to blush.

"He is quite well, thank you."

"And more than ever in love with a fickle thing who broke my heart, or nearly so."

"A fickle thing who would be most penitent but for that finale of 'nearly so,'" retorted Madeleine laughing.

"Be quiet, you unfeeling butterfly. And does he come as formerly on Sundays?"

"Yes, he does."

"And when is the wedding to be?"

"On the same day as yours; good-bye, I must be off," and away she scampered.

I went and paid a visit to my favourite summer-house, finding which occupied I loitered about the grounds at random. While inspecting some new rose-trees in the vicinity of the two pieces of artificial water, I heard myself called by name by an infantine voice; and turning round, I saw Mdme. Collet with her little ones; the eldest of whom, a boy, had recognised me. We exchanged salutations and greetings, and went on talking and walking until the second bell for dinner warned us to go in and take our places. We had in our stroll picked up others of the boarders, we met more in the passage on their way to the hall, and found others waiting there; all of whom, most of them ladies, welcomed my companion and myself with great friendliness.

Mdme. Collet called my attention to the Ruolz forks, which had replaced the former steel ones.

"Wonders will never cease," said she; "this is a change for the better, which is entirely owing to you."

I answered that it was so far true, as I had advocated it for years, but had almost despaired of ever seeing my advice followed. We made some more comments on this improvement, and on the spirit of progress which had suddenly descended on the owners of the establishment, after which Madame Collet observed, "We are already a goodly number, I think we had better take our seats. Some ladies, you know, are never ready." And suiting the action to the word, she sat down at the head of the table, her boy and girl right and left of her. The rest of the company present followed her example.

I was going over to the opposite pole to Mdme. Collet — that is, to the farther end of the table, the place of the last arrivals — when I heard a great rustle of silk, and in came, with the step of a Juno, a tall fair-haired lady, handsome, but looking extra size, and dressed in a fashion the French call *mirobolante*. I much regret not having sufficient technical knowledge to enable me to give a scientific description of it. I can only state that it was very rich, very showy, and

that its good taste was rather questionable to my mind.
A little over-dressed boy had hold of the big lady's
hand, and a maid followed with two equally over-
dressed little girls. The nurse or lady's maid had
enough to do to perch her charges on their chairs, and
compel the three sets of voluminous petticoats, especially those of the mother, to remain in limits not offensive to next neighbours. By the time this was accomplished, the seats were occupied almost all by ladies
and children, with an additional sprinkle of gentlemen,
three or four of whom had followed in the wake of
the grande dame, whose carriage and grand dress, and
fuss and waiting maid, jarred too violently with the
traditional simplicity of our Spa not to be rather disagreeable to me.

We were forty-one guests at table. I counted
heads, eight gentlemen, eleven children in various
stages of growth, the rest ladies — old, elderly, middle,
and young. The end of the table where I sat was occupied exclusively by Germans, and the talking there
was loud and unceasing; while at the end opposite,
where Mdme. Collet had her seat, conversation lan-
guished sadly, indeed it would have died outright but
for the children of the big lady, who were constantly
asking for this or that dish, and crying and scolding
whenever it was refused them by the maid in attendance. An air of constraint pervaded that part of the
table too marked to be overlooked. I made an advance towards my *vis-à-vis*, an absent-looking elderly
matron, and was repulsed. I then tried to make friends
with a little German girl of six or seven on my left,
but I discovered she could not speak French. Neighbour I had none on my right, and so I ate my dinner

in silence; nor was I sorry when I saw Mdme. Collet
rise and leave the room followed by a good many of
the company. I quickly joined them.

Mdme. Collet led the way to a row of tables with
benches all round, almost facing the entrance door,
and to the left of the garden gate. As we were seat-
ing ourselves, I remarked with some surprise, that all
our party consisted of those same persons, excepting
some very few additions, who had gathered about
Mdme. Collet before dinner, and who, on her proposal,
had seated themselves at table. A few minutes after,
those we had left behind emerged in a formidable
column from the house, stopped awhile at the foot of
the steps, talking and laughing, then moved on in the
direction of the garden gate. The big-skirted lady was
at their head.

"Won't you join us, Frau Hermann?" asked Mdme.
Collet; "it is so charmingly cool here."

"Thank you, madam," was the large lady's answer;
"we prefer the Belvedere on account of the beautiful
view," and on she swept. Belvedere was the name of
that bit of rising ground close by with the two summer-
houses, one of which you remember was mine.

"There is no making head or tail of those blessed
Germans," said Mdme. Collet in a whisper.

"I see," said I, "that we are divided into Monta-
gues and Capulets."

"Rather into French and Germans," she returned.

"And pray, how and in what did this split originate?"

"That is more than I can answer. Half at least
of the ladies and gentlemen present can bear witness
to the perfect peace and harmony which prevailed
among bathers of the two languages so long as Frau

Hermann was not here. She came, and all was changed as if by magic. A drop of vinegar, you know, is enough to spoil a bowl of milk."

"Still," insisted I, "there must have been a special cause or pretext to have brought about this state of things. Have you and Frau Hermann never come into collision?"

"Not exactly; but there has been a quarrel with the heads of the establishment on my account, or rather on account of the room I occupy. I must tell you that I had long bespoken Mdlle. Sprungli's room. Frau Hermann, ten days after I had taken possession of it, wrote to desire that it should be kept for her, and without waiting for an answer, arrived and claimed it. Of course, I neither could nor would give it up, but on my honour I refused with courtesy and good humour. Frau Hermann was extremely disappointed, found fault with Frantz and Madely — even spoke of going away; and from cool, which from the first she has been to me, has become icy, not to say downright hostile."

Mdlle. Sprungli's room, or rather salon, — so called from the lady its constant occupant as long as she lived, — was very large and well furnished, and it had besides an alcove, an advantage which made it much prized by ladies with a family. These spacious chambers, of which there were three or four in the establishment, often proved apples of discord.

A few days of observation showed me the depth and breadth of the social split. There was not only absolute separation, but open hostility between the two camps. The leader of the German party, numerically far the stronger, let no opportunity slip which allowed of politely vexing and crossing the leader of the French, a task in which she was well seconded by her followers. To give some idea of the pettish spirit by which they were actuated, suffice it to say that they formed a conspiracy, and carried it through successfully, to oust me from the summer-house which bore my name. Whatever the hour at which I went there, I always found it occupied. Their great number rendered this an easy undertaking, and I had to yield.

The leader of our camp on her side, though generally forbearing and to some extent conciliating, had hot blood in her veins, and a sharp-edged tongue, and when provoked, would use it freely, and give a Roland for an Oliver. Her quiet and ladylike way of managing this did great execution in the enemy's ranks. She made a rule of inviting Frau Hermann and her company, whenever the opportunity offered, to come and join us — did this with a gentleness and sweetness, which, though quite irreproachable, yet had a sting in it, under which the others could not help smarting. There were several points of natural antagonism between Mdme. Collet and Frau Hermann. Both were tall, handsome, and commanding, and either would have been the queen of the establishment but for the other. Each had thriving and beautiful children, and would have been the envy of all mothers, but for the other. Each was rich and well dressed, and either would have been the richest and the best dressed but for the other.

Add to this that Mdme. Collet came from Neuchâtel, the somewhat aristocratic capital of the Canton of that name, while Frau Hermann came from Lachauxdefonds in the same Canton, — a rich industrious democratic village, to which nothing was wanting of a

city but the name. Now it must be known that Neuchâtel and Lachauxdefonds were like cat and dog at
the time I am writing of — the former looking down
upon the latter as a set of revolutionists and parvenus,
the latter looking down upon the former as a nest of
good-for-nothing aristocrats, and moreover as the
usurper and retainer of the title and rights of a capital
— a title and rights which ought to belong to Lachauxdefonds in virtue of its greater population, industry,
and wealth.

This feeling of rivalry and jealousy between the two
places will explain how it came to pass that when on
fête-days the retinue of both leaders was increased by
husbands, brothers, other male relatives and friends;
these, I am sorry to note it, were absurd enough to
espouse the quarrel of the ladies, and turn up their
noses at each other. And more than once when the
two hostile columns happened to meet in some secluded
spot, I was not without apprehension that the purposely
exaggerated ceremony of raising of hats, and of bows
(for no forms of politeness were ever dispensed with)
might lead to a round of fisticuffs; and in which, as
Neuchâtel was only two to three of Lachauxdefonds,
we might come off second best.

Such was the uncomfortable state of things pre-
vailing in our little colony, and towards the cessation
of which I would fain have made any sacrifice, if I
had only known what. Had Herr Konrad been at the
Baths, I felt sure that under his auspices matters would
have immediately mended; but Herr Konrad was not
there, nor was he expected. While I was racking my
brains in search of a peace-maker, a family arrived
from the town inhabited by Louisa and her mother,

loaded with all sorts of affectionate messages to the
proprietors of the Baths. "Louisa's mother was not
well," said the new arrivals; "she had had half a mind
to come and make some stay at Schranksteinbad, when
some other Spa had been recommended to her, and she
was undecided whither she should go."

When Madely mentioned Louisa's name to me, it
was like a flash of lightning which shows his path to
the benighted wayfarer. Louisa was the peace-maker
I had been longing for; Louisa would restore harmony
to our distracted Spa. I well recollected the irresistible
charm possessed by the little pet, and the wonders of
humanization which I had seen her achieve on the
most refractory natures. Mdme. Collet, who was really
a most kind and motherly soul, entered fully into my
views and hopes, and Frantz and Madely were easily
converted to them. Thereupon Madely wrote to Louisa's
mother, pressing her in the kindest and warmest terms
to give the preference to her old friends, and come
to Schranksteinbad with her little daughter as soon as
possible.

When I said that Frantz had been easily won over
to my scheme, I went too far; I ought only to have
said that he did not oppose it, for at the most he
only passively acquiesced in it. Since the failure
of his speculation with the goats, Frantz had had
neither enthusiasm nor sympathy left in him for anything or anybody; or if any particle had been left, a
second disappointment, that at which Madely had darkly
hinted on the first day of my arrival, treading on the
heels of the first, had trampled out his last sparks of
friendly zeal. Frantz on his way to Appenzell upon
his unlucky errand for the goats, had visited some

other baths with the intention of adding to his own such improvements as he found elsewhere, provided they did not go beyond his powers. Frantz, to his honour be it said, was not without having had some ambition developed by the unprecedented affluence of visitors the previous year, and was not unwilling to make a certain outlay in order to realize his new-born ambition. Now, in most of the establishments visited by him, no steel forks were to be seen; they were either of real silver or Ruolz, and Frantz resolved that forthwith steel forks should disappear from Schranksteinbad, and be replaced by those of Ruolz. This change applied to hundreds and hundreds of forks was rather expensive, but Frantz reasoned thus: If I spend my money freely that my boarders may benefit by such and such an improvement, it would not be just that they should enjoy it without in some small way repaying me. I cannot manage that they should do this by raising the prices, for they won't hear of such a thing. But I can and will make them repay me by introducing a new item into the Schranksteinbad bills — a charge which is made everywhere else, that is so much for service. I will make it as low as possible, only twenty centimes a day (twopence) for each person.

Considering his logic unanswerable, Frantz passed and promulgated a decree to the effect aforesaid — I mean that he inserted in his best writing this additional article in all the copies of a tariff of the prices of the establishment together with the regulations. This tariff was hung up in every room and passage of the house: "Every boarder will be charged twopence a day for service." This trifling innovation was no sooner per-

14*

ceived by some of the first comers than there arose a
perfect uproar. Every voice protested against such an
imposition; on the one hand, threats of leaving were
resorted to, on the other, threats of staying, and re-
fusing at all risks to pay the obnoxious pence. In
short, Frantz had, like Charles the Tenth, to withdraw
his *ordonnances*, and with his own hand to efface the
freshly-drawn article. This second blow was poor
Frantz's finishing stroke.

The answer from Louisa's mother came in due time,
and was favourable — even the day and hour of their
arrival were mentioned. Mdme. Collet, her children,
two other ladies, and I went to the station to meet
them. Many more would have done so, but we dis-
suaded them; we wished to avoid anything like a fuss
which might give umbrage to, or prejudice the hostile
party against our intended little peace-maker. Louisa
was no longer the wee thing I had parted from some
years ago, still her growth had not been considerable
enough to rob her of any of the charms of childhood.
She had scarcely completed her tenth year. She was
a little marvel of beauty, grace, and intelligence. She
recollected both my name and person quite well, threw
her arms round my neck with a warmth of feeling
that went to my heart, and spoke of poor Suldi with
a mixture of terror and attachment. Her reception by
the whole household was a positive ovation. Even
disconsolate Frantz brightened up at sight of her. We
took her to see the goats, with whom she fell in love
at once; we made the tour of the establishment —
cows, poultry, bees, ponds, springs, jets d'eau; and for
everything animate or inanimate connected with her old
associations she had a word of welcome and endear-

ment. In the garden she pointed out to me two beds
of heartsease, one all yellow, the other all purple, opposite to one another like two rival forces drawn up in
battle array, and she reminded me that I had told her
the yellow were Austrians, and the purple Piedmontese.
Mdme. Collet was delighted with Louisa, and her children speedily fraternized with her.

Before we had ended our stroll, we met Frau Hermann's maid with Master and Miss Hermann; we invited them to come and walk with us, which they did,
and both were soon excellent friends with Louisa,
especially the boy. Everything promised well.

Shortly before dinner Madely came and told us
with great glee of a contrivance she had hit upon in
furtherance of our plan of peace-making. She had
arranged that Louisa's place at table should be between
Mdme. Collet's daughter and Frau Hermann's son, and
that Louisa's mother should sit between Mdme. Collet's
boy and Frau Hermann's girl. By this clever plan,
went on Madely, Louisa would be almost Frau Hermann's *vis-à-vis*, — a situation most favourable for the
exercise of Louisa's softening influence on the big lady.
This arrangement I opposed with all my might. I
argued that it would be a barefaced infringement of a
very strict rule only fit to create jealousies, and that
Frau Hermann was more likely to take it ill than well.
Madely replied that Louisa and her mother could not
be reckoned as strangers, and therefore the rule did
not apply to them, or, if it did, it might be waived
once in a way in consideration of the good end we had
in view. Mdme. Collet, in spite of all I could say,
sided with Madeleine, and all my objections were, as
a matter of course, overruled. What woman wills — I

believe every male reader knows the conclusion of the
proverb; and where there are two female wills combined, I should like to see the man who can carry his
point against them.

The second dinner-bell rang, and in we went. Frau
Hermann was more behind her time than usual, and
almost every one was seated when she entered. My
heart beat loudly at the sound of the rustle of her
silk. She stalked up to her usual seat, saw the new
arrangement, exclaimed, "These are not our places!"
and wheeling suddenly round, turned her back upon
the table, and walked straight out of the room, followed
by the children and her maid.

The first impression was one of general consternation. Madeleine turned as white as the napkin she had
on her arm, and nearly spilled the plate of soup into
the lap of the lady she was about to serve. Then a
loud murmur arose from the offended camp, and Frantz
and Madely were openly accused of, and held responsible for, an intentional slight to a respectable lady
and her family. It was a shame; such whims were not
to be borne; a rule was a rule to be held good by
everybody. Madeleine made a very feeble defence.
Louisa's mother, with tears in her eyes, protested that
she was not to be blamed, it was none of her doing;
she had sat down where she had found her name, that
was all she had had to do in the matter. Louisa felt,
and looked most indignant; she took her own and her
mother's knife and fork, and without a word carried
them to the other end of the table, near to me. Frantz
carved violently with a devil-may-care expression of
countenance, whistling under his breath. Our party
was much taken aback, and held their tongues. The

act complained of, whoever the author, was one not to
be defended.

Madeleine went to seek the offended lady, and did
her utmost to propitiate her, but in vain. A second
deputation, composed, at Madely's earnest entreaty, of
Louisa's mother and Louisa, this last most reluctant to
go, and half dragged by main force, was more fortunate.
Frau Hermann condescended to return with them to
the dining-room, and to resume her former place, but
did not sit down until she had seen the mother and
daughter take their new seats; then speaking loudly
enough to be heard by every one present, she said that
it must be perfectly understood that the cause which
had prompted her to withdraw had nothing personal in
it to the newly-arrived lady and her charming daughter.
My own impression was that Frau Hermann was conscious of having pushed matters too far, and was anxious
to put herself right by a show of graciousness. But
whatever her feelings, it was now too late to hope that
Louisa would work on them to the restoration of harmony. Louisa already hated her. "*Je la déteste*," she
whispered in my ear, with a concentration of passion
positively appalling in so young a creature.

Still the beneficial influence of Louisa's presence
made itself felt indirectly. Louisa was a capital hand
at all sorts of games, and full of inventions and contrivances for making time pass agreeably, so that she
was much sought after by our little folks. Frau Hermann's son, the tallest and most influential of the
squad, could not do without her, and naturally the
mothers, whose children were playing together from
morn to evening, could not be at daggers-drawn, and
thus there ensued some relenting, a slight thawing, a

degree or two more of communication among them all.
But Frau Hermann's boy had a will, and so had
Louisa, and one fine day there came a clash between
the two wills, and then a quarrel ending in a pitched
battle, in which spirited Louisa gave more than she
took. This led to angry words between the respective
mammas, followed by a command to the children not
to play together, and by a recrudescence of universal
ill-humour.

Nothing, so it is said, like a common misfortune
for healing feuds and reconciling jarring spirits. The
young generation at our Spa proved the truth of the
dictum. A terrible and unforeseen blow fell upon them.
One eventful morning the beautiful goats, their hearts'
delight, were missing; they were searched for down
the vale and up the hill in vain. Where could they
have gone? Who could have taken them away? They
had gone back to Appenzell. Frantz had sent them
away, and he stood forth to answer for what he had
done. "But why send them away?" "Why deprive
the children of such an innocent amusement?" cried
the mothers in chorus. Frantz answered the query by
showing a few dry figures, which demonstrated that
the "innocent amusement" made him a loser of three
francs per diem. Why not say this in time? Had
they only known! Frantz's only reply was whistling a
tune under his breath; this whistling had become a
habit with him of late. He had his revenge.

The departure of the goats created so great a void
in the young ones' sports, that it brought about a
renewal of friendship between the children of the two
camps — a peace which lasted as long as it could.
Of subjects of jealousy there was no lack, God knows!

Louisa was the spoilt child of the Old Mutter, and as
such enjoyed immunity and privileges, which were as
gall and wormwood to the rest. I remember an ex-
plosion taking place on its being ascertained that
Louisa had been seen, actually seen, within the sacred
precincts, so unmercifully closed against all profane
feet, where the stork lived. The Old Mutter and the
stork, here are two new personages that I beg to introduce to the reader.

The Old Mutter, or Alte Frau, as the dame was
called, was Frantz's and Madely's grandmother. It
took me two whole seasons to penetrate the mystery
of this relationship; not that any attempt was made to
dissemble it, God forbid! but the grandmother's department in the establishment lay so entirely away
from that of her grandchildren, and her business kept
her so much out of doors, that there was scanty opportunity for such intercourse between them as might
have enlightened me. Then the fact of her dress being
that of a peasant, and of her being always engaged in
some out-of-door work, had made me take up the
idea that she must be an old and confidential servant
of the family. She was indeed very old; she did not
know her exact age, but was positive as to being past
eighty, when I first became acquainted with her. She
was very old, as I was saying, very thin, and slightly
bent, but still strong and hale, and able to brave all
weathers. Her features, somewhat Dantesque, were
regular and handsome. Hers was a hopeful nature,
nay, inclined to optimism, which was the more remarkable in one, the early part of whose life had been a
series of trials, hard toil, and deprivations. Be it that
it rained, or that it was dry, the Alte Mutter held to

it that it was good for the crops; and when forced out
of her opinion by evidence, she would go on for an
incredible sequel of days predicting fine weather or
wet, according to the requirement of the moment. We
were on the best possible terms; and whenever we
met, which we did very often in the grounds, and
infallibly every morning in front of the barometer,
which, when she chanced to be engaged in-doors she
consulted every ten minutes; well, whenever we met,
she always made me numerous little speeches, to all of
which I could only reply with a volley of *Jas* and *Guts,*
alte Mutter.

She wore a big crinoline, and declared it to be a
most beneficial invention for womankind, whose skirts
when wet, which hers often were, it kept from dangling
about the feet, and from communicating their humidity
to the nether limbs of the wearer. She, who frequently
chose to squat on the ground to dig up potatoes, or
pick up fallen fruit, was peculiarly alive to this benefit.
But a crinoline was the only innovation in dress she
had permitted herself to adopt; she adhered strictly
to the costume of the Canton, and she had never quite
forgiven her granddaughter for dropping it. I never
saw her idle; she was either looking after the labourers,
or seeing to the cows, or to the swine, or the rabbits.
But where she reigned alone and supreme was over
the poultry. No everyday hen-house, I assure you, was
this of hers. She had had it built expressly for her,
after her own plan, and under her own superintendence.
It stood in the field behind the house, a small wooden
building painted white, a kind of gigantic doll's house,
having a castellated turret at each end, and the front
ornamented by two rows of glazed miniature Gothic

windows. This Lilliputian castle occupied the centre
of a grassy space, surrounded by high palings, and in
which there was a pond. On two sides were large
poplar trees, throwing far and wide a grateful shade.
Within this enclosure perambulated at will the fowls
and ducks, which had their roosting quarters in the
castle.

One of the wings was, however, entirely devoted
to the service of one feathered biped, and the ground
in front of this wing was railed off from the general
play-ground of the poultry, with a wicket on the outer
side to allow of this favoured inhabitant to go forth at
will, and roam about if so disposed, instead of merely
taking the air on a toprail adjusted on the inner railing
for its convenience. This gate or wicket was, however,
strictly tabooed, and the bird never allowed to go out
during the season. Nay, even the railings surrounding
that part of the enclosure exclusively destined for him,
were boarded up for additional security against any
missiles that might be launched at him by any mis-
chievous passer by. No child, save Louisa, was ever
admitted within this sanctum.

The bird lodged in so princely a manner, you are
already aware, was a stork — an unfortunate specimen
of his kind, for he limped, one of his legs being shorter
than the other. It is not at all unusual to meet with
storks thus domesticated in Switzerland. There, as
everywhere else, storks are much respected, and considered as omens of good. As an instance of how
strong this feeling is, I can quote a fact which was
attested to me by all Schrankstein. When the works
for the railroad, which was to pass by the village,
were first begun, it was found that the proposed line

would necessitate the cutting down of a tree, in which from time immemorial there had been a stork's nest, which had never failed to have yearly tenants. The superintending engineer was much disturbed at the circumstance, and actually for an instant thought of modifying the course of the iron road. This being found impracticable, he gave orders that the tree should not be cut down, but transplanted with every care, and without disarranging the nest, to a few yards backward, in a straight line from the spot where it had been. The birds had already migrated when the translocation of the tree was effected. The following spring, the return of the storks was anxiously looked for, and, to the joy of the village, back came the usual tenants of the nest, and resumed possession of their old home as if nothing had happened.

Now, was it only the traditional respect for the race, or was it some peculiar and almost superstitious feeling connected with some important event in the annals of the family, which made the stork of Schrank-steinbad an object of so much care and veneration? The answer to this grave query will be found in the next chapter.

CHAPTER XIII.

The Stork and the Squirrel.

AFTER Ucli and Suldi, the stork had most interested and puzzled me on my first discovery of Schrankstein-bad, and if I did not sooner introduce him to the reader, it was owing to the wish and the hope I entertained of some day being able to give at one and the same time the riddle and the key to it. For to me, this grave, meditative, melancholy lame stork was a riddle, and the more I looked at him the less I could bring myself to believe that beneath so impressive, suggestive, and truly solemn an exterior and demeanour, there was to be found only an instinctive, irresponsible bird.

I recollect one morning being surprised by Madeleine while in deep contemplation of my riddle, and being asked by her what I was doing. "Interrogating the sphinx," I replied. Sphinxes not being migratory birds, Madely was thoroughly unacquainted with them, and so she looked up vacantly into my face. "I mean," resumed I, "that I am trying to pump his secret out of your stork."

"What secret can a bird have?" quoth she, with so innocent an air — the artful dissembler! — that I took it for granted that if there was a secret connected with the stork it was unknown to Madely. It was long afterwards, indeed only the season preceding the one of which I write, that I acquired the certainty of Madely having then and there taken me in. One day, as I was passing by the stork accompanied by Herr Konrad, I happened to say something about the mysterious effect produced on me by the bird, and of my impression that some legend or story must be attached to him.

"You have made a good guess," said Herr Konrad; "there is indeed no legend, but a *bona fide* story, and one not without interest concerning this very stork. Years and years ago I wrote it down at the request of the grandmother, and from her own dictation. She had good reasons for wishing to leave after her some written record of the circumstances of the case. So I made two copies of the alte Frau's statement — one in German and the other in French. I will ask Madely for the French one, and, with the grandmother's permission, give it you to read."

"Then Madely knows all about it?" said I.

"Of course she does, and Frantz also; on coming of age they were each told. Two other persons were acquainted with the story, but they are dead." The Old Mutter having made no objections to my being trusted with the MS., Herr Konrad handed it to me, and the reasons which were the cause of the story being kept secret having by this time ceased to exist, I subjoin here, with the leave of all concerned, a little translation. It is given as nearly as possible in the grandmother's very words.

THE STORY OF THE STORK.

It was the year 1831, late in the month of September, the season when storks take flight. A large number of them gathered together here, and for some

days they were wheeling round and round, flying in
compact bodies this way and that, just as if they were
drilling themselves for a long journey, and ended by
perching in a line all along the edge of the roof of
our great barn; they looked as usual, grave and wise;
the leaders, still wiser and graver than the rest, seemed
for all the world as if they were consulting together
about their plans. At last one morning off they set in
ranks like a regiment with captains at their head, and
were seen no more that year. I must here note that
the month of September had been uncommonly warm
and dry for these parts, and the morning of the day
on which the storks took flight had been positively
hot; but a little past midday the weather changed to
stormy, and I was sorry on account of the poor birds.

As I was going my rounds of the farm in the afternoon, what do you think I found at the foot of the
poplar, close to the end of the barn, but a poor stork
wounded and helpless. Whether it had been fighting
with some of its brethren, or had got hurt by some
mischance, of course I can't say, but there it lay with
both a leg and a wing broken. It was a pitiful sight,
and your heart would have ached to see it, even had
it been any other dumb creature, let alone a stork. I
took it up, poor thing, as gently as I could, and
brought it into the kitchen, and then I did my best to
set its leg, and washed the wound in the wing, and
put some oil on it. Perhaps it had been stupefied by
its fall, or perhaps it felt that I was doing it good:
however that might be, it scarcely struggled against
me, and when I put it into a basket, it lay quite
quiet; a little later, when I brought it food, the poor
thing took it very willingly.

When my husband and the labourers came in for
their four o'clock meal, I told them how I had found
the stork, and all that I had done for it; and they
said it was quite right, for a stork cannot be killed
and put out of pain, as any other bird may; and that
no one would ever turn a stork away from a house, as
storks always brought good luck. I had always heard
say so, and I know that the saying has proved true
for us. We were not always prosperous as we are now,
and on the very day that I saved the stork we were in
great trouble.

When my husband and I married, we had but a
very few fields, and this farm-house, which was then
very small. It contained just three rooms and a kitchen,
divided by the entrance passage as they remain, and
to which the outer steps lead up. Below, on each
side of the steps, were other rooms, which were
used then as now for cellars and storerooms. Their
windows open, as you know, into the verandah
covered with creepers. My husband one year had a
very bad cough, and after having swallowed a deal
of doctor's stuff without getting any good of it, he
took a whim to drink nothing but the water of our
spring, saying that what was good for cleaning the
outside, was good for the inside, and sure enough
he was very soon cured. Then the labourers began
to do the same, and as they found that the water
cured their ailments, it came to pass that our spring
was much talked about, and the sick people in the
village came to drink of it. Sometimes after their walk
they wanted some other refreshment than water, so we
set up a sort of public-house *(Wirthschaft)* in addition
to our farming. Little by little the fame of the virtue

of our spring spread, and the sick country folk from all the villages round would come hither to stay for a fortnight or three weeks. This made us determine to add a storey to our house; so we built four rooms for the use of boarders during the summer months, and it answered well.

You must know that at that time my eldest son, God rest his soul! the father of my grandchildren, Frantz and Madeleine, was a miller to trade, and had kept a mill in the next village, in partnership with his father-in-law, for the last couple of years. The two did not agree, and they resolved to separate. Just when this happened there was a mill to be sold at Schrankstein. Our son had saved a little, but not sufficient to buy the mill, and he asked his father to give security on our land for a part of the purchase-money, and his father did so. But the mill had not been bought a year, when one unlucky night it took fire, and ere help could be had it was burned to the ground. Then the creditors fell on my son, and in his default upon us. Not that they were very exacting; on the contrary, they would have willingly given us time, could we have paid the interest of the mortgage, and yearly a little of the capital. But that we were unable to do. We had had two bad years running, the crops had been almost all lost, and out of our three cows one had died. The last two summers had been wet, and scarcely any boarders had come to us. It was all we could do to keep our heads above water, without having debts to pay, and when that trouble was added to the rest, there was no help for it, our land and house must be sold. The very day before I

found the wounded stork, notice had been served upon
us that the sale was to be in three weeks.

Well, the evening of the day on which the storks
had taken flight closed in dark and stormy. A high
wind was driving the heavy clouds and the slanting
rain before it. The poplars in the avenue tossed about
and moaned like wild living creatures in pain. I had
just done feeding once more my foundling of the
morning, and I was standing weary and sad at one of
the windows, when I fancied that I heard between the
blasts the sound of wheels at a distance. Presently
the sound became more distinct, and then I saw a carriage driving up the avenue, the bells on the horses'
necks jingling cheerily. In less than two minutes the
carriage stopped at our door. My husband and I ran
down the steps with umbrellas, and opened the carriage
door. Out jumped a tall gentleman with dark hair
and mustaches, and handed out a lady who leaned
heavily on his arm as they went up the steps, followed
by a pretty little boy. All three were dressed in an
outlandish fashion, and were in deep mourning. You
would have said three drops of ink.

Well, it was perhaps foolish of me, but the moment I saw them, I said to myself, Here is our good
luck coming! I lighted a candle quickly, and then I
saw that the lady, who had sunken into a chair, was
very pale and breathless, and looked as if she were
going to faint. Her husband said something, but we
could not understand a word of what he said. I told
him in return, in my Swiss German, that we could not
speak French, but he could not understand me a bit
better than I could him. We all looked and felt
puzzled. At last the gentleman pointed to his wife

and made signs that she ought to lie down. So I took
up a candle and beckoned to him to follow me, and I
led him up-stairs to our best bedrooms. When he saw
two of them opening into each other, and that one had
two beds in it, he looked quite pleased, and nodded
and smiled. I made up the bed in the singlebedded
room, and he got the lady up-stairs, and as soon as
she was in bed, I brought her a cup of good hot coffee,
which seemed to revive her. Then I set something
more substantial before the gentleman and the little
boy — a handsome child he was, and greatly relished
his bread and honey-comb.

It was very awkward, as you can believe, not to
understand a word the gentlefolks said; but somehow
we managed pretty well by dint of smiles, and nods,
and signs. I had determined that the first thing next
day I would send for the postmaster of the village, he
being the only person near who could speak French.
Our doctor, who can, was still absent, and as for Herr
Konrad, who speaks all languages, he did not make
his appearance hereabouts for some years afterwards.
I supposed it was French they talked, though it did
not sound quite like some French I had heard. Sure
enough I sent for the postmaster next morning, but he
had gone only the day before to the Oberland for a
month's holiday on account of his health, and the
deputy he had left in his place could not speak French.

The gentleman came down with the little boy quite
early, and found me feeding the stork. They looked
at the bird with great curiosity, and I showed them
the poor thing's broken leg and wing. The gentleman
shook his head compassionately, the child took some
of the food out of my hand, and the stork ate it as

15*

well from him as from me, which made the little fellow clap his hands and caper with joy; nothing would
serve, but he must feed the bird again and again. At
last the papa went away with his pretty boy for a
walk, and during that time I carried up breakfast to
the lady, who was still in bed. When the father and
son returned, they went and sat with her. I must say
I never saw a husband so attentive to a wife; he
stayed with her all day, except when he went out for
a walk in the morning, and during the night I could
hear him go ever so many times from his room to hers.
Once or twice I even thought I heard him come down
stairs, but as he did not call for any one, nor did I
find that he had carried anything up-stairs, I supposed
I had been mistaken.

After a few days the lady was well enough to
leave her bed, and even to come down and sit in the
garden. We had a beautiful warm autumn, and all
three of them used to sit out of doors for hours during
the day; and the little boy coaxed me to set the stork
in its basket near them, and he fed it, and they all
three petted it. I used to point to it and say to them
Gut, gut, and I think that at last they understood what
that word meant. At least, they would look at the
stork and then at me, and smile and nod quite pleased.
By degrees the bird got better, and began to hop out
of its basket and limp about the garden, and was quite
a playfellow for the child. The lady and gentleman
were always satisfied with whatever we gave them,
and were very good-natured, but very shy of strangers.
They had the grounds quite to themselves alone, as
boarders we had none, and occasional visitors were
rare at that late season. But when anybody did chance

to come, I observed that all the family kept out of the way.

The gentleman was handsome and kindly in his looks, and the lady was downright beautiful; she had the softest voice in the world. I liked to hear her speak, though I could not understand her; and she smiled so sweetly, and yet in a way that gave you half a mind to weep. Both husband and wife were pale and thin, as though he as well as she had been ill, or as if they had both suffered much in their mind. The boy was the very picture of his mother, only rosy and hale, and would amuse himself with anything. In a little while I grew quite fond of them all.

One morning when I came to lay their breakfast in the parlour, I was surprised to see a second gentleman added to the party. I had not seen him come in either by the front or the back door. I stared not a little. The lady and gentleman made me signs that he was to breakfast with them. I hoped he might understand our language, but no — he did not. When night came, the visitor was gone, without my knowing how or where. This happened twice — each time he came very early, and always managed to come and go without our seeing him. It looked rather odd.

Another discovery which I made within a week after puzzled me still more. Two shovels and two pickaxes had been found missing by the labourers, who had sought for them early in the morning. They asserted most positively that they had put them the evening before in their usual place, a dark recess under the stairs, where all such implements were kept. Every corner was searched for the missing tools, but to no purpose; nor were they to be found at the place

where the people had been at work the day before.
Thieves we had none; what then could have become
of the shovels and pickaxes? Well, sir, I did the
lady's room about noon — think what was my surprise at discovering the four missing tools concealed
between the head of the bed and the curtain!

But this was nothing compared to the shock I got
at a very strange scene which I was destined to witness on the very night of that very day. One of our
cows fell ill, and had to be looked after. My husband
sat up till midnight with the poor beast, and then I
told him to go to bed and get the rest a hard working-
man needs, and I would take my turn and see after
the cow. Some time later, I took her a warm mash,
and stayed to watch how she was getting on. As I
was just coming out of the stable, a sudden gust of
wind blew out the candle in the lantern, for I had forgotten to hold towards me the side where the glass
was broken, and so I had to find my way across the
yard in the dark; there was no moon, but a sort of
glimmering light from the stars. When I had got half
way up the steps to the door, I heard a slight noise in
the verandah on my right hand. I stooped down and
tried to peep through the Virginia creeper that clustered
thickly over the verandah, and the iron rails which
shut it in, as you know, on one side. It was so dark
inside that I could see nothing, but I heard a stealthy
step, and the next moment I perceived our boarder
issue forth in front of the house. I recognised him at
once by his figure, and his foreign coat and hat. He
walked very gently, and passed into a path under the
apple-trees to his left. He had something on his
shoulder. I was so surprised I could not say a word,

and I stopped to watch him. Presently I fancied I saw the twinkle of a light before him, as if he were carrying a small lantern, and was doing his best to hide it. A great desire seized me to find out where he was going, and what he could be doing out of doors at this time of night; so I stole after him, keeping at a certain distance, and getting on the grass as soon as I could, that he might not hear my footsteps.

He walked on cautiously, looking about him as if he feared to miss his way, until he came to the grove of fir-trees, which is above the little spring that flows over a rock into a basin, and falls from thence into the brook crossing our field. Well, when he got as far as that, he turned in among the trees, and there it was so black that I lost sight of him, and I could only tell where he was by the rustling he made in forcing his way through the brushwood. I crouched down behind a bush just outside the grove. In a minute he uncovered the lantern and set it upon the ground, and then I could see him perfectly, as also another man, who must have been already waiting there. This second person was the stranger gentleman who had come so mysteriously twice to the house. He stood there, and at his feet lay a long box which I recognised instantly as being one I had seen habitually under the lady's bed. The two men said a few words to each other in a low voice. Then our boarder threw down what he had been carrying on his shoulder, and I saw our missing pickaxes and shovels. My heart beat like that of a mouse caught in a trap.

They presently took off their coats and set to work to dig a large deep hole. This took them a good while; at last, however, it was done; then without

waiting, out of breath as they were, the two lifted up
the box, which seemed very heavy, and laid it into
the pit they had dug. After that they both kneeled
down on the edge and prayed. I heard them quite
distinctly say three *Paters* and three *Aves* just as our
priest does out of his mass book, and they looked up
to heaven and crossed themselves, and cried like
children, and prayed over and over again. After a
time they got off their knees, filled up the hole as
fast as they could, levelled the earth, scattered dead
leaves and branches over the place, so that no one
could see that the ground had been moved, and that
done, they again knelt down and prayed, sobbing
aloud; then they embraced, spoke a little, and took
leave of one another, each going his separate way.
Our boarder came back as he went, and actually
brushed against the bush, my hiding-place. I held my
breath, and he passed without discovering me. It was
some time before I could stand steadily; then I broke
off a twig from a tree, stripped it of the leaves, and
stuck it into the grave, so that I could recognise the
exact spot in the morning, and this done I hurried
homewards. As I got near the house, I descried the
figure of our boarder some way in advance of me; he
turned into the verandah, and presently I heard a
window of the ground storey which opened into the
verandah softly closed. That was how he managed to
get in and out of the house unobserved, and no doubt
the other gentleman had come and gone that way.

I was bewildered by what I had seen, and unable
to collect my thoughts. Only one thing was clear to
me, and that was that I must have an explanation
with these people, whoever and whatever they were.

Yes, an explanation I would have, even if I had to go to the town and bring back some one able to speak French. With this determination, and still trembling, I went to bed, though in a couple of hours it would be time to get up again. I'll tell my husband the first thing in the morning, said I to myself, no use waking him now; and thinking thus I fell asleep, and when I awoke my man was already gone to his work.

In spite of all that filled my head, I did not forget to feed the stork.

When our boarders came down to breakfast I hardly knew how to look at them. The gentleman made signs that he wished to pay his bill and go away. I was half glad, half sorry at this, and altogether puzzled; but what could I do but make out the bill? I took it to him, he looked at the sum total, and then at me, smiling, and said something to the lady which made her smile too. The gentleman paid me at once. There were a few francs of change, but when I offered them to him he gave them back to me. Presently I heard sounds of wheels, and a carriage stopped at the door — our boarders were all ready to go. The luggage was brought down and put on the carriage. I took an opportunity of asking the driver where he had come from, and he named the best hotel of the nearest town. When our boarders came to the door, the gentleman took both my hands and pressed them kindly, the lady kissed me, and the boy hung about my neck. All at once he ran after the stork, caught it in his arms, kissed it, and put it down gently. I don't believe there was a dry eye among us. Father, and mother, and child got into the car-

riage, the driver cracked his whip, and away they
went. Just before turning out of sight, they all put
their heads out of the window and waved their hands.

That was the last I saw of them — they had been
just seventeen days with us — nor have we ever heard
of them since. When I went to town the next market
day, I asked at the hotel mentioned by the driver
who they were and where they went. No one knew
anything about them except that they had gone away
in the diligence to Berne, and though I have inquired
of many persons from that town, none had ever known
such a family.

But to return to the day of their departure. A
little while after they were gone, I went to clear their
rooms and set things to rights, and, bless me! what
should I find on one of the tables but a small packet
directed to me (they knew my name from having seen
it written in my prayer-book), a packet containing a
thousand francs in gold! A thousand francs, only
think! A sum I could not have hoped to save for
Heaven knows how long — enough to get time from
the creditors, and stop the sale of our land. I fell
down on my knees and thanked God, and then ran
down-stairs like a creature mad with joy as I was. I
met my husband just coming in, I pulled him into the
parlour, shut the door, and showed him our treasure.

"Where did you get that?" he asked, breathless
with surprise.

I told him, and he gave a jump crying, "What
good people! what excellent people!"

"I think so, I hope so," said I, for the recollection of the night's work I had witnessed came over me
just then.

"You think so! you hope so!" exclaimed my husband. "Why, wife, you have lost your wits with joy. What better proof than this can we have of their being good? they are angels come down from heaven to us."

"But listen to me first," said I; and then I told him all I had seen with my own eyes the night before. He grew very serious as he listened, and when I had finished he said, "It is odd, to be sure, but people who had been after any wickedness would not have prayed and crossed themselves as they did. Besides, our gentleman looks as honest and noble a fellow as ever I saw. I thought so before I knew what a good turn he was going to do us. No, no, wife, there is no harm in that man. And if he is generous and likes to pay for his board like a prince, why should we fear to take what is fairly given? If you had minded your own business instead of spying after other folk's secrets, you would not be troubled with all these doubts and scruples."

"Well, well, but suppose there was anything wrong?" interrupted I.

"Wrong! what wrong could there be?" cried he, "I see no wrong but what you did yourself. Suppose the gentleman has many more thousand francs, and thinks it safer to bury them than to travel about, stranger as he is, with so much money, where is the harm, I should like to know? And if he has chosen to bury his gold in my land, it is in a safe place. I am not one to take the advantage of him."

"That's true as gospel," answered I.

"Well then, leave off talking nonsense, and, God willing, no later than to-morrow afternoon I will go to the town, and settle matters with the creditors' lawyer, and have the sale of the land stopped. Oh wife, what a blessing that will be! what a weight off my heart!"

Truly I felt this as much as he, but for all that I could not rest satisfied in my own mind. However, I said no more. What was the use of spoiling my poor man's joy, if he was not troubled with any of my scruples? So I gave him his dinner, and afterwards he went out as usual to his work; but before he went, he gave me a hug and a kiss that did my heart good. All the same, I had no peace. I was afraid there might be some great evil hid under this mystery. It was no use my saying to myself that the two gentlemen would not have prayed as they did if they had been criminals; and that if I were to say anything, I might injure people as innocent as I was; and God forbid I should bring sorrow on that sweet lady and her little son. Yet it seemed wrong to hide such unaccountable doings, and to take what was perhaps hush-money; for, after all, how could I be sure that the gentlemen did not see me behind the bush?

In this difficulty I determined to ask the opinion of one who would know how to advise me, and who, I was certain, would not speak of the affair to any human being. So off I went to the village, and told everything in confession to our parish priest. After I had ended my story and answered several questions, he said that our best course was to go together, dig up the box, and see what it contained. It was only after seeing the contents that he could safely advise me what to do. He desired that my husband and I should come to meet him in the grove next day, bringing with

us pickaxes and screw-drivers. We were to choose the
hour when all the labourers were sure to be in the
fields. We did according to his bidding, and met him
at nine next morning in the grove of fir-trees. We
went to work at once, digging hard. It was a long
business, for the box was buried deep; at last we came
upon it, and a pretty job we had, first to lift it out,
and then to open it, for it was locked. However, the
curé managed to unscrew the lock.

When the lid was lifted, the first thing we saw
was a crucifix, as if put there to guard all that lay
beneath. Our curé reverently raised the sacred emblem,
and leaning it carefully against the trunk of a tree, he
proceeded to draw forth a much-battered flag, riddled
by shot, and with the staff broken. Below the flag
was a uniform coat, much cut and torn about the breast:
there were spots on it like blood stains. Under this
uniform there was a second one, quite complete, much
richer than the former, and in a better state of pre-
servation. Under this again, at the bottom of the box,
there were four pistols, two swords, two sets of epau-
lettes in their cases, a much-worn Bible in French, and
in a corner a big packet carefully wrapped in sheets
of tinfoil. The priest opened this, but there were only
papers inside. These were all the contents of the box.
The curé stood for some time silent lost in thought,
and eyeing sadly the things strewed about. Then he
gave a deep sigh, and began to pack them again into
the box with respectful care. They were put back in
the order they had been taken out.

When this was done, he turned to me and said,
"Frau, you are a conscientious good woman. I respect
your scruples; but on examination I find no trace of

crime or wrong doing, rather of wrong suffered. None
but the innocent would place their secret under the
protection of this holy emblem." As he said these
last words, he reverently replaced the crucifix upon
the flag, and fastened the lock again. "Many of those
persecuted for their opinions," continued he, "take refuge, as you are aware, in our happy Switzerland.
The persons you have had in your house may be some
of these exiles. At all events, I see no reason why
you should divulge their secret. Respect the wishes of
the unfortunate. You have done well to speak to no
one but me of this matter; for an indiscreet word might
have got innocent people into trouble. Continue to
hold your peace, with an easy conscience. As to you,
my worthy man," addressing my husband, "use the
money these strangers have generously bestowed on
you without scruple, and employ it as wisely as you
can. Now help me to lower the box, and fill up the
hole."

This time we worked with a light heart, and had
soon got the job done. We covered the spot with dry
leaves and broken branches, and no one ever found
out a tittle of the adventure. Many and many a time
did I go to look at the place: it has always remained
untouched. Only now the trees have grown much
thicker around, and grass and weeds hide the buried
box better than the dry leaves and branches.

The afternoon of that same day my good man paid
enough to keep the creditors' lawyer quiet for the time
being. Within the two next years we had saved money
enough to pay off the whole mortgage. Everything
has succeeded with us, and all has gone more and more
prosperously ever since the day the dear stork brought

luck to our door. You can understand now why I love and pet the stork.

————

To return from the record of the past to the daily occurrences of the present, I must say that of all those, who petted and spoiled Louisa, as did every one of our party, and even some of those belonging to the opposite faction, none did so more assiduously and resolutely than Herr Telliker on Sundays. Besides the bonbons and toys with which he came provided, and of which she had the lion's share, he was indefatigable in making her swings, and garlands of flowers, and wreaths of leaves; and as for little baskets, dolls, chairs, and what not, out of chestnuts and walnuts, and best of all, pipes out of reeds, there was no end of them. When not engaged to Madeleine, as was sometimes the case, he would choose Louisa for his partner in the dance. She had a wonderful facility for learning all sorts of dances, and was never out of time. This marked preference could not fail to make the other boys and girls jealous, and none showed the feeling more than Frau Hermann's boy, who was by nature both envious and jealous, and who would have had Louisa, as the best dancer, all to himself.

One Sunday, what novelty do you think Herr Telliker brought for his pet? Why, a squirrel, a live squirrel, a beautiful tame squirrel. This was the drop which made the cup overflow. The squirrel and its fortunate possessor became the focus of the rancour of all the young party. Louisa felt this, and watched over her treasure with maternal solicitude. She flatly refused the proposal made to her by Frau Hermann's son, as mouthpiece of the juvenile community, to let them play with the squirrel, and have it, as it were, in common. Whereupon the cue was given to disparage and find fault with the squirrel, and Louisa was formally excluded from all the games of the others. What need had she of other playfellows? argued the little rogues; had she not her squirrel for playfellow?

She took her exclusion most philosophically. In fact, she had not only her squirrel to play with, but two or three faithful allies of her own age, and not a few grown-up people, among them your humble servant, who was like the rest, but too happy to make himself a child again in order to please the little beauty. The scheme of the taboo not answering, Frau Hermann's boy opened fresh negotiations with Louisa, this time to the effect that she would permit them to look at the squirrel, he and the small squad pledging themselves not to touch it. Children are children, and Louisa was not a little vain of her pet; so, in an evil moment, she consented, but added as a *sine qua non* condition to her concession, that the squirrel should be viewed from a certain distance, and which, upon no pretext, was to be passed. The negotiator agreeing, the squirrel was exhibited on the lawn, Louisa mounting guard over him, holding him by a chain attached to his collar. Several of these exhibitions had taken place without any breaking of the peace, when one morning . . .

But to make what is to be related clear, it is necessary to give an account of a very stirring incident, which had rendered memorable the preceding day. No less than two snakes had been discovered and pursued,

pelted with stones, and finally killed by the bravest of
the young band. This extraordinary adventure, which
had caused great commotion among the children, and
not a little elated Frau Hermann's boy, who had
played the most prominent part in it, had also been
the occasion of bringing to light what I shall call —
begging pardon for the long word — an idiosyncrasy
of Louisa's, but what all the infant world stigmatized,
of course, as Louisa's cowardice.

No sooner did she catch sight of the alarming
reptiles than she began to scream desperately, flying
in a paroxysm of terror as far as her legs would carry
her. The persons who ran to her rescue found her as
white and cold as marble, and trembling from head to
foot. It was one of those inborn antipathies over which
reason has no control; for in other cases Louisa had
shown that, far from being of a timid, she was of a very
courageous disposition. But all creeping things struck
her with unconquerable horror; her mother had seen
her nearly faint at the sight of a toad; a frog, a lizard,
was enough to chase all colour from her cheek. However, this weakness having been found out, it offered
too good a chance to be let slip for her companions,
who knew nothing about idiosyncrasies, to assert their
superiority, and to take revenge by ridiculing the little
coward.

Well, on the morning of the morrow, Louisa was
doing the honours of her squirrel to a numerous young
audience, when something was thrown so as to fall to
her feet. It was one of the dead snakes. No one but
children being by at the time, it was only by their
after-confessions that it was ascertained that Frau Her-

mann's boy was the perpetrator of this practical joke.
Louisa gave a wild shriek, and rushed off like one
mad. When her mother and Mdme. Collet overtook
her, they found her lying on the ground nearly sense-
less. She was so convulsed with terror as not to be able
to speak, and her eyes were frightfully dilated. Her
first words, on recovering her speech, were "My
squirrel." Louisa had, in the first shock of terror, let
go the chain by which she was holding the little nimble
animal.

The theatre of the late exhibition was at once resorted to, the lawn searched, every bush and hole
peered into, but no squirrel was to be found.

In this, according to testimony, Frau Hermann's
boy was again the culprit. He had been seen trying
to catch the squirrel, chasing and scaring it out of its
wits, till at last, the poor beast, to escape him, had
fled into the copse in front of the ponds, and there
disappeared. On the strength of this information the
copse was explored, all the most overgrown parts carefully beaten, the trees climbed, all to no purpose. The
hunt was continued for hours far and wide, the whole
household of the Baths and most of the boarders joined
in it — in vain. The squirrel was lost — irretrievably
lost.

Louisa had kept quiet enough as long as she had
had any hope; when not a shred remained, the frenzy
of her grief knew no bounds. Her cries, her tears,
her passionate calls to her squirrel were positively
heart-rending. She stamped her little feet in despair,
tore her hair, threw herself on the ground, rolling on it
in her anguish. Her mother, to pacify her, promised that

she would get her another squirrel, one far handsomer. This only served to add to Louisa's wretchedness. What did she care for all the other squirrels in creation? It was that one, her own, her pet, the delight of her heart, that she wanted back. There was only one squirrel in the world for Louisa. "Oh, mother, let us go away, let us go away from this wicked place! — it will break my heart to stay here a day longer; it will indeed."

The mother was scarcely less frantic than the daughter. "Yes, my love, it is a wicked place, we'll turn our back on it, and shake the dust off our shoes. We will go immediately, but not before I have told my mind to this worthy lady." And addressing Frau Hermann, she said, "You don't deserve to be a mother, for you don't fulfil the duties of one. Your boy will grow up to make you shed bitter tears, and it will be only justice; because, instead of discouraging, you have fostered and encouraged his wicked propensities. You carry with you wherever you go the curse of your selfishness and pride; and thanks to you, this peaceful retreat is transformed into a hell of discord, and people henceforward will ask before they venture to come hither whether Frau Hermann is there; and if she is, they will avoid it as a pest-house."

Louisa and her mother departed in the evening of the same day. All the boarders warmly expressed their regrets, but none tried to persuade them to stay. The place jarred too much with Louisa's feelings for any, even of her great friends, to wish to detain her. Frau Hermann went away two days later, and with her vanished, as if by magic, all dissensions and heart-

16*

burnings. The weather was superb, and our enjoyment of the remaining fortnight of the season would have been perfect but for the shadow left by Louisa's misadventure.

CHAPTER XIV.

"There's nae Luck about the House."

A PIECE of bad news was awaiting me next year at Schranksteinbad. The stork, alas! had migrated to the land from whence there is no return. Dead! gone! *gestorben!* Such was the triple exclamation which burst from my three kind welcomers, Frantz, Madely, and the old mother, on my inquiring after the Socratic-looking bird. Had the establishment or the Alps been missing, the intelligence could not have taken me more by surprise.

How dead? I could not help asking, as if there were more ways than one of being dead. Few were the particulars I could glean about the stork's exit. He had died, like an old Roman, standing. One morning of hard frost in the previous February, the old mother had gone to look after him, and found him on his one leg in the middle of his enclosure stark frozen. A thick coating of ice covering his claw and riveting it to the ground, accounted for the erectness of his position. Why he had roamed forth in such inclement weather when close at hand he had a shelter and refuge in a comparatively warm hut, nobody knows. Perhaps he felt the approach of the supreme hour, and chose to die in sight of heaven.

The old Mutter took me by the sleeve and led me to the Great Hall, and there, fronting the entrance, and supported by a shelf fastened to the wall se-

parating the great from the lesser room, she pointed
out to me the bird stuffed, and looking more meditative and solemn than ever on his one leg. It had
been a fancy of the old dame's, and carried into execution in spite of much opposition, that her pet should
stand after death in the same posture in which she
had most often seen him in life. During this survey
she never ceased talking to me, and gesticulating with
much animation. I could not have repeated a syllable
of what she was saying, and yet I gathered from a
word caught now and then, and above all from the
dirgelike tone in which it was all uttered, that she was
predicting no end of evils as the natural sequence to
the stork's death; in short, pronouncing a funeral
oration over the establishment. I did my best to comfort and re-assure her. I tried to laugh her out of
her dismals, but nothing had any effect; she would
not be consoled. All that I said she met with angry
Neins and *Ihr wird sehe* ("Noes," and "You will
see.")

This vehemently desponding, nay, hopeless mood,
struck me the more in one hitherto of such an optimist
turn of mind, and I felt much disquieted; for I have
not unfrequently seen it occur, that a deep-rooted anticipation of evil creates and brings to pass the evil
itself. I cross-examined Frantz during the day, and
was sorry to perceive, in spite of his denials, that his
imagination was travelling at a good trot on the same
gloomy track on which his grandmother's was galloping. But there was yet still worse in store. A few
days' observation made me aware of the fact that the
old grandmother's despondency had infected to some
degree most of the bathers, and that by dint of having

it sung to them in every key that the establishment
was doomed, a general impression prevailed that such
might probably be the case.   If even the boarders,
who in general belonged to the educated class, had received a slight taint of the kind, I leave you to imagine
how imbued with it must have been the dependants of
the household, most of them ignorant rugged peasants,
and therefore easily accessible to superstitious impressions.   In the pantry, the kitchen, the cowhouse,
the doom of the establishment was an article of
faith.

There was only one *esprit fort* among us, and that
was Madely.   She laughed at all the current notions
as nonsensical, and gently upbraided her grandmother
for giving way to them.   But Madely, you know, was
in love, and love is an infallible talisman against all
kinds of superstition, save those which concern itself.

The prospects of the season, though not promising,
had nothing, however, so threatening as in the least to
justify the old Mutter's sinister prognostications.   On
the day of my arrival, the 5th of June, I had found at
the Baths eleven boarders, children included; one more
arrived on the 10th, and two on the 14th — in all
fifteen, counting myself.   June marks the beginning of
the bathing season, and in ordinary times this number
would have been considered not unsatisfactory.   What
made it rather so now, was the precocious and really
extraordinary heat of the season.   Papers mentioned
the great rush of visitors to all Spas; at such a one
scores of arrivals had been refused admittance, at such
another tents had had to be erected for the temporary
accommodation of bathers.   Commercial travellers and
tourists, who happened to stop at Schranksteinbad for

dinner or for the night, spoke of the hundreds they
had met at A. and B., and marvelled with some pity
at our scanty number. How did it happen? Why
were our Baths an exception to the rule?

Certainly, short of adopting the old Mutter's inter-
pretation of the case, it looked rather odd; still, as I
said before, the posture of affairs was not such as to
preclude the reasonable hope of yet having a good
harvest. Matters might change for the better from one
day to another; and, to a certain extent so they did —
for three days running we had fresh arrivals — a
bachelor past-fortian, an old couple, and a mother with
her two girls. At every fresh arrival I never failed
to go and wish the alte Mutter joy, and prognosticate
in my turn that the house would soon not be large
enough to hold the applicants. I put scraps of German
together, and prepared formulas to such like effects.
All labour lost. The good old soul was as tenacious
now of her gloomy ideas as she had been in times of
yore of her sunny ones. Her answers were always,
*Nein, nein; Es macht nut; wartet ein wenig; Ihr wird
sehe* — ("No no; It don't signify; Wait, you will see.")

Chance seemed bent upon humouring her gloomy
anticipations. A few days after the last triple arrival,
I found her about breakfast time waiting for me in the
passage leading to the dining-room. As soon as I appeared she came up to me and imparted something
'— what, I did not understand; but, from the tone of
voice, both excited and grimly triumphant, I at once
guessed she must be telling me some bad news. Nor
was I mistaken. One of the finest cows in the stables,
about to calve, as Madeleine explained to me, had been
taken ill in the night. Something going wrong with

her, the cow-doctor was sent for, but his skill proving
ineffectual, and the poor animal sinking fast, he had
decided that the only thing to do was to kill her immediately. This was done in the early morning with
as much secrecy as the roaming and prying of children,
those terribly early birds, would allow of, the upshot
being that by breakfast time everybody was acquainted
with the catastrophe, which made a painful impression
on us all.

The worst of the affair was, that this untoward accident became the occasion of a second and not less
unfortunate one. Here is the how. You must know
that at Schranksteinbad, as in many other places, the
system of never letting the cows out in the fields has
prevailed from time immemorial. The partisans of this
method contend that cows kept in the stable give more
and better milk, and are easier to manage. However
this may be, the cow-doctor sent for in the night was
of an opposite opinion, that is, he averred that fresh air
and exercise were as necessary for the health of cows
as for that of human beings, and even hinted that the
poor cow, whose death-warrant he had had to sign, had
she enjoyed the benefits of fresh breezes and of fresh
pasture, she would in all probability have been still
alive, with a fine calf to boot. More especially at this
moment, the cow-doctor went on to say, when sudden
and not unfrequent deaths had been noted among the
cattle, and fears were entertained of a coming epizooty,
was it necessary to be doubly careful about keeping
them clean, and allowing them plenty of air and the
free use of their limbs. The cow-herd was emphatically
of the same opinion. The doctor, our old friend, being
also consulted, gave his vote for exercise and fresh air,

and Frantz and Madeleine were very willing to try
the experiment; but their grandmother opposed any
change with might and main. She was sure nothing but
ill would come of it. The cows had never been let out
in her father's time, nor in her husband's, and they
were none the worse for it; quite the contrary. What
was the use of trying new ways, when the old had for
so long answered well? No novelty found grace in
the old Mutter's eye but one — the crinoline. At last,
however, her grandchildren wrung from her a reluctant
consent, and on the very day of the death of the cow,
the cow-herd received orders to lead forth her milky
sisters into the pastures.

We were all on the watch to see them go, and a
melancholy sight it was. The beautiful animals, as
they were led forth, stared suspiciously and timidly
about them, and, evidently frightened by the glare of
day, faced round to their stable. And when driven at
last into the green meadow, most of them seemed to
have unlearned how to graze, and after a few languid
attempts gave it up, and stood disconsolately, lowing
piteously, and stretching their necks with longing eyes
towards their stable; then, as if roused to sudden determination, rushed back and planted their heads in a
row against the shut door of their house just like so
many applicants for prison. The cow-herd was soon
at them, and by dint of shouts and cracks of his whip,
they were scared from their post, and sent in lamentable
confusion and terror back into the field. In one of
these terrified flights a poor beast slipped and fell on
the stone pavement which bordered the stable door;
she tried to get up again and again, but could not,
and lay there panting and groaning in a way most

grievous to hear. Upon examination it was found that the thigh was dislocated, a case allowing of no remedy, so that the only thing to do was to put her out of pain on the spot, and as soon as possible. Now the accident had occurred in full view of the house, and all the ingenious devices resorted to, in order to conceal the ignoble execution which ensued, were of little avail.

The effect on the minds of the boarders was deplorable. Together with the very sincere commiseration which every one felt for the family who had experienced two such severe losses in one day, there mingled a sense of disgust quite conceivable. I heard a lady, otherwise very kindly disposed, observe with some bitterness, that she had fancied herself at an establishment of baths, and not at shambles. The lady with the two daughters was so overcome by the incident, that she took her departure on the morrow. I need scarcely add that no further attempt was made to turn the cows out to pasture.

The disagreeable impressions produced by the double execution had scarcely worn away when a fresh cause of discontent arose. Really, it seemed done on purpose to confirm the alte Frau in her superstitious *parti pris*. Not a drop of rain had fallen for a whole month, and this, combined with the great heat, had made water scarce at our Spa as elsewhere. Instead of fine columns, mere threads of water flowed from the two springs, and the bathers had to be reduced to half rations, that is, only to have a bath each alternate day instead of one daily. This real inconvenience, which was nobody's fault, excited a good deal of ill-humour. What was the use of staying at baths when no baths were to be had? Some went away; those that remained

indemnified themselves by grumbling and declaring
right and left that the old mother was right — the
whole affair was going to the deuce.

Our number had dwindled to fourteen. Day after
day heavy masses of black clouds rose from behind that
indenture of the Jura from which rain was wont to
come, tantalizing us with hopes of an imminent storm;
hopes which vanished with the clouds, as evening after
evening closed in with a flaming sunset, harbinger of
a still hotter morrow. The weather-glass had lost all
credit, and we sneered at it and called it names when
it fell down to storm.

The storm came nevertheless, and when we least
expected it. It was on a Saturday; we had just done
dining, and were lingering over the dessert. All on a
sudden, without a note of preparation, a tremendous
blast of wind shook the house from top to bottom,
banging shutters to and fro, and setting all the windows in a rattle. By the time the sashes had been
secured the rain was falling in sheets. What a blessing! real, actual rain. We could scarcely believe our
eyes and ears, and but for the dread of wet jackets,
would fain have gone out on the balcony to make assurance doubly sure. Within a minute every trace of
anything like landscape, except the poplars of the
avenue, had disappeared. Hurrah! we shouted and
sung, as we danced for joy.

Every eye being busy with what was going on outside, no one had observed that the commotion caused
by the slamming of the windows had knocked down
the stork from his pedestal, until one of those boys
who have eyes for everything noticed the prostrate

bird, and lifted it from the ground. The party was too elated to receive any strong impression from this incident. On the contrary, it was little dwelt upon, and that little was only to agree on concealing the bad omen from the alte Frau, and Frantz at once set about restoring the injured bird to the high station from which it had been precipitated. But our chari-table intentions were frustrated. Some how or other, the old mother came to the knowledge of the circum-stance, and to all appearance drew her own conclusions from it. For from that time there came a change over her dream. She no longer sought to play the part of Cassandra to me or any one else, but held aloof in silence, only, whenever she met me I could hear her mutter, *Ja ja*, *Gut gut*. I confess I would rather have seen her in her former excited mood, rattling on and denouncing all day. However, let us not anticipate.

It did not rain, but pour all that day, and through the night, and all the following day, by which time the enthusiasm for rain had singularly abated. On the third morning, the rain still continuing, and the glass being steady at "great rain," the omnibus was put in requisition, and five of our ladies took their departure. The temperature had of course fallen con-siderably, and the boarders remaining began to com-plain of the cold. By the middle of the fourth day, the rain still falling heavily, there was a sortie *en masse* of the rest of the company. They went, promis-ing to return as soon as the weather had settled to fine again. On the morning of the fifth day the rain ceased, and the sun shone gloriously on the wrecks of the party, FOUR in number — an aged and infirm lady, who kept her bed almost the whole day, the deaf pro-

fessor, Herr Telliker, and myself. For once the ugly
sex had the majority at Schranksteinbad.

Yes, Herr Telliker had been with us for the last
eight-and-forty hours. On the second night of the
rain, at half-past eleven, every one of course being in
bed, we had been roused by loud and repeated knock-
ing at the entrance door, which, after a parley, had
been opened and somebody admitted. This somebody,
to our great surprise, we discovered next morning at
breakfast to be Herr Telliker; we had seen him only
a few days before, on the preceding Sunday, and did
not expect him so soon again. For all explanation he
coolly said that he had felt the want of rest, and had
come for some. Some one jokingly observed, that instead of a wish it must be a rage for rest which could
prompt a Christian to come through such a deluge as
he had done, and on foot too. Herr Telliker replied
in the same jesting tone that it was true, but whenever
he had set his heart upon anything, he could brook no
delay to possessing it, and so here he was to enjoy
rest. Were we sorry he was come? The general and
hearty protest against any such supposition sufficiently
testified to the popularity of the man. Herr Telliker
had continued to be a constant visitor to the establishment on Sundays, and had as rapidly ingratiated himself with the boarders of the present, as he had done
with the boarders of the last season.

To be candid, I have to own that the unexpected-
ness of this visit made me at first suspect some embarrassment in Herr Telliker's affairs. The old deaf
rector's odd grimaces and ironical ejaculations when
Madeleine had boasted of the solidity, extent, and
lucrative nature of Herr Telliker's business, had re-

mained deeply impressed on my mind, and I was prepared to hear any day that his prosperity had burst
like a bubble. I accordingly kept a little watch on
him — I had plenty of opportunity for this, as we
were most part of the day together — and very soon
I became convinced of the groundlessness of my suspi-
cions. Not only did his money flow as freely as ever,
but he was always calm and playful, which, as it
seemed to me, it is not in human nature to be when
under pressure of money difficulties. Even in his most
unguarded moments, never did I detect the smallest
wrinkle of anxiety on his mouth or brow, nor perceive
a shadow of care cloud his cheerful face. He was uncommonly attentive and affectionate to Madely, and
spent hours in the kitchen chatting to her, helping, or
perhaps impeding her, and pretending to be taking
lessons in cooking.

How, then, did it come to pass that, with so much
reason to be happy, my nymph Egeria did not look
so? I could not hide from myself the fact that with
Herr Telliker's arrival had coincided a change for the
worse in her humour and appearance. She was pre-
occupied and restless, talked little, smiled less, and
seemed to have forgotten all those small attentions and
small ways with which she used to keep the boarders,
especially of her own sex, good-humoured and contented. Single people of both sexes at Spas like to
be made much of, and courted, and flattered; of all
which arts Madeleine had been mistress. She used to
be the providence of shy people, made them feel at
home at once, and knew how best to break down the
barriers of ice between new comers and old. All this
was changed now; she was civil to every one, but she

made herself agreeable to nobody. She had grown
taciturn even with me, her old friend, she avoided me
rather than not, and the little conversation she granted
me never approached the confidential tone to which
she had so long accustomed me.

A series of observations which, so to say, forced
themselves on my notice threw me into new perplexity.
Madely, lately always nervous and restless, was never
so much so as when any new people came. At the
sound of approaching wheels she was on the threshold
in an instant, anxiously on the lookout. On all such
occasions Herr Telliker, as a rule, went into the house
of his own accord, or if he did not, Madeleine invariably called to him; and the result was, that he would
keep out of sight for some time. One forenoon, after
one of these admonitory calls, he did not show himself
during the rest of the day, in fact, not until two gentlemen who had made their appearance had taken their
departure. Having noted these peculiarities, I invo-
luntarily returned to the old conclusion that there was
something out of joint in Herr Telliker's affairs. But
how then could he put such a good face on the
matter?

Meanwhile the season dragged its weary length
along. None of the bathers scared away by the rain,
who had so faithfully engaged to return, kept their
promise, and new arrivals were few and far between,
and in nothing resembling angels. During the whole
month of July our number never exceeded eighteen,
and ordinarily oscillated between twelve and fifteen.
An assemblage of more morose and ill-to-please individuals could hardly have been got together. Among
them were two rich peasant dames with their daughters,

five persons in all, and a more exacting, more arrogant, self-conceited set of genuine upstarts it was never my lot to meet. They bore a grudge to Madely, and let slip no occasion to show it, because she did not pay them as much attention as she did to fine ladies, everlastingly assuring her that their money was as good as that of a royal princess. Poor nymph Egeria grew more wan and thoughtful every day.

The pulse of Schranksteinbad was thus beating languidly and irregularly, like that of one in the last stage of consumption, when an unexpected infusion of fresh blood suddenly restored it to fuller animation. One eventful morning in early August, three carriages with postilions came dashing up the avenue in great style, and stopped at the entrance. A gentleman in the first carriage, without getting out, asked the people of the house assembled at the door to meet the unexpected guests, if they could promise dinner for twelve persons by two in the afternoon. On receiving an answer in the affirmative, the spokesman and all his party left the carriages, and dispersed themselves through the grounds. There were two ladies, two young girls, three gentlemen, three lads, and a couple of babies with their nurses. It was long since Schranksteinbad had had such a banquet for its curiosity, and the excitement was great among the bathers and every member of the household. The postilions were questioned, and soon fame proclaimed through his hundred trumpets that it was a Russian prince, name unknown, coming from Berne with his family and suite, who had stopped at our Spa for dinner.

Now, whether it was that the fare, together with Frantz's champagne, had found grace in his highness's eyes, or that the beauty of the spot had struck her highness's fancy, or whether it was only a *caprice de Grand Seigneur*, certain it is that about five in the afternoon fame was busy with his trumpets again, and this time with the still more marvellous news that the Russian prince, his family and suite, had decided to make a sojourn at Schranksteinbad. In confirmation of which wonderful intelligence, the postilions shortly after took back to Berne three empty carriages, and at nine in the evening the prince, family, and suite betook themselves in a body to the respective quarters which had been assigned to them. The arrival next morning by the early train of a mountain of luggage silenced the sceptics, two in number, who knew for certain that the strangers were to start after breakfast.

On this same day, the 5th of August, we had the honour of dining with the princely guests. They were made to occupy the upper end of the table, our former and legitimate place, we being removed at one fell swoop to the lower end. This glaring infraction of all precedents, this authorized usurpation, was bitterly resented by all our party, except myself and Herr Telliker, although none chose then and there to express their resentment openly, save the two rich peasants' wives, who protested loudly against the new arrangement, and even aimed some poisonous shafts at the unconscious usurpers. At least this is what I was told by my neighbour Telliker, who of course understood the patois of his country-women, and I am inclined to believe that the prince and company, albeit they were never heard to speak but in French, also understood and took note of the sarcasms.

Dinner over, I sought Madeleine, and remonstrated

with her rather warmly on the egregious blunder she
had committed. For the first time the good girl took
my interference in bad part, and, for the first time, I
in my turn, I am sorry to say, got angry with her.
Nor did my displeasure diminish when I saw her day
after day play the agreeable, and lavish *petits soins* on
all the Russian party, oblivious as it were of all the
other boarders. It is true the Russians formed the
majority, and spent more for champagne in one day
than all of us put together in one week; but was that
a good reason for utterly ignoring us? I thought it
mean of her, quite a new trait in her character, and
accordingly I remained distant with her.

The Russians kept very much to themselves, as
was natural; they were, however, very civil to us all,
except to the rich peasants' wives, whom, with their
daughters, they overlooked and cut unmercifully. They
seemed much to enjoy the animated scene presented
by the Baths on the Sunday following their arrival, repeatedly paid long visits to the ball-room, looking on
with evident amusement, but refraining from mixing
among the dancers, until about nine. The noisiest and
least aristocratic of the company having departed by
that time, leaving only a sprinkle of strangers with the
boarders and the people of the house, they then condescended to dance, but only with one another.

At half-past ten, just before going to bed, I had
the curiosity to go and take a peep at what was going
on among the dancers. To the right and left of the
principal door of the Grande Salle were two closets or
pantries, with glass doors opening into the big hall.
These pantries would have been quite dark but for the
slender rays which streamed into them from the chan-

17 *

delier in the hall. I took up my position behind one
of the glass doors, whence I could perceive the dancers,
like figures in a magic lantern, flitting rapidly across
the ball-room beyond the hall. I had expected to see
Madely among them with her usual partner Herr Telliker, but I looked in vain for her. Herr Telliker had
Anna, our apprentice table-maid, on his arm. This
girl was better known as "*la belle Sommelière*," and fully
deserved the appellation. She belonged to a respectable family of well-to-do peasants in the Canton of
Lucerne, and was undoubtedly a beautiful creature.

The generation of our day is so devoted to the
beautiful, so artistic and thoroughly Athenian in its
tastes, that a *sine qua non* condition of success for such
places of public resort as cafés, restaurants, baths, and
knick-knackery shops is, that the customers should find
there lovely faces, and elegant figures to wait on them.
Civilisation at our Spa had not yet such artistic re-
quirements. Good-looking or plain, we took the cham-
ber-maids and table-women as we found them, though
we were able to discriminate beauty where it existed,
and to pay due homage to it when it reached such almost ideal proportions as it did in Anna.

Well then, after having duly admired the splendid
bust and noble profile of the "*belle Sommelière*," the
Juno-like majesty, and yet perfect pliancy of her figure,
not overlooking the richness of her black tresses gathered
into a knot at the back of her head as we see in Greek
statues, I could not help thinking that, were I Madeleine, I should be jealous of Anna. On the heels of
this thought came a second — who knows whether she
is not, and whether the change I have noted in her is
not owing to jealousy? While engaged in these specu-

lations, I heard behind me a sound as of stifled sighs. I lighted a match and saw Madely. At first I thought she was weeping; another match and a closer inspection convinced me that she was gasping painfully for breath; in fact, to all appearance, she was labouring under a strong fit of asthma. Her eyes were lustrous, and her cheekbones vermilion red. She looked in a fever. "What is the matter, my poor child?" said I; "can I do anything for you?" She put her hand to her throat, pointing to some water. I poured out a glassful, and handed it to her, but she could not swallow. I wetted a corner of my handkerchief, and bathed her temples. I remarked, as I did so, that her eyes were constantly wandering in the direction of the dancing-room. "Shall I fetch Herr Telliker?" She knitted her brows portentously, and shook her head violently. The fit, whatever it was, gradually subsided, and she was able to rise.

"I am better, thank you; not a word about this to Herr Telliker, if you please, it would be alarming him for nothing."

In spite of her wish to the contrary, I would not let her go alone. But at the foot of the stairs leading up to her room, she gave me a decided "Good-night," and I heard her lock her door.

The first thing I did in the morning was to go and search for Madely. To my inquiry how she was, she answered with a shade of petulance that she was never better in her life. "Have you ever before had such an attack as that of last night?" asked I.

"Attack! I had no attack," returned she. "I was a little drowsy when you saw me. I believe I had fallen asleep in an uneasy posture, and did not know what I was about when you awoke me — that's all."

Seeing that she was bent on evasion, I put no more questions, and quitted her more than ever satisfied that jealousy had something to do with the late alteration in her looks and humour.

On the morning of the Thursday following, I heard it rumoured among the bathers that the nobility (poor nymph Egeria never designated the Russian family otherwise) had hired the village band for the evening, and were going to have a ball on their own account. There was nothing extraordinary in the statement, it being known that Russians of every class are fond of all sorts of gaiety, and above all of dancing. In the course of dinner, the prince politely mentioned that he was about to have a small *soirée*, and he gave invitations by name to Herr Telliker, to a young lady lately arrived, and to me; in short, to all the able-bodied among us — only leaving out the peasants' wives and their daughters. These, according to his wont, he entirely overlooked, just as though they had not been in existence. I was for my part much obliged to him, but at the same time it seemed to me rather odd that he should, as it were, take possession of the dancing-room as if it were his own apartment. The room was the public property of all bathers, and even the temporary exclusive use of it could not be conceded to some, and denied to others.

Well, evening came, and with it the village band, and after supper the ball began. I had not profited by the prince's invitation, and loitered in the hall with the presentiment that some disagreeable complication would arise. I was not wrong; dancing had not been going on for more than a quarter of an hour, when

the peasants' wives and daughters in their best array
skipped past Madeleine, who made vain efforts to arrest their progress through the great hall, invaded the
ball-room, and at once began to foot it merrily among
themselves. The intrusion was no sooner perceived by
the prince than he sat down, as did all his family and
suite, and so did Herr Telliker and his partner, the
young lady lately arrived. Thus, within a minute or
two of their entrance, the five peasant women had all
the dancing to themselves. This state of things being
at last noticed by the orchestra, the music suddenly
ceased, and the intruders had no alternative but to
cease also, and to seat themselves on the nearest bench,
which they did in some confusion.

The prince beckoned to Madeleine and said, "Will
you be so good as to ask those persons who invited
them here?" The answer was quick, and to the point.
They needed no invitation to admit them to a room,
to the use of which at all times every boarder was
entitled.

"May I ask you," said the prince, addressing me,
I suppose, as the oldest of the gentlemen present, "may
I ask your opinion of the case?"

"I must in justice say," I replied, "that the right
alleged by these ladies seems to me incontrovertible,
much as I may deplore the manner in which it was
asserted."

"Why did you not explain this to me before?"
asked the prince, turning to Madeleine; "or rather,
why did you tell me quite the contrary?" And without
stopping to hear Madely's diffuse explanations, he rose,
and bowing, left the room, with all his party.

On the following morning the Russians asked for

their bill, paid it, and bade us farewell with much politeness. They had remained eleven days with us. At
noon of the same day the peasants' wives and daughters departed in high dudgeon. Madely, I regret to
say, gave me covertly but clearly to understand that
she laid this double catastrophe to my door. In vain
did I patiently explain to her, that being directly appealed to, I could not, without prevaricating, conceal
my way of thinking on the matter — a way of thinking,
the soundness of which I abundantly vindicated, and
justified over and over again. I should probably have
been less patient, had not the disastrous condition of
the establishment made me sorry for her. All the *personnel* of the baths was reduced by this time to Herr
Telliker, the young lady mentioned above, and myself.

But I might as well have pounded water in a
mortar as argue the point with Madely. She was
utterly impervious to reason, and kept on saying that
those who paid for the music might claim the exclusive enjoyment of the dancing-room on all or any day
of the week, excepting Sundays. Telliker, divided between logic and love, sided with me when in my company, and with Madely when in hers. Frantz was entirely demoralized by the breaking to pieces of the
concern, and had no opinion on any subject whatever.
The old Mutter kept aloof more than ever, and muttered
to herself her usual *Ja ja* and *Gut gut*, with a glee as
lugubrious as that of an owl raising his wild cry on a
stormy night.

All this was not exhilarating, and — must I say it?
— made me long for a change. And so I thought I might
as well hasten my departure by a couple of weeks, and
go and join a dear friend then at Les Plans, over Bex.

The leave-taking between Madely and me was most constrained. At one moment I hoped that she would give way, and be friends with me again. Unhappily she made an effort, and succeeded in keeping down her emotion. Altogether, the feelings with which I left Schranksteinbad this time were different from those with which I had quitted it for a number of years past.

CHAPTER XV.

Served Right.

HAD. I been Julius Cæsar instead of only the obscure old bachelor that I am, and had I had to go to
the Senate instead of to the Paris terminus of the
Strasbourg railway, the odds are that I should have
recoiled before the evil omens which crowded on me.
True it is that the Ides of March were long past. First
of all, in shutting my trunk, I had the irreparable
misfortune to crush a well-beloved meerschaum; then,
the day was rainy and windy, and no coach was to be
found, and when one was got at last, the horses were
so worn out that they could hardly make head against
the weather, and my heart was in my mouth lest I
should miss the train; then I had a narrow escape of
losing my portmanteau, which was actually slipping
off the roof of the coach when some good genius inspired me to look after its safety, and to have its
descent stopped in the very nick of time.

Oh! the luggage, the luggage! What tourist's heart
does not ache at the mention of that inexpressible
nuisance? Oh! discoverers and inventors of the nine-
teenth century, which of you will liberate us from that
galley-slave's chain, from that hindrance to all our
pleasures? The one who does so will have a right indeed to the title of benefactor of mankind. I don't
ask that it should be entirely suppressed, but reduced
to portable proportions without inconvenience to the

traveller. For, from the moment you cannot yourself carry your luggage you are its slave. Don't answer that the thing is not possible, for indeed it is. When we go to take a bath, do we carry with us the towels and other *et ceteras?* No, we find them ready for us at the establishment, and we willingly pay for the convenience. Why should not the traveller find, on some similar principle, at his halting-places, such articles of clothing as he may require, ready to be hired, instead of having to burden himself with what would furnish a bazaar? I do not enter into particulars, but I recommend my hint to more fertile brains than mine. It contains the germ of an entire social transformation.

My ill luck followed me even on Swiss land; in changing carriages at Basle, who should I find as my *vis-à-vis* but the choleric gentleman who had years ago quitted Schranksteinbad in a pet because no fowl's wing remained in the dish when presented to him!

"Glad to see you looking so well," said he; "on your way to Schranksteinbad as usual, eh?"

"Yes — that is to say — I am not really quite sure."

This rather incoherent phrase portrayed to perfection the muddled state of my mind in regard to my ancient haunt. I was on the road to it — of that there was no doubt; but was I positively going thither, and if so, did I intend to make any stay there? I could have answered none of these questions. The nine months intervening between my last visit and the present moment had softened, but not obliterated, the uncomfortable feelings with which I had left it. There were two opposing currents in my mind, that of the old, and that of the recent recollections — the one drawing me thither, the other repelling me from it.

However, in proportion as I approached the once favourite spot, the current of attraction strengthened, and at the last station but one I had a sudden perception that I could not decently go by Schrankstein without paying at least a passing visit to my old friends of the establishment. As to my remaining there, that was quite another matter — the odds were against it . . . unless — in short, much would depend upon circumstances. In pursuance of this resolution I alighted at the station of the village, saw my portmanteau and bag safely locked up in the luggage-room, and perceiving no omnibus, I set off by the short cut across the fields to the Baths.

And as I strode along, fancy rehearsed before me the scene of my arrival. First would run out Madeleine (better inspired, of course, by time and reflection) — Madeleine all smiles of pleasure at sight of her old friend; then came Frantz and the alte Mutter vying with each other in cordial demonstrations of greeting. The picture was completed by the servants bustling to shake hands with their old acquaintance. I saw myself the centre of a group of beaming faces. Presently would arise the question of "Where is your luggage?" followed by a cloud of disappointment on every countenance as I replied that I had come to see how they all did, but not to stay. Not to stay! Was it possible? It could not be true. Why, the establishment would not look like itself without its oldest frequenter. Was I too going to forsake them in their difficulties? — and here a final chorus of prayers and entreaties, which there was no withstanding. I was conquered.

In this relenting mood I reached the last undulation of the gently raised plateau which intervenes between the village and the Baths, and the long, ugly, dear house, the verdant vale in which it nestled, and the surrounding grounds rose into view. It opened on me like the face of an old friend. Not a fold, not a knoll, not a tree, not a stone, with which I was not familiar. The stately avenue, the jets of water, the balcony, the gable of my room, the dinner bell on the roof, the two summerhouses to the left, one of them *my* summerhouse, the velvet-like mamelon to the right, with the blackbird's cage on the summit, the three oaks higher up, a walk I had discovered named after them and made popular; all the spots that long habit had endeared to me seemed to beckon me on and welcome me. Memories crowded upon me, sweet memories of quiet days spent in meditation, in study, in close communion with Nature, in wholesome interchange of thoughts and sympathies with genial or lofty minds, and I felt positively ashamed of having ever contemplated to desert a place with which I had such associations — to desert it, and for what? For a few pin pricks, a few moments of annoyance which weighed so little — I acknowledge it now, oh! so very little — against the sum of placid enjoyments with which it had blessed me. And so on I hurried (I would have run back for my luggage but for the scorching sun), on I hurried, anxious, as it were, to make amends for my ingratitude.

As I entered the avenue I observed that the meadow on my right had been partly dug up, and a pretty large piece of water had been formed in its centre, and on this piece of water floated a smart boat. Here is a

270 A QUIET NOOK.

famous novelty, thought I. Frantz has not lost heart,
I see; quite the contrary. Bravo, Frantz! The grounds
were in excellent order, the garden trimmer than I had
ever seen it. Better and better. Nobody about though.
I inferred from this solitude that the boarders were as
yet scanty in number. I cleared my throat noisily as
I climbed the flight of steps adjoining the verandah.
No one came to see who was the new arrival. I
opened the parlour on the left, Madely and Frantz's
place of resort when they had nothing to do — it was
empty. The walls had been newly papered, and it
had acquired a new air of comfort. I pushed on to
the kitchen situated at the end of the passage. The
kitchen too had been renovated, and looked all the
better for it. The only person there was an elderly
woman. I inquired after Madeleine and Frantz. I
could make nothing of her answer in German, seeing
which she motioned me to follow her, and knocked at
a door opposite to the parlour which I had already
searched. A young man appeared at the summons
and asked me to walk in. The room which, when I
had left the year before, had been a tap-room, was
now transformed into a nice little study. Could this
person, so like a gentleman, be a butler, or was he
a boarder on whom the old woman had forced me to
intrude? Whoever he might be, I said, "I beg your
pardon, sir; I am an old frequenter of these Baths,
and finding no one to receive me . . ."

At this point the young man interrupted me, saying,
I suppose, that he did not understand French, but that
he was going to fetch somebody who did. He went,
and very soon came back accompanied by a gentleman,
who shook me by the hand, said, in excellent French,

that he was very glad to see me, and asked if I had
had a good journey. "Very good, though rather too
hot to be pleasant," replied I, wondering the while
who this unknown cordial gentleman could be. To
sound the ground I added, "Not many boarders yet,
I fear?"

"I beg your pardon," was the reply; "almost as
many as the house can hold — upwards of fifty, not
reckoning those we are expecting."

"Capital!" cried I; "I am heartily glad to hear
this. I had anticipated quite the reverse from seeing
no one about."

"The boarders," explained the gentleman, "are just
now at their tasks." The word "task" made me feel
a little odd; it seemed a rather inappropriate equivalent
for bathing. "By the bye, I hope my room is not
occupied," said I.

"Your room is ready for you," answered the gentleman; "shall I show you to it?"

"Need I give you that trouble?"

"No trouble, I assure you," and he led the way
up to the second storey. So far all right — but he
stopped at No. 27.

"This is not my room," I said; "mine is No. 31."

"No. 31," returned the gentleman, "is occupied by
the Professor of Mathematics."

"I am sorry to hear this, for I hold very much to
No. 31." My conductor looked puzzled, and said,

"You have then been here before?"

"Have I?" said I (with a little swagger, I fear).
"Why, of course, for a succession of years. I am
one of the oldest *habitués* of the house, probably the
oldest."

"Then you are not ... the Professor of French that I am expecting."

"No, indeed; and I suppose you are not..." I was going to say the head waiter of the establishment, but I altered it into "the gentleman deputed by the family to receive the bathers."

"No," said the gentleman with a smile at my not very felicitous periphrasis, "I am the new proprietor of the house, and head-master of the school which has taken the place of the Baths."

I stood petrified, struck dumb, feeling like one in a dream. "A thousand pardons," I said, rousing myself; "and pray can you tell me what has become of the family who kept the Baths?"

"They are living at the village yonder; that is, they were when I saw them a week ago."

Nothing remained for me but to take my leave, which I did with many apologies and thanks. The polite head-master would have shown me the improvements he had made; and pressed me to stay to dinner, but I declined. I was not in a frame of mind to be an agreeable guest.

And so it has come to this, thought I, as I passed down the great avenue. My quiet nook has vanished. I have but what I deserve. I turned up my nose at it, and it has given me a cold shoulder. We are quits. I may go and roam in search of a new retirement, and roam long ere I find the equal of the one I have lost. It was not good enough for me forsooth, fool that I was! And as I reached the extreme edge of the slope which would rob me of its sight, I turned back and embraced in one fond last gaze that beautiful corner of earth to which I was indebted for so many joys

— the more beautiful, and lovely, and loved, for being now, alas! lost to me for ever. I bade it a long farewell. It was as if a part of my life was wrenched from me.

I went straight to the doctor's house: he was fortunately at home.

"Ah! here you are, and by your looks half broken-hearted too," cried the good-natured but incorrigibly sarcastic doctor. "You were not aware of what great change had taken place in our part of the world, and the surprise has been too much for you."

"I have just been enlightened in an interview with the head-master of the new school," said I; "but tell me of Madely and Frantz, and the alte Mutter."

"All safe and sound in a lump at Schwafelberg."

"Schwafelberg! what is that?"

"A mountain above Thun, where pure Alpine air and excellent sulphuric water may be imbibed *ad libitum*."

"Any of them ill?"

"Madely was but poorly, and I ordered her thither. If you ask me her complaint, I tell you candidly I don't know — a temporary sluggishness in the flow of life, such as that which last year afflicted the springs of Schranksteinbad, the consequence and result of long wear and tear of mind and body."

"Is she in any danger?"

"Not in the least. I expect that a few weeks of rest and mountain air, and lots of sulphuric water, will remove the sluggishness I have alluded to. She will remain delicate, that's all; but with proper care may live to be a hundred."

"Did she ever tell you of the fit of asthma I found her labouring under last year?"

"Not a word — tell me all about it," and so I did.

"It was very foolish to conceal such a thing from me," said the doctor, who had listened to my tale with much gravity. "Doctors ought to know everything about their patients, but women always will keep back something. I shall scold her for this."

"And how about the sale?"

"It was decided on principle that there should be a sale two or three years ago, but six months back imperious circumstances precipitated the consummation of the project. First of all, the family was no longer equal to the task of managing the establishment — a task that latterly was rendered impossible by Madeleine's failing health; and Madeleine, you know, was the life and soul of the concern. Secondly, the disastrous season of last year, owing principally to the monomania of the old mother, who, like another Cassandra, never left off predicting the fall of our Troy, and who, unlike her prototype, was believed. Well, the last disastrous season, as I was saying, depreciated thirty per cent. the presumed value of the establishment, and a second disastrous season, which was inevitable, would have reduced it fifty per cent. at least. So the best way was to hurry the sale, which was done."

"But why not have sold to some one who would have carried on the Baths?"

"For the simple reason, my dear sir, that no speculator of the kind was to be found. Formerly there had been plenty of such applicants, but after the failure

of the last season they withdrew in a body, and very
fortunate it was that our friends lighted on this professor, who wanted to set up a school, and who had
ready money to pay for the premises."

"By the bye, what of Herr Telliker?"

"Herr Telliker first got into difficulties, and secondly into the Gazette, and lastly ran away, then
appeared when least expected, and paid all his creditors
in full, with whose money I needn't say. He is now
settled at Bouffarick, in Algeria, at the head of a
farming business, which may God prosper better than
the other! He is betrothed to Madeleine, and will
return as soon as his affairs permit, marry her, and
take her to his new home. The climate of Algeria will
suit her very well."

"So there will be an entire break-up of the whole
family; for I do not expect the old Mutter long to
survive the loss of her old home, and of all the associations of all her life."

"It is not likely, but old age becomes sometimes
uncommonly tough."

"I will go and see them at Schwafelberg."

"Yes, do; it will do them good, and you too: you
have no idea how affectionately they all talk of you,
Madeleine especially. You may take a peep *en passant*
of the great gathering of singers at Berne, between
four and five thousand. There are to be illumina-
tions, and rejoicings, and processions of·torches without
end."

"Thank you for the hint; but, my dear doctor,
gatherings and all such things are little to my taste."

"Nonsense! try them, and the taste will come. The
odi profanum vulgus et arceo is nothing but the profes-

18*

sion of morose selfishness. Mix with your fellow-creatures, and try to draw amusement from what gives
pleasure to the greater number."

The doctor never missed an opportunity of com-
bating what he termed my morbid propensity to misan-
thropy. Perhaps he was right in his judgment. At
all events, I promised to follow his suggestion, and
after a pot-luck dinner, as freely offered as accepted, I
left by the next train for Berne.

The unusual length of the train, and the great
number of passengers that we picked up on our road,
made me anticipate a lively competition for rooms at
the end of the journey. Consequently, on reaching
Berne, I left my luggage at the station, and hastened
in quest of a resting-place. I was fortunate enough to
secure, without much difficulty, a single-bedded room
in a hotel of third rank, near the station. This done,
I retraced my steps leisurely, and brought my luggage
to my quarters. And having smartened myself up a
little, I locked my chamber door, put the key in my
pocket, and sallied forth with a quiet heart to enjoy
the fête. I willingly admit that the stern old city
looked most bewitching in its array of green boughs
and flowers; that the *coup-d'œil* exhibited by the *Cantine*
or *Festhütte*, a temporary building capable of accommodating five thousand persons at dinner, was second
to none in point of gorgeousness and good taste; that
the long cortège of singers, enlivened by bands, and
chequered by picturesque old costumes, had an interest
of its own; that the singing in the old Minster, such
scraps of it at least as reached me from a distance,
was most beautiful. But, oh! the price paid for all
this! oh! the heat, the dust, the noise, the throng, the

crushing, the utter impossibility of procuring any seat, or anything to eat or drink in this Babel! At the end of a couple of hours I had more than enough of it, and when, by dint of superhuman exertions, I succeeded in getting out of the whirlpool, and found a seat in an out-of-the-way house, half café, half tavern, and obtained something like a dinner, I thanked my lucky stars indeed. There's no forcing nature, my dear doctor; it is not everybody who is organized to enjoy monster festive gatherings.

After a long rest I set out again, this time into the country, roamed through fields and meadows, sat down now and again to rest, and did not return to the town until towards dusk; had an ice and a paper at a café, took a stroll under the arcades, and as ten was striking made for my hotel. I was tired and rather out of spirits, and was looking forward with fond desire to a good night's rest. But I had reckoned without my host. On opening the door of my room, what to my horror did I see, but a second bed, and some one in it, loudly snoring! I retraced my steps in search of the landlord or landlady to remonstrate on the liberty that had been taken. The waiter who had given me my candle, I knew to be past remonstrating with. I could discover no one but a kitchen-maid, who told me that all the family had gone to the *Festhütte*. I wished them joy of it, returned to my room, went to bed, and spent the night in listening to the music of my companion's nose.

Fortunately, he was a very early riser, and I made the morning do duty for the night; in fact, I overslept myself, and, not to miss the train for Thun, I had to get up, shave, pack, and breakfast in a hurry — a thing which I detest. I had scarcely time to get my luggage booked, and had to run for my life to get a seat. The train was chokeful, as all trains are to and from Thun at this season. Up and down, up and down, up and down, I searched through nine carriages, and found no corner free; in the tenth at last there was the half of a seat; that is, it was only half filled by a bundle of alpenstocks, which in my hurry to occupy the vacant space, nearly knocked me down. I was quite out of breath with the race and the anxiety, my heart was thumping like the engine. I don't wonder that railways should develop diseases of the heart.

I had lighted on an English colony. I heard no language but English spoken on all sides. My immediate neighbours were a family of five persons, the proprietors, as I soon discovered, of the alpenstocks, all of them very handsome and very quiet. There was even a shade of preoccupation upon the very fine countenance of the still young-looking pater-familias. I fancied, for writers must always be fancying, that he had just paid his bill at the Bernerhof, and finding it heavy, was calculating the possible gap which, at the same rate, this Oberland tour would make in the family income for the year to come. The young people, a full-grown girl and two lads of fifteen and sixteen, were on their side probably enjoying in anticipation the conquest of some untrodden Alpine peak. My seat being next the window, and to the right of the carriage, I had the full benefit of a scorching sun upon me all the way. It was bad enough while the train was in motion; positively intolerable when it stopped, which it did five or six times. The curtain, a delusive palliative, could not be made to

keep down. Let all travellers from Berne to Thun by
the train of 2.20 P. M., in the month of June, profit
by my sad experience, and choose seats on the left of
the carriage — if they can.

I arrived half baked, and wholly incapable of any
exertion beyond that of panting in the shade, and
wiping away the cascades of perspiration flowing from
my brow. In this state of semi-annihilation, I handed
my luggage ticket to a porter (*Dienstmann*), meekly
begging him, when he had got my boxes, to take them
and me to any hotel he pleased, excepting that of
Bellevue. I have already lodged at Bellevue. I know
every inch of its beautiful grounds. I admire its situation and its magnificent view over lake and Alps. It
has only one drawback in my eyes, that of not being
quiet and homely enough for what may probably be
considered my perverse taste.

By-and-by my *Dienstmann* (such is the designation
embroidered upon their caps, by which these meritorious public servants are known) — well, my *Dienstmann*
brought me word that the luggage was on the roof of
the carriage, would I get in? Certainly I would and
did, and within five minutes we stopped at a house of
tolerably good appearance; it was the inn chosen for
me by my guide. I went up two short flights of stairs,
and was shown into a long capacious room, which, as
far as I could judge by the dim light admitted by the
sun-blinds closed against the glare, looked clean and
decently furnished enough. I desired the waiter to let
me have dinner as soon as possible, and washed and
cooled myself to my heart's content.

Dinner was presently announced, and I followed
the welcome messenger down a staircase, along a pas-

sage, and through a *Salle à manger* into a balcony
covered by a gaily striped awning, and pleasantly
decked on the outer side of the balustrade with a rich
fringe of green formed by the round heads of a row of
acacias growing on the edge of the water below. Besides being ornamental, this verdant screen had the
advantage of agreeably softening to the eye the mad
rush of the Aar prancing and foaming beneath like a
wild horse.

"I have laid the cloth here," said the attendant
Sommelière, "thinking it would be more agreeable."

"And so it is," I answered; "I am much obliged
to you." This solicitude for the comfort of travellers
was of good augury. The Sommelière made me think
of Madely, such as Madely was on the day I first saw
her. She was as obliging, but far less handsome than
my nymph Egeria. This miniature balcony too reminded me of the magnificent one at Schranksteinbad.
Notwithstanding these recollections of the happy past,
I ate a hearty dinner. I had been in a bustle ever
since getting up in the morning, and this was my first
moment of quiet, real quiet. A sense of well-being
stole over me such as I had not yet felt since my
arrival on Swiss soil. The fine prospect before me
had its share, no doubt, in producing this comfortable
disposition of mind. I had right in front of me the
most jagged and fantastic of mountain ranges, that of
the Stockhorn. Sideways to which rose the massive,
grim, often cloud-capped Niesen. Farther yet to
that side, that is to my left, the splendours of the
lake, of the Jungfrau, and Blumlis Alps sparkling
in the sun like mountains of silver. The broad
expanse stretching between me and them was as rich

and varied in colour as in form; a mosaic of hill, slope, and vale; of black forests, tender-hued pastures, yellow corn fields, green meadows; the whole studded with hamlets, steeples, villas, and châlets.

With the dessert came also the landlord to pay his respects and chat with his new guest. He played the part of cicerone most obligingly. "Can you tell me," said I, "whereabouts is Schwafelberg?"

"There," said mine host, pointing to two peaks on the right of the Stockhorn range, "in the hollow between those two points lies Schwafelberg."

"High up enough," observed I; "and pray, what sort of a road is there to it?" My landlord opened his grey eyes very wide. "You are not meaning to go there, are you?"

"Why not?" asked I; "is it dangerous?"

"Oh, dear no, not dangerous; only the way is terribly rough, and the place is not fit for strangers. We have plenty of baths more easy of access, and far more comfortable, in this neighbourhood. To name only a few, there is Gürnigel, Blümenstein, Heustrich, Leuk, Wissenburg. At Wissenburg especially, but a three hours' drive from this, you will find excellent accommodation, and the best company — English, Russians, Americans, and what not. The waters of Wissenburg are sovereign in all complaints of the chest."

"I have, thank God, no complaint of the chest, and I have friends at Schwafelberg."

"That alters the case," replied resignedly my host. "Well then, since you must go there, mark that oblique line formed by black firs, that is the road to Schwafel-

berg; it keeps always along the skirts of the forest, you
could not miss your way if you tried."

"As far as I can judge by my eyes, about a couple
of hours' ascent," said I, giving myself the airs of a
thorough connoisseur.

"Add another couple, sir, and you will be nearer
the mark."

"I suppose there are mules or horses to be hired?"

"Nothing of the sort, I regret to say; the road is
too rugged even for mules; no means of going but
on foot, unless you choose to be carried like a
cheese."

"Like a cheese!" cried I.

"Exactly so — you must know that the dwellers
in the châlets along the mountain side use for carrying
cheese a kind of high thin board, slung like a knapsack
on their back, and crossed by a narrow plank, on
which rests the lower edge of the large round cheese.
This machine (*raef* we call it) the mountaineers are
willing enough to put at the disposal of such customers
as chance may send them. Ladies never make the
ascent otherwise."

All my pride of manhood revolted at the bare idea
of being treated like a cheese, and the *raef* scheme was
then and there rejected without appeal. Let my legs
suffer, provided my honour be safe. On inquiring in
the evening at the post-office, I learned that a vehicle
of some sort started every morning at 10 A.M. for . . .
I forget the name of the place; and that this cart or
coach would put me down at the foot of the mountain
I had to ascend, and within five minutes' walk of the
road, if road it could be called, to Schwafelberg.

I slept soundly all night, and got up wonderfully

refreshed. The morning was cloudy, a thick mist
enveloped the top of the Stockhorn, and much as I
was tempted to spend another four-and-twenty hours at
least in my present cozy berth, upon second thoughts,
I determined to turn to account the cloudy state of the
atmosphere, and set out without delay on my mountainous expedition; for, if there is one thing which I dread
more than another, it is a long walk in the sun.
Accordingly I threw a few articles of linen and my
Mackintosh into a knapsack, armed myself with my
umbrella, and applied to the post for a place in the
coach, which went so far my way as the foot of the
mountain. There was no place vacant, but thanks to
that blessed regulation of the Swiss post, which never
sends back a traveller disappointed, I was provided
with a supplement in the shape of a round box of
leather, *alias* a *char-à-banc*, having between the shafts
a very long and lean horse. The post-boy, a real post-
boy with red facings to his jacket, squeezed himself
with difficulty into a narrow niche before me, and we
jogged along lustily. The appearance of the equipage
was nothing to boast of, nay, if truth must be told, it
cut rather a sorry figure, as far as I could judge from
its shadow in the sun, peeping now and then from the
clouds. It might have been the shadow of a monster
snail or spider, choose whichever of the two you like.
And yet it was something novel in these our railway
times, and almost exciting from its novelty, to be drawn
by a flesh-and-blood horse, and driven by a *bona fide*
post-boy, with no piercing whistles in one's ears, no
burning soot in one's eyes, no fear of being behind
one's time for the corresponding train. Sure it is that
I enjoyed my drive exceedingly. My Automedon was

one of the ugliest and best-natured fellows that ever
sat on a box; he was for ever willing to listen to the
queries, or news, or whatever it might be, of the first
carter, or traveller in a gig or on foot, who chose to
stop him, and he indiscriminately accepted with the
best grace all such messages, and parcels and baskets,
and what not, as any of the male or female cottagers
on his road chose to load him with. He then grinned
at me — his only mode of communication, in a signi-
ficant way, as much as to say, "poor people, they are
so easily obliged."

At a certain point he bade me alight, and pointing
out to me the opening in the forest through which my
course lay, he added a host of instructions and recommendations for my further direction, entirely lost upon
me, I regret to say, but all given with an eagerness
which could not have been greater, had I been his
own brother. We parted company with a hearty,
though on my part inarticulate, reciprocation of good
wishes, such as is seldom come to by fellow-travellers
of little more than an hour.

CHAPTER XVI.

Uphill.

BEFORE entering the forest I looked at my watch — twenty minutes past midday — then up at the rocky peaks, my exalted goal. There they were, sure enough, only so much bigger and higher than they had seemed last evening from the gay balcony, that I somewhat regretted my precipitation. Regrets or no regrets, it was too late to draw back now, and so on I strode.

The commencement was not so bad as it might have been; the path crept up by short zigzags, far from easy, yet practicable. The hard work began with the ceasing of the zigzags, and the opening in front of me, steep and abrupt, of a gully, ravine, or goat-track, or whatever other name expressive of difficulty you choose to give it. Breakneck would be the most appropriate. This gully, as is too often the case with its like, was graced with a stratum more or less deep of rounded pebbles of different sizes, every step over which brought about an avalanche. Incredible were the gymnastic feats I had to accomplish in order to avoid a catastrophe on this dominant difficulty of the ascent. Hard as I found it to preserve my balance over slabs of naked rock smooth as glass, which every now and then intercepted my progress, harassing as it was to climb over huge boulders occasionally blocking up the gully, extremely disagreeable as it proved to

stick ankle deep in marshy patches, and have to fight
for my shoes, all this being only transitory, was as
nothing to that perpetual tread-mill of the pebbles.
Nature seemed to have accumulated difficulties in the
way to this Schwafelberg with the same jealous care
as though it were a second garden of the Hesperides.

To complete my distress, shortly after my confronting the gully, the curls of mist hanging on the
mountain began to dissolve in rain, which, although
very minute, was not the less penetrating, and I had
to don my Mackintosh, open my umbrella, and stumble
on in this accoutrement, than which a more awkward
and more incommodious one for uphill work I don't
know. At the end of a couple of hours of this toil, I
was fairly done up, and exhausted to a degree that,
had there loomed far or near one of those machines
for carrying cheese, from which I had recoiled with
horror, I don't know to what depth of degradation I
might not have descended. But, as my good angel
would have it, there was neither peasant nor portable
pillory in sight, though two châlets were, so I was
saved the possibility of demeaning myself further
than to sit down on a wet stone, wrap my Mackintosh
round my legs, and lower my umbrella as closely
as practicable over my head and shoulders, — a pitiful object to behold certainly, had there been any be-
holder.

A series of loud shouts above my head interrupted
my melancholy meditations. I looked up, there was
no one visible, and I mechanically answered the shouts.
The counter shouts became louder and louder, and
presently a man's figure appeared to my right on the
outskirts of the forest. On my left, all trace of forest

had ceased at the entrance of the gully. The paletot and round hat which this person wore showed clearly that he was not an aboriginal of these wild regions. I stood up and telegraphed to him, and he telegraphed to me in return, and up I strode to him at a quicker pace than three minutes previous I could have believed myself capable of. The voice and sight of a fellow-creature had acted on me like a tonic.

"What is the matter?" cried I in French, as soon as I was within speaking distance of the stranger. The answer, thank God, came in French.

"One of the ladies of my party has fainted away for the second time, and I have been shouting with all my might to try and bring some of those folks from the châlets to help to carry her."

"I am very sorry for your plight," said I; "I wish I could be of some use. Where's the lady?"

"There," with a backward nod towards the forest, "under a tree yonder," said the young man, helping me to ascend the bank on which he was standing. In a minute we were by the side of the sufferer. She lay with her head in the lap of another lady (her sister from their great resemblance), who sat on the wet ground. My stock of little comforts for ladies — a stock, alas! useless now — I had left with the rest of my luggage at the much-regretted inn below, but by a happy inspiration I had taken from it and put into my waistcoat pocket a bottle of eau des carmes. This I produced, and pouring some drops of the contents on the corner of a handkerchief, I gently wetted the lips and temples of the invalid, who immediately revived, half opened her eyes, glanced round, and murmured something which sounded singularly like "*que c'est bête*," and which I took for granted to be something else, until I heard it again most distinctly repeated, and this time accompanied by a little burst of laughter. Whatever her ailments might be, the lady, I was glad to see, had not lost her spirits, upon which I took the liberty of complimenting her.

Remarking the look of surprise, almost of alarm, with which she eyed the unexpected addition to their party whose unfamiliar voice had just struck her ear for the first time, I hastened to add, "Don't be alarmed, madam, he who stands before you is neither an inhabitant of the moon, nor a *genius loci*, but simply a common mortal ill advised enough to be on his way to Schwafelberg."

"And so are we," answered three voices.

"How lucky for me, if you will allow me to join your party."

"With great pleasure," was once more the unanimous answer; "that is, if we can manage to go at all," added the young man, "which in Amalia's state seems problematical."

"Amalia will do wonders if you will only have faith in her," said that spirited invalid, rising. "I assure you I am not ill — how can I be since I feel absolutely hungry? I never fainted since before in my life. It was only a passing weakness, a tribute paid to this abominable cassecou. Did you ever see anything like it before, sir?"

"Never," I replied with energy; "and I was told that ladies never ventured on it unless they were carried."

"Yes, like a cheese; *quelle horreur!*" cried Miss Amalia.

"Horror or no horror," said the gentleman, "who wills the end must will the means. I warned you in time, but no, you wouldn't, and now we should be only too lucky if we could light on one of those *horreurs.*" Whereupon he fell to shouting again, louder than ever, but to no purpose.

"Come along, you cousin of little faith," said Miss Amalia, and set off up the ascent.

"Don't, don't," cried Cousin Charles, running after her.

"Tut, tut, I will," answered Cousin Amalia.

"At least take my arm," urged Charles.

"Tut, tut, I won't," and up she went. Mr. Charles shrugged his shoulders, and followed in her wake as closely as was possible, the other lady after him, and I after her. Truth to say, had the rebel accepted of his arm, he would have been much puzzled how to give it to her. The way at that crisis did not admit of two persons walking abreast. It was strewed with *débris* of rock, some of such long standing as to be overgrown with moss, and obstructed by stumps of trees sometimes so crowded together that it was all you could do to squeeze yourself through the narrow interstices. Umbrellas had long become impracticable, and we received the rain as God sent it. Wonderful to see Miss Amalia glide over and through the impediments as light as Atalanta. It was too beautiful to last, her spare little body was not equal to the strength of her soul. She paused on a sudden before a rock, which there was no turning, leaned against it, and ... Cousin Charles was scarcely in time to receive her in his arms, and hear her whisper *"que c'est bête,"* before she had again fainted. We made a couch of stones as best we could, laid her on it, and the eau des carmes was brought again to the rescue, and with the same success as before. Miss Amalia was not long in recovering consciousness.

Meanwhile, Mr. Charles had been consulting his watch, thrusting his hands repeatedly through his hair, with the gesture of one on whom uneasiness gains apace. At last he turned to me, and said, in an undertone, "Our only chance of getting to Schwafelberg before night, and get there before night we must under penalty of breaking our necks; our only chance to manage this is to find a carrier for my cousin with the smallest delay. Evidently there are none in those two châlets. I know, however, where to find one; but, make what haste I can, it will take me longer than an hour, and I cannot leave my cousins here alone...."

"My dear Sir," interrupted I, "go on your errand with an easy mind, I will stay and take care of the ladies; we began our acquaintance by my expressing a wish that I might be of use to fellow-sufferers, and I thank my lucky stars that I can be so." Upon this he shook hands with me, and without further parley, save a jocular threat to Cousin Amalia of bringing back presently, for her service, one of those beautiful contrivances, to which she was so partial, he set off. Poor Miss Amalia was so worn out that she did not accept the challenge, only smiled wearily.

As soon as he was gone, I went into the thicket, and came back presently with a load of fir boughs sufficient to make a seat for the ladies — a little less wet and hard than the naked stone. And so we three sat looking disconsolately at one another, Miss Amalia dropping now and then into a doze, the elder sister

and I doing our best to keep up a little conversation,
which soon flagged and went out of its own accord,
like a fire of damp sticks. The sisters were manifestly
uneasy about their cousin, and I was uneasy about
them; that is, on account of the consequences, which
a long halt in the damp might entail on delicate women. Fortunately the rain stopped soon after Mr.
Charles's departure, and a bright sun came out to warm
and cheer us.

At last, after an anxious expectation of an hour
and three-quarters, every minute of which I counted,
a succession of double shouts — that is, from Mr.
Charles and from the carrier with him — came to give
us welcome intimation that help was at hand. Another
quarter of an hour, and Mr. Charles himself appeared
followed by a robust mountaineer with the famous conveyance on his back. Miss Amalia allowed herself to
be perched on it, and strapped to it with the best grace
imaginable; and the long-interrupted march was at
length resumed. Of this second part of our journey, I
shall only say that it was beset by the same difficulties
as the first, *plus* an infinity of boggy places of unprecedented depth. To me it proved infinitely more
painful — for the long rest had stiffened my knees to
such a degree that every step forward cost me an effort
and a pang. It wanted ten minutes to nine when we
reached our destination, a dismal-looking plateau with
a dismal-looking châlet on it. This was the establishment of the Schwafelberg.

Being aware from our previous conversation that I
had not bespoken a room, and that I could not speak
German — the only language spoken by the mistress
of the premises — Mr. Charles kindly took upon him-

19*

self to secure a bed-chamber for me; and having ushered me into a *Salle à manger*, bade me wait there till he came to report progress. The *Salle à manger* was of moderate size, low pitched, and stiflingly hot; its atmosphere, impregnated with the smell of stale tobacco, was little calculated to give one an appetite. Its only occupants for the nonce, save a servant girl who was clearing away, were some peasants smoking their pipes over a bottle of wine. I was not sorry to see none of the family I had come to look after. In my present frame of mind and body I was heartily glad to postpone our meeting till the morrow. I was so dreadfully tired, and my knees ached so, that I had no want, no desire, no dream of bliss, except to stretch my legs at full length in a horizontal line. By and bye Mr. Charles brought me word of the happy conclusion of his negotiations — only happy in this respect, that he had secured a bedroom for me, but it was one of the least eligible in this very primitive establishment. Such as it was, he had had to battle for it, the house being full. "You wonder at my statement," he continued in answer to my looks of surprise; "you must know that Schwafelberg, in spite of the extreme difficulty of its access, and of the absence of all comfort in its arrangements, is much resorted to, principally for its powerful curative waters and most salubrious air, and also a little on account of its fabulous cheapness."

While Mr. Charles was giving me theseex planations, a hot dish was placed on the table, which turned out to be a sort of unsavoury panada. I swallowed some spoonfuls of it, had half a glass of very indifferent wine, and then prepared to withdraw. Mr. Charles called for a light, and the servant-maid, all in her good time, brought us a square block of wood with a hole in the centre, in which a tallow-candle was stuck. This candlestick was typical of the degree of civilisation which prevailed at this elevation. I received the primitive instrument with the supreme indifference of one who cares for nothing in the world but a bed. The penitentiary aspect of the room allotted to me, and to which Mr. Charles had insisted on conducting me, was as though it were not. There was a bed, and I had no eyes except for the bed. I had no wish beyond. And so, after saying good-night to my fellow-traveller, and sending my best wishes for the same to the two ladies, who had at once gone to their rooms and never re-appeared, and after an ineffectual attempt to lock the door, which boasted of not even a vestige of a lock, I took off my clothes in a twinkling and glided into my bed.

I was not sleepy, and I was glad I was not, for sleep would have deprived me of the keen enjoyment of full indulgence in the horizontal line. A progressive tide of warmth stole over me, and inundated me with a delicious sense of comfort. Had this blessed condition remained a *statu quo*, the night it promised would have indemnified me for the hardships of the day. But a change did come — the tide of warmth continued to rise, and I soon had too much of a good thing. At the end of a certain time the pleasant glow had augmented to a stifling heat. Withal I felt pricked on all sides as though I was lying on a bed of nettles. I searched the bed thoroughly, and could discover no enemy — I was indubitably its only tenant. I learned afterwards that the substance with which the mattress was stuffed, a kind of lichen peculiar to the locality, played the same trick to all new comers. As for the source of the extreme heat, there was no mistaking that; it was caused by the mountainous eiderdown quilt covering the bed. Everybody knows that eiderdown, when in contact with animal heat, is apt to develop after a while an enormous amount of caloric.

I removed with all haste the obnoxious coverlet, and once more breathed freely. But the nights, even in June, are chilly at the height of five thousand feet, and I was not long in finding that a mere sheet interposed between me and the ambient of my room was an insufficient protection against the cold; and so I was compelled to have recourse to the eiderdown, only in a few minutes to kick it away again. In this agreeable exercise I spent the night. The needles of which my bed seemed composed were all the while busily at work. Such snatches of sleep as I could get were filled with the wildest fancies, which, however, must have had their starting point in the reality. I dreamed alternately that I had fallen into the *crevasse* of a glacier, and that I was making my escape from a house on fire. Towards dawn I fell, from pure exhaustion, into a somewhat more profound slumber, out of which I was suddenly startled by a series of loud knocks above my head, just as if somebody was felling a tree.

I sat up in bed and listened, and presently made out that the noise was caused by the tramp of very heavy boots — half-a-dozen pairs of heavy boots, on the most sonorous of wooden floors forming the ceiling of my room. Who the deuce could be getting up at such an impossible hour! Afterwards I learned it was the class of *baigneurs sérieux* of Schwafelberg, a numer-

ous class as it seemed, who went to drink at the spring
at daybreak. The noise proved infectious — knock-
ing at doors, clearing of throats, fits of coughing, of
sneezing, of singing, of splashing of water, succeeded
and crossed each other in a sort of grotesque fugue
reverberated by all the echoes of the house. The *baigneurs sérieux* went out like an avalanche, and returned
like a charge of cavalry. Useless to think of sleeping,
I gave up the attempt, and read instead, and smoked
cigar after cigar until my little room acquired a striking resemblance to a vapour bath. I got up to open
the single window. Impossible! it was not made to
open. As I returned to my bed, I made at a glance
an inventory of the contents of my chamber — there
was a bed, one wooden stool, a deal table, and on it
a large basin of common reddish earthenware, and a
bottle of water standing in the basin; and that was all.
Not a scrap of towel was to be seen.

Towards eight o'clock, considerate Mr. Charles came
to see how I was. How could one be in this most
wretched of holes but ill, very ill, as ill as possible!
— and I gave him a list of my grievances and mis-
fortunes. Mr. Charles listened to me with a half smile,
and said, "Exactly the impression I received the first
time I came to Schwafelberg, and spent my first night
in this identical room. And yet I got acclimatized
to it."

"Which I never shall or will," returned I. "I am
for simplicity *quand même*, but not for nakedness, and
discomfort, and the absence of the first necessities of
life — air, for instance."

"Come and enjoy the air out of doors," said the
young man as he prepared to leave me, "it is as

good as a cordial; it will restore your energies at once."

"Would you be so good," said I, "as to tell some one to bring me a couple of towels? they have forgotten to put any in my room."

"I will bring you some of mine," said Mr. Charles, "I have a stock with me. The establishment, you must know, does not furnish any linen."

"Deuce take it!" I could not help exclaiming in my exasperation. "I should like to know what it does furnish."

"I have already told you," said Mr. Charles sedately, "excellent curative water and excellent air — the result of both being health restored to the ailing. Is that so little?"

It was, in fact, something, and I held my tongue. Mr. Charles was a Swiss, and not for the world would I have wounded his national pride. Better accept his advice and his towels, which I did with thanks.

CHAPTER XVII.

Dropped Stitches taken up.

THE first person my eyes encountered, as I shortly
after came out of the house, was Madely seated on one
of the benches which stood on either side of the entrance
door. She was busy writing: she looked pale and
thin, and, though exposed to the rays of a warm sun,
was carefully wrapped in a thick shawl. I said in a
quiet voice, "Writing to Bouffarich, I'll bet a wager."
The sound of my voice acted on her like an electric
shock: she jumped up, turned all colours, and cried,
"Good gracious, you here!"

"Just so. I have come all this way, and what a
way! to seek after you, you ungrateful little thing, who
have not so much as thought of embracing me." (In
other days we used always to embrace at meeting and
parting.)

"Pardon me, I did think of it, but . . . I dared
not after . . . behaving so shamefully to you as I
did."

Two big drops of moisture trembled on her eyelashes as she spoke. "We will wipe out all traces
of the past along with those sweet proofs of repentance," said I; and I actually did wipe away with my
lips her gathering tears. She kissed me in her turn
most affectionately, and kept on saying, "How good
you are!"

"Don't assure me of my goodness, but tell me how

you are. I have come all this abominable way precisely
to know that."

"Better — almost entirely well, thank you — we'll
talk about that presently. But first listen to me, I
have something to say in extenuation of my wrong-
doings."

"I will listen to nothing of the sort. I have just
wiped away what you call your wrong-doings. Am
I to recommence the process, and if I do what will
Mr. Telliker say? By the bye, give me some news
of Mr. Telliker. When did you hear from him
last?"

She told me of Mr. Telliker — the subject proved
a rich mine, and not easily exhausted. Ah, me! how
that young man had coiled himself about her heart!
Then she gave me an account of her health that was
altogether reassuring. At one period, she said, she
had felt very ill, and thought all was over with her,
and she had not much regretted that so it should be.
But now she felt quite strong and anxious to live; the
air and waters of Schwafelberg had done wonders for
her. I related in my turn how I had been to Schrankstein, and seen the doctor; then I told her of the
hardships of the ascent of the day before, and of the
sufferings of the night; and by a little exaggeration
I obtained from my listener a great success of laughter.
Presently Frantz hove in sight, and was hailed by us,
then sent to fetch the "alte Mutter," who came in high
glee. There was no end to the cordial greetings and
mutual congratulations. It went to their hearts that I
should have thought so much of them as to seek them
even at the cost of some little personal inconvenience.
They made much of the fact.

Frantz who once, in point of leanness, might have personated the apothecary of Romeo and Juliet, had grown almost fat; and the cloud of discontent which had obscured his countenance for the last two years had vanished, and in its stead now shone the benevolence and contentment which nature had intended to be there. As for the grandmother, she looked, as I told her, the daughter of her former self, positively twenty years younger. What a flow of spirits she had! It was a real treat to hear her rattle on in her usual lively way as if I had understood every syllable of her patois. She was informing me, as her grandchildren explained, how she had taken a horror of Schrankstein-bad ever since the death of the stork, and how happy she had been to turn her back on it, as she hoped for ever. Here was a notable instance of the force of early associations! And I, who, in my simplicity, had supposed her all but dead of a broken heart! Never were sinister prognostications more fully and categorically belied, nor did ever "proving right" give more pleasure than this "proving wrong" afforded me.

The dinner was gay, if not good; Mdlle. Amalia's wit was better than champagne. She handed about two very clever caricatures she had made of herself, at which it was impossible to look and not to laugh. In the one she was represented perched on the cheese conveyance with dangling legs, in the other lying in her bed holding an open umbrella over her head. The second of these humorous sketches was the representation of a comic episode of her first night at Schwafelberg, which she told with great effect. She had been awoke towards break of day by something falling at irregular intervals on her pillow — which something,

on examining it by the light of her candle, she discovered to be a succession of drops of water oozing
through the crevices of the unplastered ceiling. All
her efforts to change the place of her bed being unavailing, she had sought the help of her umbrella, and got
what rest she could under its protection.

Let me not forget to add here in a parenthesis, lest
the present proprietor of Schwafelberg should sue me
for a libel, that the establishment has changed hands
since the days of which I write, and is said to be much
improved, so that the traveller adventurous enough to
scale those heights has every chance of meeting with
better accommodation than fell to my share, inclusive,
let us hope, of towels, and windows that can be opened,
and exclusive of stillicides.

After dinner my kind old friends did me the honours of their temporary residence, that is, took me to
see its big gun — the springs. A strong smell of sul-
phur, at a considerable distance from these last, bore
witness to their powerful nature. The view, on the
whole, was monotonous and uninteresting — a succession of peaks higher than Schwafelberg shut up the
horizon on all sides. The vegetation was scanty, no
trees save here and there a sprinkling of poor firs. The
only thing to gladden the eye was every now and then
a patch of pasturage lower down, so green, so smooth
and rich, as to make one almost wish, especially after
such a dinner as ours had been, to be one of the cows
grazing lazily thereon.

My legs not having yet recovered from the strain
of the forced march of the day before, I gladly acceded
to Frantz's proposal to seat ourselves near the house
and have a bottle of genuine old Margraviat from the

late cellar of Schranksteinbad. While thus genially occupied, we noticed two gentlemen so like each other in all respects save age, that we instantly set them down as father and son. It was impossible not to be struck and prepossessed by the comeliness of their appearance and the natural dignity of their bearing. But for the square caps they wore, a fashion exclusively Polish, I should have taken them for English. The new arrivals went into the house, and almost immediately reappeared upon the threshold with one of the maids, who pointed in our direction. The elder of the two — he could not have been less than sixty — put up his eye-glass, took a rapid glance at the group of which I formed part, came deliberately towards us, and taking both hands of the "alte Mutter" in his, called her by her name, adding in German far from fluent, "How heartily I rejoice to find you looking so well, dear madam! you don't recollect me, I see."

"Nor me," cried the younger stranger, stepping forward and kissing the old lady on both cheeks; "I have altered too much, but I remember you quite well and the dear wounded stork. Now I speak of him, surely you recollect me. How is the dear old fellow?" The son's German, unlike that of his father, was perfect, at least so said Madely, to whose rapid translation I am indebted for the comprehension of the dialogue.

"I see now, I see now," broke forth the "alte Mutter," clapping her hands, "you are the foreign gentleman, I recollect you now: it was you who came and stayed at our house so many many years ago; and this tall young man must be your son, the boy who was so fond of the stork, and used to play for hours with it. And how is your dear, sweet lady?"

"Quite well, thank you; she is just now in Paris."

"And what of the stork?" again inquired the son.

"Dead — alas! dead; and everything has gone wrong with us since."

"We went to look for you at Schranksteinbad," said the father, "and were grieved to find you had parted with the establishment."

"True; but your box is all safe: you may have it whenever you please. It is under my bed at Schrankstein."

The two gentlemen looked at her as she said this, then at one another, then at her again, with the most amazed look that two very intelligent and mobile countenances can wear. Thereupon the old lady briefly related the circumstances which had made her a witness of the burying of the box, together with what had followed the discovery.

"God's finger was in all this," said the elder gentleman, crossing himself devoutly. "And pray," added he to the "alte Mutter," after a rather dubious look at me, "might I say a few words to you in private?"

"As many as you please," replied the old lady, "though there's little occasion for secrecy; these two," pointing to Frantz and Madely, "are my grandchildren, and helped me to dig out the box when we were leaving Schranksteinbad, and, of course, know all about it; and so does this gentleman," turning to me, "an old friend of our family."

"Allow me to explain to you, gentlemen," said I in French, "that this good lady, with a view of securing your claim to your property, in case you did not come for it till after her death, took the precaution of having a record written of all the occurrences of

your arrival and stay in her house in 1831. This
document I have read by her permission, but you may
rest assured that your secret, if secret there be, is safe
with me. I am an Italian, and for many years ate
the 'salt bread of exile.' I guess that you are Poles,
gentlemen — need I say that your noble country has
my heartiest sympathy and good wishes?"

They both grasped me by the hand with an emotion too deep for utterance. The elder was the first to
recover himself; he said, addressing me, "Yes, we are
Poles, and, as such, we cordially thank you for your
sympathy and good wishes; indeed, we believe we
possess those of all true patriots, for, whatever our
shortcomings, none can accuse us of loving our country
by halves, or of grudging our blood in her service. It
was my good fortune to shed some of mine for her in
my youth, and every day of the endless thirty years
that have since elapsed, it has been my constant prayer
that I might still spill its last drop in her behalf. The
moment for this has at last, thank God, arrived. I
suppose you know that Poland is once more in arms
against her oppressor. We are going to join in the
struggle, to conquer or die, no matter which. To die
in a holy cause is to forward it. But if to stake our
lives in the deadly contest is a duty we hold in common with all our fellow-countrymen, there is another,
and a special one, which devolves on us alone, that of
restoring to our dear country a sacred legacy, of which
we are the depositaries. I mean the contents of the
box of which we have been speaking. You will understand its full value to us and to every Pole when
I tell you that all the things in it belonged to our
great Kosciusko, who bequeathed them to my father

(at that time the great man's young *aide-de-camp*), with the injunction to use them whenever Poland should again take up arms. My father, General ——, did, in fact, use them during the whole campaign of 1830-31, and it was in one of Kosciusko's uniforms that he received his death wound in the battle in the suburbs of Warsaw. These relics thus doubly hallowed are held in great veneration throughout Poland, as great as authentic relics of William Tell or Winkelried would receive in Switzerland. They are to us a real force. The care of these heirlooms devolved upon me at a most dangerous moment. Warsaw was once more within the clutch of Russia, and life and property lay at the mercy of her savage bands. A God's miracle alone could and did keep my precious deposit from falling into their hands, and enabled me to carry it safely beyond the frontier. From thence to Switzerland the task was comparatively easy; what made it so was the number of sympathizers we met everywhere, even among those in office, and all ready to help. From Switzerland to Paris, our final goal, I anticipated no serious difficulty, but in this I was mistaken. In fact, I learned that a written information had been lodged with the French authorities on the frontier, and by them transmitted to Paris, to the effect that an attempt was about to be made to introduce into France a box full of Polish uniforms, arms, and manifestoes, to be forwarded to the capital for revolutionary purposes. Russian agents are unsurpassed at this sort of thing; and it must be borne in mind that Poland, at that time, was the watchword of a party of French malcontents, who used her grievances as a weapon against Louis Philippe. As it was, there was little

chance of my being able to pass the chest openly, nor
was it worth while to run the risk of smuggling it, for,
after all, it would not be safe in Paris, where Poles of
distinction, and French sympathizers with Poland, had
just had their houses searched by the police. Such
was the substance of a communication which reached
me from the Polish Committee in Paris. Then, for the
first time, the thought crossed my mind of trusting to
mother earth what the wrath of man threatened. My
wife being worn out with fatigue, I made inquiries for
some quiet place close to the frontier where we could
stop in peace, and I was advised to go to Schranksteinbad. I studied the locality, and fixed on the
grove of young fir-trees as a spot suited for my project; which, however, it was physically impossible I
should accomplish with only the feeble aid of my sick
wife and little boy. To overcome this difficulty I had
no other resource than to summon to my help one of
my cousins who had preceded us into the land of exile,
and who had fortunately taken up his abode in a small
French town on the borders of Switzerland. He came
by appointment, and I got him into the house through
the storeroom window which opened into the verandah.
My cousin had to elude the vigilance of the police in
order to cross the frontier, and this he could best do
by night; hence the mystery of his movements. You
know the rest."

As the father gave us this explanation in French,
the son translated it into German to the "alte Frau,"
whose wonderment and interest were equally intense.
Few, however, were the remarks proffered, or the
questions put by her or by any of us. We were too
deeply and sorrowfully impressed by the strange and

solemn predicament in which these two noble beings
stood to find much to say. They announced their
intention of starting by break of day next morning;
on hearing which I proposed to be their companion in
the descent, a proposal which was readily accepted.
The object of my visit being by this time satisfactorily
attained, Schwafelberg had no inducements of its own
to keep me there any longer. Frantz gave the gentlemen a few lines to his married sister, desiring her
to give up to the bearers of his letter the box left in
her care. Previous to withdrawing for the night
(Frantz had obligingly given up his room to them,
though of that they were ignorant), the Poles took
an affectionate leave of the family, and so a little
later did I, not without emotion on both sides. Parting at a certain age is fraught with melancholy reflections. Poor Madely was deeply affected; so much
so that, in order to comfort her a little, I had to
listen to what she had to say in extenuation of her
past offences.

She had much to say, and said it more at length
than I am at this moment inclined to repeat. Her
excuse for all I had once blamed her for, to sum it up
in a few words, was the great distress of mind under
which she had been labouring at the time. When
Herr Telliker came to the Baths in the month of
August his affairs were slightly embarrassed, not from
any fault of his — of course not, but in consequence
of the wicked conspiracy of rival houses. A trifle, ten
thousand francs, would have put all to rights, but he
could not raise that sum, nor could she without her
grandmother's consent. This the grandmother absolutely refused, and did her best to make Madeleine

give him up. The poor thing was living in daily terror of seeing Telliker arrested when the Russian family arrived, and what do you think she took into her head? She allowed now that she must have been positively crazy to harbour so wild a fancy. Well, she took it into her head that she might possibly be able to borrow the sum that she wanted from these Russians. Ten thousand francs seemed such a paltry sum, a mere nothing for a Russian Crœsus. That was the reason why she paid such assiduous court to those foreigners, that was the reason of her shameful neglect of everybody else, that was why she humoured their fancy for having the ball-room all to themselves, and took my advocacy of the opposite side so ill, and openly laid at my door their subsequent departure, for all and each of which sins .... She was going to add that she begged my forgiveness, when I interrupted her, saying, "Since you are making a clean breast of it, tell me truly, Madely, when I found you so dreadfully breathless on *that* evening, was there no . . . jealousy at work?"

She reddened, hesitated a moment, then said, "Yes — to you I will confess there was — not that Telliker had given me any cause for it, but I was jealous of 'la belle Sommelière.' She was so much younger and handsomer than I was; and to see him dance with her was more than I could bear. It was partly with the wish to exclude her from the ball-room that I gave it up so readily for the use of the Russians. Don't think too ill of me, pray — a woman who loves can be very good and very bad." This confession, and my absolution as father confessor, eased her mind completely, and we parted better friends than ever.

20 *

witness a last request she made, and my ready acquiescence in it. You guess what the request was —
that I should be present at her wedding, whenever it
took place.

By ten o'clock next morning my two travelling
companions and myself were breakfasting in the gay
balcony of the cozy inn at Thoune, and an hour
later I had seen the last of them in all human probability on this side the grave. My blessing went with
them.   ▪

I spent another couple of days at the little inn,
and then a great longing after fields and woods seized
on me, and I determined upon a tour of exploration.
Many were the places I visited — kulms, spas, pen-
sions, hotels great and small. In each and all I
found something to sympathize with, in some few
much to admire in point of grandeur or loveliness
of prospect. But nowhere did I find such ample
scope for roaming, such a happy combination of simplicity and comfort, of privacy and life in common;
in one word, nowhere did I experience that feeling
of home which had so endeared to me the "Quiet
Nook."

THE END.

PRINTING OFFICE OF THE PUBLISHER.

www.ingramcontent.com/pod-product-compliance
Lightning Source LLC
Chambersburg PA
CBHW031406270326
41929CB00010BA/1342